The Genesis
of
Ethical Leadership

What makes a great leader?

The Genesis of Ethical Leadership

What makes a great leader?

Guy Forsyth

Dedication

To Katherine - for the inspiration

About the author

Guy Forsyth is an advisor and consultant to some of the world's leading corporations and also provides his expertise at the Federal and State Government level. Specialising in the area's of leadership and management, business consulting and organisational change, he has worked with numerous organisations in both the public and the private sectors. Graduating from the Universities of NSW and Canberra with qualifications in Commerce, Law, and a doctorate in management, he has lectured in leadership and management, and conducted training in leadership and ethics at the Australian War College. He is presently an Officer in the Navy Reserve and has been awarded the Prince of Wales Award for his services. A keen student of military history, he has read widely on the various campaigns of many leaders with a primary interest in the Napoleonic period. He also has a deep interest in leadership development and leader personalities. Guy's work as a consultant also involves him with firms that deal with leadership, performance, change management and ethics. He lives in Australia.

Table of Contents

Chapter 1 - **Introduction**

What is great leadership? Think about it — how do you know when you see an example of great leadership? What appears to be a seemingly innocuous question is not so obvious when you really think about it. The difficulty in being able to identify great leadership stems from the conjunction of great and leadership (and to some extent the conjunction of great and leader), which implies that a great person in a leadership position is a great leader. A leader might be perceived as great because they have achieved a significant feat, or even attained a prominent position, but it does not follow that just because they became such that they also exercised great leadership, indeed they may not have even exercised good leadership. The illogicality here is evident yet we seem to accept that a leader that has achieved a great feat is also a great leader when this might not be true. The problem remains that we need to understand what is really meant by good and great leadership.

Great, or even good, leadership should result from the manner in which a leader exercises leadership. In saying this it must be recognised that the leadership, and not the leader's attributes that needs to be considered in making this assessment. The failure to separate the two elements leads to the illogical conclusion that if a person is great in terms of eminence or achievement, and they are in a position of leadership, then ipso facto they exercise great leadership.

It is natural for a leader to want to be seen as a good leader, and possibly even as a great leader. In order to be a good leader one must do good. This is the essence of ethical leadership - being a good person is not enough, although as Plato would say, a necessary precondition. You might be a good or virtuous person, but being a good leader requires the demonstration of leadership that conforms to the principles of ethics and also demonstrates leadership – no easy task.

We can all point to what we regard examples of good leadership, who have become renown as great leaders of their era. People such as Martin Luther King, John F Kennedy, Nelson Mandela and Margaret Thatcher might come to mind. We can also point to abominable examples of leadership such as Adolf Hitler, Idi Amin, Josef Stalin or Augusto Pinochet. But before reaching the conclusion that one leader is "great" and another "abominable" it is necessary to look at their track record and understand why we tend to strip some leaders of the epithet "great" when they were, at one point, regarded by their followers as great leaders. Without doubt, the most controversial of the aforementioned leaders is Hitler. Prior to the commencement of World War II the German people revered him. He was recognised as a saviour, someone that had led them out of their post WWI humiliation. What he and his party achieved for the country was exceptional in the 1930's and his leadership was at that time labelled great by his countrymen with an almost cult-like reverence. Similarly, JFK was regarded in glowing terms by most of his countrymen during the early sixties, and to this day his leadership and achievements are seen as extraordinary in a tumultuous time. But can we compare Hitler to JFK in terms of great leadership? The problem with doing so is not so much one of comparison of the two individuals from an ethical perspective but the legacy of their leadership. Understanding what constitutes good or ethical leadership is necessary if we are to have a basis for comparison.

Until now, the success of these and similar "great" leaders has been attributed to the notion of them possessing inherent abilities.

[1] This perspective has been the situation for over half a century, with the trait theory of leadership maintaining the belief that leaders possess "the right stuff" for them to become leaders, and indeed great leaders. Take for example the quality of intelligence. This is still widely regarded as an antecedent for leadership. We seem to insist that our leaders should be intelligent and possess certain mental and physical abilities yet we pay less attention to their beliefs and values, in fact in some areas we do not even know these attributes. Even though we may recognise aspects of our leaders backgrounds as supporting their inherent qualities or behaviours, even accounting for their success or "greatness", other influences such as the ideologies, culture and philosophies to which they have been exposed receive scant attention. This is peculiar when it has been proposed that all leadership is ideologically driven or motivated by a certain philosophical perspective.[2]

Do great men possess the inherent capabilities for leadership? Unsurprisingly, research has identified that the emergence and effectiveness of leadership cannot be solely attributed to the possession of certain traits. Traits might be a precondition for the emergence of leaders but they are not solely responsible, and they are certainly not the sole source of a leader's effectiveness. Researchers have therefore turned to investigate a range of other factors to understand how leaders emerge and succeed, leading them to conclude that certain behaviours and abilities are equally important as traits. Some of these behaviours can be learned but, by and large, most of them still seem to be innate in some people.

The Great Man theory of leadership

Despite its somewhat politically incorrect name the Great Man theory took root in the early nineteenth century as a way of explaining why some leaders achieved greatness. Open any leadership textbook and you will find the theory given prominence as the father of all leadership theories. Given the amount of literature that has been devoted to this one theory one would be excused for thinking that it is the source of our modern understanding of leadership. In a nutshell the Great Man theory proposed that the qualities of certain men (great men) were innate. The theory derived its name from the study of leaders at the time who were, predominantly if not exclusively, men. One such proponent of the notion that certain men possessed the qualities for greatness was Thomas Carlyle, a nineteenth century Scottish philosopher. Carlyle was fascinated by the French revolution that had only occurred just before his birth. Perhaps the Scottish struggle for independence from the English inflamed his interest. Nonetheless, he went on to write about the French revolution and began to formulate his ideas around it. One of these ideas was the notion that certain cataclysmic events in human history are the work of great men. His most obvious denouncement on this idea is to be found in his most famous work - On heroes, Hero worship and the heroic in History in the statement: "the history of the world is but the biography of great men". His book analysed several great leaders such as Napoleon Bonaparte, Oliver Cromwell and even the prophet Mohammed to conclude that these men all possessed the qualities for their greatness and were the agents for change in human destiny.

Where does a leader's approach come from?

Leadership is, at core, a relationship[3] between a leader and followers – a social influence process.[4] A leader is able to influence followers towards some end. How they influence followers has been the subject of extensive academic enquiry and emerges in the form of numerous leadership theories. In this regard, leadership theory has predominantly been descriptive – we know how the influence process works and why it is effective, but we do not know how it comes about. How, for example, does a person's ability to influence others develop and why is it effective in some situations but not in others? What we need to know is how the leadership abilities and behaviours develop, and whether they can be learned. Chapter 2 will expand on this aspect of leadership approach development.

Leadership research has determined that leaders possess certain traits and behaviours but neither of these are any guarantee for success as a leader. They may be preconditions for leadership emergence and they may contribute to a leaders success but they are by no means the sole determinant. The traits of intelligence and persistence are two widely touted leadership qualities. Yet there are numerous people with these traits that do not become leaders, and there are some leaders that do not succeed even though they possess these attributes. The genetic (nature) argument in relation to leadership is largely inconclusive and, contradictorily even tends to suggest environmental influences (nurture) as being more determinative.

The environment argument has proposed a range of influences as contributing to leadership behaviours. Factors identified within the family and outside it may indicate certain behavioural tendencies but these do not suggest what type of leadership approach will manifest – they are only a possible precondition for leadership emergence and effectiveness.

This leads us to look elsewhere for how a leader's approach develops. If genetics has failed to provide us any reliable means of predicting leadership emergence or effectiveness then it would seem futile to continue down that path. This leaves environmental factors as the only option capable of providing some indication of the type of leadership approach that may emerge. If we accept that leadership is at core a social influence relationship then it follows that we should look to what factors impact upon the formation of our understanding of that relationship. Undoubtedly, personality attributed play a role in leadership emergence and success but it does not fully account for the type of leadership approach that the person displays.

In order to understand what environmental factors influence the development of a persons leadership approach then we need to know how the underlying beliefs, attitudes and values of a leader towards others form. We will explore the role of philosophical influences and how some of these philosophical influences have acted on people throughout history in Chapter 3.

The soldier statesmen
The key to understanding how leaders exercise leadership is revealed through an understanding of how their leadership approach develops. Why does one leader seem initially to be our great hope for change only

to become irrelevant, or worse, a monster? What separates the competent leader from the outstanding leader? Why are some leaders regarded as great and leaving a positive legacy?

To answer these questions we need to delve into the backgrounds of certain great leaders to find out. We could choose any leaders for this analysis but the four selected leaders are from a category that are generically known as soldier statesmen.[5] These leaders have been selected not simply because of their universal recognition as great leaders but because they have successfully led in two different domains – military and political. To be successful in two separate spheres indicates a high degree of leadership career autonomy, that is, they are not leaders in their field simply because of the skills that they have developed in that field. It is not a simple matter to be a leader in one sphere and succeed in another. There are not many people that achieve the high point in one career and do the same in a completely different one. For example, many business leaders succeed as leaders of their organisations in part because of their specific suitability to a particular industry.[6] Doing the same thing and doing it well for a long time gives a person credibility and judgement that is often sought out for leadership roles. But the very same person may not be suitable in a different profession or even a different industry. We often see successful people move from the business sector into politics but the truly a great leader in one sphere is not necessarily perceived as great in another. The soldier statesmen, on the other hand, demonstrate that they have successfully led in two separate domains, and in the case of the selected leaders they have done so notably. Discounting that they may have had an aptitude for both the military and political environments, the likelihood is that their leadership has a universal quality.

The soldier statesmen selected are somewhat comparative contemporaries from two different eras – one pair from the eighteenth century: George Washington and Napoleon Bonaparte and the other pair from the twentieth century: Dwight D Eisenhower and Charles de Gaulle.

The similarities and differences between these leaders are intriguing. Washington was effectively the first leader of the US republic while Napoleon was the same for France; both fought against the British and were influenced by similar ideologies that were instrumental in the development of their Constitutions.[7] Similarly, Eisenhower became President of the United States of America (USA) after WWII while de Gaulle became President of France's Fifth Republic; both fought on the same side against a common adversary and emerged out of bureaucracy with very different influences directing their destiny, both presiding over similar regime change and social turbulence. Of course, all four leaders were successful military leaders but in distinctly different circumstances. All became the leader of their nation, through force or acquiescence: some left a positive legacy while others did not. How did they approach leadership, and why did they succeed in both the military and political context? Chapters 4 through 7 will address these questions to identify the influences that determined their leadership approach.

It is also worth noting that most of the leaders pre twentieth century have not taken courses in leadership before they become leaders: this would suggest that environmental conditioning must play a role in the types of behaviours and abilities that they develop. Through an understanding of how the soldier statesmen's leadership approach forms we can then address the question of what constitutes good, and therefore, ethical leadership. Chapter 8 will look at the leadership approaches of each of the soldier statesmen and consider what gives rise to the claim of their leadership being considered ethical. We will see that great leadership results from the *manner* in which leadership is exercised. What distinguishes the competent from the incompetent leader is not what distinguishes the competent from the good or the great. We will revisit the conundrum of good and great leadership in this final chapter but also evaluate why the selected leaders succeeded and why their reputations have endured.

> The world has always seemed curious to know how its great men received their learning and training, how and where they were educated, who were their teachers and trainers, and what moulding influences gathered about their childhood and youth and fashioned them for their fate to be.
>
> Harrison, *George Washington: patriot, soldier, statesman*

Chapter 2 - **Leadership approach development**

Despite the vast amount of literature on leadership there has been very little research into how a person's leadership approach develops. As we have seen in the previous chapter leaders are not necessarily born, as there are many attributes of leadership and we certainly are not born as ethical leaders. The conundrum surrounding how one becomes a leader falls into three camps. The first (nature) is that some people simply assume that leadership is genetic - how we lead is a function of our personality and character derived from our parents (and perhaps some other predecessors). The other camp (nurture) assumes that it is the result of environmental conditioning – how we are raised and the type of environment we are raised in. And of course there is the hybrid of these two constituting the third. Nonetheless the debate between genetics and environment has raged for over a century and has become known as the nature-nurture controversy.

> ...some natures..ought to study philosophy and be the leaders in the state; and others..are meant to be followers rather than leaders.
>
> Plato *The Republic*

The nature argument (that is, the perception that leaders are "born") emerged with the early Greek philosophers.[8] The perception of being born with particular characteristics that either predestined you for greatness or mediocrity persisted well into the late nineteenth century.[9] The Great Man theory emerged out of this notion that particular traits predestined a person for greatness and that only a few extraordinary people were endowed with more of these elements than other mere mortals.[10] This view was promoted in the nineteenth century by philosophers such as Thomas Carlyle who not only saw human nature as inherent but immutable, that is, humans were largely predictable and stereotypical. However, other philosophers of the time rejected this perspective. John Stuart Mill, proposed in his 1848 work *Principles of Political Economy,* that such thinking impeded social reform.[11] After all, if human nature was so fixed then this would simply ensure the status quo forever. Such a concept suited the paternalistic and aristocratic society of the time. To Mill such a state was ridiculous and he rallied against the rampant discrimination endemic in English society - in particular against women's right to vote.

While philosophers were divided on the nature argument it was an age when science was in the ascendant. The scientific community weighed into the debate and it would achieve significant notoriety under Charles Galton. Galton was something of a polymath. His diverse scientific background exposed him to a wide range of disciplines – biology, criminology, psychology, statistics, to name a few. His focus, though, narrowed in his later career on the role of hereditary traits in humans: piqued by the work of his uncle, Charles Darwin, who had proposed several years earlier that human beings genetically mutated from an ancient ancestor. Galton subsequently wrote *Hereditary Genius: an inquiry into its laws and consequences*, in 1869, proposing that a whole raft of human characteristics were inherited: intelligence, persistence and even civic worth! It was an instant hit among the well to do. Of course prominent

> ...not all men of superior ability achieve success or fame. Historical and social conditions determine which men of superior ability are to succeed or fail.
>
> Charles Horton Cooley in Pastore *The nature nurture controversy*

men sprung from prominent men – it was only natural. The upper class ruled because they were naturally superior and the lower class were downcast because (even though no one said it) they were naturally inferior – and neither the twain should meet. So successful was Galton's theory that he became know as the father of Eugenics – the practice of improving the human race through genetic selection. Half a century later the Nazis even tried to adopt it.[12]

Following Galton's work, the scene was set for genetics to be at the forefront of scientific research into human behaviour for the next century. So certain were the researchers that genetics was the source of human behaviour that it became almost heretical to advocate otherwise. Yet heretics always have a nasty habit of popping up, and in the late 1940s a researcher by the name of Nicholas Pastore decided to review 24 studies undertaken since Galton's initial research. He found little conclusive evidence for genetics being solely responsible for human development and in fact identified that the Galtonian "hereditarians" were contradicted by the "environmentalists". Eminent sociologist Herbert Spencer concurred, proposing that it was absurd to think that a Newton, Milton or Beethoven could emerge in a family or society not conducive to such a person's development.[13] That made people think – imagine if Beethoven was born in Africa! Could he have composed the Eroica symphony without the inspiration of Napoleon or ... a piano. It seemed only logical that environmental factors must play a role in a persons development and that great men could not only be the result of genetic attributes. Interestingly, the scientists analysed by Pastore were equally split on the importance of nature versus nurture. The only determinative factor on whether one subscribed to either theory was founded on one's socio-political orientation – hereditarians being predominantly conservative (nature) and environmentalists being progressive (nurture).[14]

Research conducted into the influence of environmental factors on human development gained some traction in the early twentieth century but was overshadowed by the focus on genetics. Of distinct interest to some of the researchers was whether Galton's hereditary greatness claims were true. This naturally sparked interest in whether the people that achieved greatness possessed certain traits that predestined them for their achievements. A number of researchers quite predictably went down the trait path trying to identify personal qualities. As most of the great men analysed were leaders, in some respect, the research adopted an element of identifying the traits of leadership. The research into environmental factors proceeded in parallel but failed to attract as much attention.

Research into the environmental basis of leadership has identified several factors that were found to be predominantly associated with influences from the family (or extended family) and society. The *familial factors* identified birth order,[15] family size[16] and parenting as playing a role in how leaders emerge while[17] the *societal factors* identified career/life opportunities[18], degree of marginalisation, heterogeneity,[19] and educational standards.[20]

In relation to birth order, research identified that first- and last-born siblings have a higher preponderance for leadership.[21] Birth order, as a non-genetic determinant in predicting the emergence of future leaders, is based on the differences in per-

> The standards imposed at home, the drives engendered there, the values inculcated, the models found in parents, all affect the later emergence of potentialities for leadership
>
> J.W Gardner *On Leadership*

sonality between first-, middle- and last-born siblings.[22] Family size has also been identified as a factor in relation to the emergence of personality traits relevant to leadership (being based on the development of intelligence and persistence – two recognised leadership traits).[23] Single-child families have been found to be of above average intelligence and average persistence, while "average" families of between two and five children have been found to be higher in intelligence but below average in persistence, and children from large families of six or more have been found to be lowest in intelligence but highest in persistence.[24] In addition to these traits it has been observed that the "optimal" family size (three–four siblings) tends to produce "group goal" oriented individuals who are more co-operative than "individual prize" motivated individuals who tend to be more persistent.[25] Parenting then comes into the equation, with nurturing, positive parents more likely to produce children with socially acceptable abilities.[26] In relation to the influence of the respective parents, research has shown that a strong mother is more likely to produce leadership-oriented males.[27] In general, family influences play an important developmental role[28] in the production of leadership skills. What is not clear is the inter-relationship between all of these factors. For example, no study has yet been performed on first-born males with strong mothers from large families to conclusively prove that the combination of these factors is positively correlated to leadership emergence. And of course, none of these environmental factors are predictors of a person's approach to leadership.

Outside the family, several societal factors have been identified as being precursors to leadership emergence. Early life opportunities for exercising leadership, such as interaction with others during early years of development, enable an understanding of group behaviours, and how to best achieve desirable outcomes.[29] The degree to which one is socially marginalised (religion, ethnicity, class) has been found to correlate with the emergence of charismatic leaders.[30] The heterogeneity of a person's background, such as family mobility and childhood experiences, tends to broaden a person's perspective and so they become able to deal more effectively with others.[31] Higher standards of education have been linked to a greater likelihood for leadership emergence based in part on the trait of intelligence and in part on the career opportunities available.[32]

Of all these factors, only one, marginalised background, provides any indication as to how a person will exhibit leadership. In this specific instance the research indicates that charismatic leaders tend to emerge from marginalised backgrounds. This finding is of interest, as it would suggest that there are sociological factors in one's environment that could give rise to a person's leadership approach.

While this finding may be supportive of this particular environmental factor contributing to the emergence of charismatic leadership,[33] the reality is that the attributes of this particular leadership approach cannot be solely attributed to the leader. Charisma is the underlying essential aspect of charismatic leadership but it is also, to a large extent, a follower perception in that "it is not what the leader is but what people see the leader as that counts in generating the charismatic relationship".[34] In other words, this leadership approach is not a unilateral display of leadership; followers need to perceive the exceptional quality that constitutes the leader's charismatic effect.[35] What this suggests is that the causal connection between marginalised background and charismatic leadership is not entirely conclusive, and so this antecedent environmental factor cannot completely account for the particular leadership approach.

> While genetic influences account for a sizeable portion of leadership variance, environmental factors are substantially important in determining leadership.

Further support for the role of environment on personality and leadership development has come from an unlikely corner. Genetic research over the last decade has in fact tended to support the role of environmental factors underpinning leadership. Such research has demonstrated that while certain personality traits are indeed heritable,[36] there has been little support for a genetic link to them contributing to leadership emergence.[37] Personality traits predisposing one for leadership is considered contestable through a range of studies.[38] For example, several twin studies have discounted the veracity of the claim that environmentally separated monozygotic twins demonstrate the correlation of genetically attributable behaviour.[39] Environmental influences play an equally significant role in other research, such as the work in the development of social cognitive theory and attachment theory.[40] This being so, there is inadequate justification for the exploration of a relationship between genetics and leadership approach as the relationship between genetics and leadership emergence has inadequate support, which of course leads us back to the environmental factors.

Continuing enquiry is highlighting the significance of environmental factors[41] and diluting the role of genetic attributes in its contribution to leadership ability.[42] For instance, Psychologist and author of "The Nurture assumption – Why children turn out the way they do" Judith Harris challenges both hereditability and nurturance by suggesting that the environmental effect of group socialisation during youth is more determinative in social skill development than the role of parents.[43] Social skills contribute to the development of behaviours essential for exercising leadership.[44] After all, if leadership is a social influence process in a group, then the impact of such socialisation may prove to be more determinative than the qualities inculcated by parents or derived from them.

Two important points emerge from the contention over the role of hereditability and nurturance on the attributes relevant for leadership: firstly, environmental factors may be more determinative in the development of leaders than genetic factors; and secondly, these environmental factors do not correlate to the type of leadership manifested, that is, the leadership approach displayed.

It is therefore important to further investigate the factors that impact upon the development of a person's leadership approach as genetics has proven inconclusive and the environmental factors identified to date have not provide us with any more reliable indication of how a person will lead. The only environmental factor (marginalised background) that has been shown to predict a particular leadership approach (charismatic leadership) does not indicate a sufficiently high causal connection by virtue of follower contingencies. It is therefore necessary to determine how and what other environmental factors contribute to a person's leadership approach. One set of environmental influences that have not received attention are those that influence a person's values, attitudes and beliefs. How do these form and from where do they originate?

The influence of philosophy

To understand how our values, attitudes and beliefs form we need to know how our conception of knowledge forms - that is, how do we form the beliefs we hold? Some people naturally tend to accept what they are told, while others seem to require proof or learn from experience. We have all seen this in children that either believe what they are told or inquisitively require justification.

You can gain an insight into your own knowledge formation by thinking about how you approached learning something in your past. Think back to your school days when you were told the value of Pi(π).

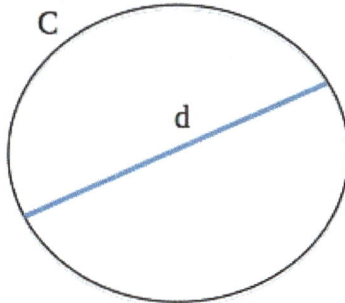

Did you just accept that Pi was 3.1415... or did you need to know why? Most people accept that Pi is a constant and that it is used to calculate certain formulae in geometry, such as the circumference of a circle ($2\pi r$), or its area (πr^2). But how many of us recall what Pi represents? Ask most people and few will say it's the *ratio* of the circumference of any circle to its diameter: *any circle* – a centimetre wide or a mile wide. Some people know this because they asked or wanted to know why. They did not simply accept that Pi was some oxymoronic infinite constant, they wanted to know how it came about. Others worked it out from the equation C=πd (as obviously the diameter of a circle is twice its radius i.e d=2r). In other words, some people will accept what they are told, and others will question it. This fundamental difference to knowledge assimilation influences how we form our conception of reality.[45] The underlying basis of this and how we develop knowledge is known as our personal belief system, or the set of relatively independent beliefs about the structure, source and certainty of knowledge.[46] This is also known as our personal epistemology – how we know what we know.

This is important because it affects how we come to form any belief that we may hold. If beliefs sound like a vague concept then consider how beliefs have changed the world and continue to do so. You only have to look at the consequences of the different belief systems between religions, countries, and political parties to know that holding a particular belief can be a serious matter.

Research into how we understand the world around us has primarily been aimed at understanding intellectual development through learning.[47] In this area it has been quite valuable. For example, if we know that some people learn by simply being told while others learn through experience then teaching can be tailored to suit the different learning types. But pedagogy is not the only application of the contribution of personal epistemology.[48] The processes by which we develop an awareness of and experience life also encompasses what we come to believe and "know" about the world around us. Our personal belief system therefore acts as a filter to determine what we believe and value underpinning our attitudes and biases, our rational and irrational concerns.[49] This system develops early in our lives, especially in relation to socially or humanly constructed facts.[50] Once this belief system is established it is relatively fixed and "unchanging" throughout life.[51]

The assumptions we form impact our perception of the social relationship and so impact the way in which we interact with others.[52] Our personal belief system forms the core set of beliefs that are considered to filter all knowledge which can be categorised in terms of being external or internal: people that form their understanding by looking outside themselves are externalists, while the people that do so by looking within themselves are internalists (this is also known as epistemic justification and can become quite complex but we will confine it to how we form our understanding of the world around us).[53]

The division between internalist and externalists is more than a semantic classification. Think of how a child's knowledge develops: at an early age a child can be quite certain of what it knows because of what it has been told and they simply repeat what they are told. As they start to learn more from the world around them they start to make claims that are based on certain facts which may or may not be true. A child will assert that it knows that Pluto is the most distant planet of our solar system but will not really know whether it is true based on any understanding of the nature of planets or based on any evidence apart from a seemingly authoritative source citing it. Unfortunately, some adults stop at this stage of epistemic development and cling to the beliefs/opinions that they form based on what they hear or observe. However, as some children mature they start to question what they are being told. They adopt a relative approach to what they know, that is, they begin to understand that what they are told is only the opinion of the holder. Many more adults do not proceed past this stage and will hold unfounded opinions based largely on the opinions of others depending on the degree of credibility of the opinion-holder. Rarely do these people see a credible opinion as a judgement that requires justification. At the final development level of some individuals the holder of a belief does so through a process of critical thinking where facts and arguments are used to construct knowledge. They might be told something and in fact believe it but they still embark on a process to determine whether it is true and whether the belief that they have formed can be justified on the basis of available evidence. This is why education is so critical – it separates out unjustified belief from knowledge.

The development of our resultant attitudes and values according to how we develop our perception of reality forms a fundamental awareness of the world around us which constitutes our worldview. These worldviews, like us, are quite independent, much like our personalities. Some elements might be shared in relation to overarching issues, such as the belief that all people are entitled to live free from oppression. You might believe that every person should be free from oppression but to what extent do you believe someone is being oppressed? How we decide between one set of values, beliefs or principles and another depends upon the influences that have acted upon us. For example, a person that abhors slavery and promotes the right of all people to be free and valued may be quite comfortable with underpaying and overworking staff. In this case their socio-political philosophy might predominate over their moral philosophy when self-interest is involved. They may even adhere to a certain moral position because of a convention, custom or law that they feel gives them the right to do so, even though holding it is unethical. Slavery for example has been justified in this way. Slave owners know that what they are doing is unethical but believe it is ethical because the law (itself unethical) deems it to be legitimate. Our resultant worldview may contain contradictions like this that need to be challenged if we are to have a congruent perspective of reality.

Our personal epistemology begins forming from before we can communicate. It is well known that a baby does not differentiate between the world around it and itself for many months. The conception of self is primarily inward focussed at a very early age – everything is about "me". This changes as we are able to interact with our environment. After this we commence interacting with our family, which is the initial source for us to determine how we relate to others. Then our school becomes an important source of social experience. Interacting with people that have their own interests at heart rather than ours becomes a particular challenge for many. As we develop independence, we generally become more involved with our local community. We might join a sporting team or a club. This exposes us to a greater diversity of people. And so the process continues and we begin to be influenced by different ideologies and cultural idiosyncrasies. We start to perceive that different people have different belief systems about a vast array of subjects. With this new knowledge we may have formed the view that our parents were conservative and that they voted a particular way because of that, or we may have found that a school friend refused to engage in rambunctious activities, or we might have queried why our society does not execute murderers. The underlying basis of all of these observations can be described as comprising a different philosophical perspective. Our parent's conservatism could be based on a particular social or political philosophy while our friends behaviour is most likely based on a moral or religious philosophy. What philosophical area is involved in a society's justification for executing or not executing criminals?

Our worldview[54] develops as an individual and subjective outlook[55] of the world around us and becomes our philosophy or view of life.[56] Understanding the ecology of its development is useful in understanding how a person's leadership approach develops as the behavioural characteristics that differentiate one leadership paradigm from another may be explained through assessing the differences in a leader's value and belief system.[57] This is because how we interpret and act towards others underpins *our conception of the social relationship*. In order to understand how our personal belief system determines our worldview it is necessary to understand what factors contribute to the development of our perspective of others. Our personal belief system may determine how we construct knowledge but not *what* we know.

To understand *what* we know about our relationship with others, it is necessary to understand the factors and influences that affect that relationship. If this were not the case then our personal belief system would simply inform our leadership approach. This is too simplistic and presumes that the way in which we construct knowledge is linked to our approach to leadership. While there may be a linkage between how we understand and form knowledge of the world around us and certain aspects of our leadership approach, it is still necessary to understand the factors that underpin the formation of that knowledge (or worldview) as a persons attitude towards others results from the worldview they form, not the manner in which they construct knowledge. As such, it is necessary to recognise that our personal belief system acts as a mediator between the philosophical influences that act on us and the resultant worldview that

	Person A	Person B
Leadership characteristic	Collaborative	Authoritarian
Worldview	People have free will and so their contributions are valuable	God/Church law is absolute and so people should follow direction
Personal Belief system	Knowledge is generated by human minds and is uncertain	Knowledge comes from an external source and is certain
Philosophical influence	Christianity	Christianity

underpins our leadership approach. This is illustrated by the example in Figure 1.

In this figure we have two sets of divergent personal belief systems but exposure to the same philosophical influence – the religious philosophy of Christianity. Christianity proposes a variety of different concepts but the personal belief system of the individual will determine which concept is accepted. For example, on the one hand Person A has an internalist personal belief system[58] and believes that knowledge can be constructed and gained through reasoning. As Christianity recognises people having free will, the internalist perception will contribute to a worldview that values the contribution of people, as all people are seen as being capable of contributing to the construction of knowledge. In a leadership role this person is likely to want to encourage the participation of others and engage with them on a deeper level, having respect for their independence and contribution. As a result their leadership approach might be characterised as supportive and collaborative. On the other hand, Person B has an externalist personal belief system and believes that knowledge is absolute and resides in authority figures. Christianity also advocates that God's word is absolute and the teachings of the Church should be followed. Given the personal belief system of this person, they would likely hold the view that what you are told by someone in a position of authority is correct and one ought to follow directions and edicts. In a leadership position this type of leader needs to exercise direction and control over followers, as they see themselves as the source of authority and knowledge. They may adopt an approach where they see themselves as the source of truth and so be perceived as authoritarian and controlling.

In reality, the complexity of a person's leadership approach will result from the interaction of the different philosophical perspectives that act on them. The philosophical perspectives which operate on us in determining our understanding of the social relationship can emanate from four broad

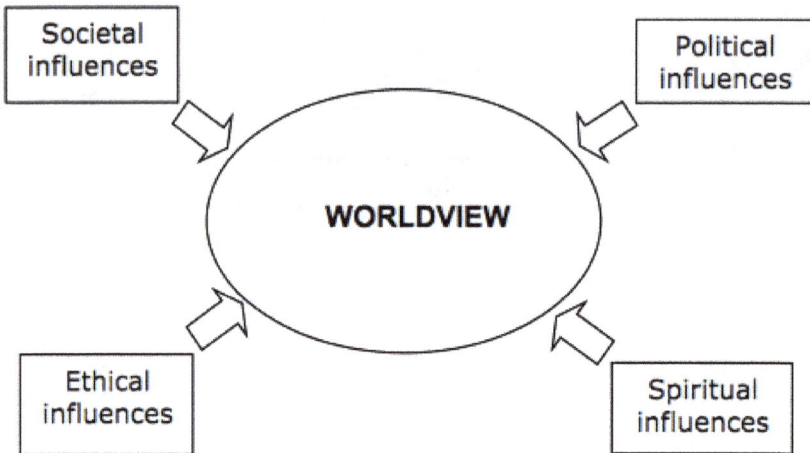

Figure 2

areas: societal, political, ethical and spiritual. Each of these has an impact on the worldview that we form and the component of that worldview that impacts on how we perceive other people. Of course, there are other elements that impact our worldview, such as the culture we live in, or even the economic system, but if we are talking about leadership then these four areas fundamentally impact the perception we form of how we relate to others.

The four areas in Figure 2 are fundamentally philosophical in nature. When we talk about philosophical concepts we are not referring to some vague, academic notion. We all deal with philosophical issues every day, sometimes in every hour of the day without even knowing it. For example, when we give advice to our children about how they should behave we are teaching them moral philosophy – what they ought to do. When we decide that a politician's new agenda is nothing more than a populist appeal we are assessing their motives from a political philosophy perspective. If we go down to the shopping centre and park in any space other than the eight disabled parking spaces out the front we are making a decision from a social philosophy perspective. Even when we give money to an indigent person in the street we might be acting out of the convictions inspired from a religious philosophical perspective. Philosophies are therefore real and not esoteric concepts – we are guided by them.

Depending on what philosophical perspective or combination has acted upon an individual, and their personal belief system, will determine the worldview that they form. For example, if one is exposed to communist doctrine during early life, then this ideology will have an influence on how one perceives others, society and one's place in society. Similarly, if one is exposed to Christian dogma, then this will have an effect on how one perceives the same. Communism and Christianity are philosophies – political and religious respectively.

The adoption of an element of a particular philosophy will be a factor in the formation of the person's worldview. In turn, this will manifest in a particular leadership approach when the need to exercise leadership arises. This process is demonstrated in Figure 3.

Leadership Approach

Affecting

Worldview

Leads to

Personal belief system

Mediated by

Philosophical influences

Figure 3

If it is accepted that leadership is, at core, a social influence process then the formation of our interaction with others must impact on that process. Since we develop our conception of the society around us through the philosophical influences that act upon us then it is of interest to understand what philosophical perspectives are relevant and how they might determine the beliefs, values and attitudes we form with respect to others. It is therefore of interest to understand to a greater extent what is meant by social, political, moral and religious philosophy in order to understand the impact that these areas might have on our leadership approach development.

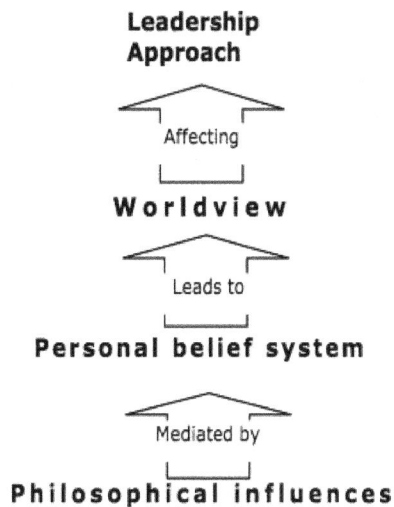

Social philosophy

Social philosophy has a lengthy history of enquiry, from understanding the nature of the Ancient Greek *polis,* from feudalism to capitalism, communitarianism to socialism. The philosophy is concerned with social issues and social behaviour; "it is about what the principles of social life ought to be and why."[59] The nature of social systems is of interest to social philosophers, with the relationship between individuals in society (how people live) of central interest.

The way in which people in society interact in different social systems underpins how we form our understanding of group interaction. Several concepts in social philosophy are therefore relevant to leadership, such as the concepts of altruism and utilitarianism, social contract theory, cultural criticism and individualism.[60] For example, contemporary transactional leadership theories consider the nature of a transactional exchange as being the basis of the relationship between leader and followers. There is clearly a "social contract" of sorts in these relationships and the concept of the social contract in philosophy has distinct relevance. Social contract theory also raises issues of rule and the role of the polity. This necessitates an understanding of power and rights, which fall within the scope of political philosophy.

Political philosophy

Political philosophy is principally concerned with the conventions that govern society.[61] It identifies "the nature and causes of good and bad government"[62] and "how the state should act, what moral principles govern the way it treats its citizens, and what kind of social order it should seek to create."[63] The rights of citizens, social justice, liberty and equality are of importance in political philosophy.[64] The notion of government is not merely about the ruling party but all the institutions of administration and execution over a society.[65] In some respects political philosophy is concerned with any situation where power is involved.[66] Political philosophers pose questions such as, "Who should rule?" and "Why do they rule?".

Western civilisation has been dominated by the religious philosophy of Christianity for the past two centuries, which has in turn impacted the cultures moral philosophy. Inherent in Christian natural law is the divine purpose and plan of God. While Aristotle proposed that all of nature has a purpose, to Christians this purpose is part of God's plan. This raises the concept of how things *ought to be*, which implies that if certain acts are not in accordance with the natural order (God's plan) then they are unnatural and hence immoral. This concept underpins Christian theology and morality but is elaborated by various other "laws" such as the Commandments and Scriptures that define the Christian moral compass.

Aspects of authority, power and control are relevant to the study of leadership. Why we choose certain political systems and how individuals behave in those systems are not only useful to understanding political leaders but why any leader emerges and succeeds.

It is apparent that political philosophy is inextricably bound up with social philosophy, as social philosophy is also concerned with man-made edifices in society and the manner in which these structures ought to operate. How something *ought* to be raises moral issues and so necessarily overlaps with moral philosophy.[67]

Moral philosophy

Moral philosophy is one of the main branches of pure philosophy – ethics. In its most succinct form it is concerned with enquiry into "how we ought to live". [68] Of central concern is "the effort to guide one's conduct by reason – that is, to do what there are the best reasons for doing – while giving equal weight to the interests of each individual affected by one's decision."[69] This philosophical area ponders the deeper questions of what constitutes the nature of right and wrong, virtue and vice, good and bad. The moral philosophy of a person fundamentally defines their value system.

Moral philosophy in leadership has obvious relevance. The evaluation of "good" leadership takes on a different dimension in the moral context, often referred to as a normative perspective of leadership. While good leadership is generally equated with effective leadership, that is, leadership that achieves a particular goal, moral philosophy would not only question whether the goal itself is morally justified but the manner in which the leader goes about leading the group. It is necessary to take into consideration both the leader's conduct and actions in relation to how the leader treats followers and the effect of their actions.

For our purposes, moral philosophy will be confined to the issues related to the formation of an individual's moral development. This will necessarily consider the role of religion and its influence in the formation of morality. As with the overlap between social and political philosophy, there is considerable overlap between moral and religious philosophy.

Religious philosophy

Some clarification of the term "religious philosophy" is required to distinguish it from the philosophy of religion. Religious philosophy enquires into the basis of a particular religious belief system, while philosophy of religion takes a more holistic, metaphysical perspective, such as whether God exists. Religious philosophy systems, such as Christianity, Buddhism, Islamism and so on, are within the domain of religious philosophy. Each of these religions has a specific philosophical perspective that influences the values and beliefs of its followers.

Religious philosophy is of interest to the enquiry into the formation of a person's attitude towards others because a person's religious beliefs contribute to the development of one's morals. If moral philosophy is relevant to the formation of beliefs and values, then religious philosophy must also be included. "In popular thinking, morality and religion are inseparable: people commonly believe that morality can only be understood in the context of religion."[70] Therefore, religious philosophy seeks to understand man's belief systems in the context of a particular doctrine. The influence of a particular religious philosophy is of concern, as we seek to understand why leaders behave in a certain way.

It is worth noting that all these philosophical areas overlap considerably.[71] Even though social philosophy is concerned with the interaction between individuals in society, if that interaction occurs between certain members of the polity then it becomes an aspect of political philosophy, such as the legitimate role of a leader and the role of the polity. If the leader's value system is called into question then the enquiry could come within the rubric of moral philosophy (if not legal philosophy). Similarly, if these values are a result of the leader's particular religious philosophy, then the philosophical enquiry could more correctly be a religious one. As a result, it can sometimes be unclear and imprecise to strictly apply one area of philosophy, but the fact remains that the influence will be philosophical in nature.

To provide some context to how philosophical perspectives contribute to the formation of worldview it is necessary to look at the different philosophies in a little more detail. While we may have developed a certain worldview it is of interest to understand its origins. What is important to recognise is that the influence of philosophy can take place through contact with those around us or through contact with different media. Our conception of our relationship with others is determined by the philosophical perspectives that act upon us, and this no less impacts on the formation of our leadership approach. The final piece of the model (at Figure 3) is the leadership approach – what is meant by leadership approach and what leadership approaches do leaders display? This is critical to the perception of our leadership as a good or ethical leader.

Leadership approaches

There are numerous leadership approaches in the leadership literature that identify with a range of different theories. Most people are aware of charismatic leadership or ethical leadership or even more specific manifestation such as Action Centred Leadership. In general, leadership theories are classified into broad approaches such as the trait approach or the behavioural approach and so on. One such example of the range of leadership theories and their classification is provided in Table 1. This table is not considered the authoritative classification of leadership theories but is one of the better examples of consolidating leadership theory into the types of leadership. Many texts on leadership refer to similar classifications used in this table as "leadership approaches" but will often include other approaches, such as the skills approach (based on a leader's skill) or the style approach (based on a leader's style).

I. Contextual		A. Trait	Tt Trait Theory	Ps Personality Approaches	II. Individual			IV. Normative	Cl Citizen Leader	Il Instrumental Approaches
Hi Historical Approaches										
Cu Cultural Approaches		B. Behavioral	Bv Behaviour Theory	Ob Organisational Behaviour					Sr Servant Leader	Tl Transformational Leadership
Cc Cross-cultural		C. Cognitive	Im Implicit Theory	At Attribution Theory	Mo Motivation Theory	Po Psychological Approaches			E Ethical Theory	Tg Transforming Leadership
Di Diversity Approaches			F Follower Approaches	Ro Role Theory	Ch Charismatic Theory	Ld Leader Development	Sf Self leadership		Va Values Approaches	Cg Change Theory
Od Organisational Approaches									Rv Revolutionary Approaches	
Gr Gender Approaches										

		III. Process							V. Method	
A. Contingency	Cy Contingency Theory	Si Situation Theory	De Decision Theory	Pg Path-Goal Theory					Qu Quantitative Method	
B. Transactional	Ic Idiosyncrasy Credits	Lm Leader/member Exchange	Tr Transactional Leadership						Ql Qualitative Method	
	Po Power Approaches	Co Communication Theory	In Influence Approaches	Gp Group Process	De Democratic Theory	Cr Conflict Resolution	Au Authority Issues		Pb Problem Based	
	Ls Leader Substitutes	St Strategic Approaches	Tm Team LDSF	Vi Vision Approaches	Sy Systems Theory	Pr Participatory Approaches	Aw Adaptive Work		Ar Action Research	

Goethals and Sorrensen (eds) (2006),
The quest for a general theory of leadership

Wren's periodic table of leadership theory

For the purpose of this book the following definition of leadership approach should be used when attempting to describe how a leader leads:

Leadership approach is the manner in which a person

consciously or unconsciously exercises leadership.

Briefly, it is *how* a person leads. This might take the form of a particular style, or an aspect of their personality, or through exercising a particular function, or empowering followers, or a combination of these approaches. However leadership is exercised, all leaders demonstrate a particular approach. The approach that manifests may be conscious, or it could emerge unconsciously. For example, a military commander may make a conscious effort to show concern and empathy for those under his or her command. This may be effective until conditions of duress, such as military combat, gives rise to a directive leadership approach which may emerge unconsciously, reflecting the needs of the circumstances, the personal attributes of the commander or their training. How they exercise their leadership will be perceived by those under their command. It might be efficient and "by the book" but is it good in the sense of being perceived normatively. A quick glance at Table 4 identifies that the normative theories have been seen as distinct classification. Yet we know that a leader can have combinations of these types of leadership, such as being an ethical transformational leader. In other words, a leader may exercise multiple characteristics and be described along lines that could fall into several leadership styles, approaches or other typographies. For our purposes what we are looking for is whether they are seen as demonstrating ethical leadership. To understand this we need to determine how our moral compass has developed and so an understanding of the origins of the concept is necessary.

Chapter 3 - **The good leader**

No area of human interaction is untouched by some form of philosophical thought, and the same can be said of leadership. Philosophical leadership theory has developed for millennia, from the early Greek philosophers to modern day.[72] This chapter will trace its development to highlight its influence on society from ancient to early modern times. It does not cover every philosopher or even some of the most eminent of recent times but provides a perspective of the influence of philosophical theory on the development of leadership theory. The range of philosophies covered is relevant to the era in which the subject leaders (soldier statesmen) lived.

Early philosophy

One of the most prominent early Greek philosophers, Plato (424-347 BCE),[73] demonstrates an initial focus on leadership in several of his works, but in particular the *Republic* (c.375BCE),[74] where he explores the interaction between the individual, society and the state. Plato was "concerned above all with discovering conditions that are conducive to social integration and equilibrium".[75] Each member of society was a valuable and independent contributor. Every person would thus perform a function that was of use to the general welfare of all. Such a society would also need someone to lead it, and so Plato recommended that the state be ruled by a philosopher king: one who had the ability to comprehend eternal truths through a desire for knowledge.[76]

The philosopher king was required to have training in a variety of areas; ranging from the intellectual to the artistic.[77] This would give them the mental acuity to deal with the rigours of governing, and an ability to appreciate "forms".[78] This ability required a leader to determine what most benefited society. To Plato, the ultimate goal of leadership was to provide happiness or the "good" for society.[79] Only the ruling class, the Guardians, were perceived as being able to attain the wisdom to understand these forms and hence the needs of society.[80]

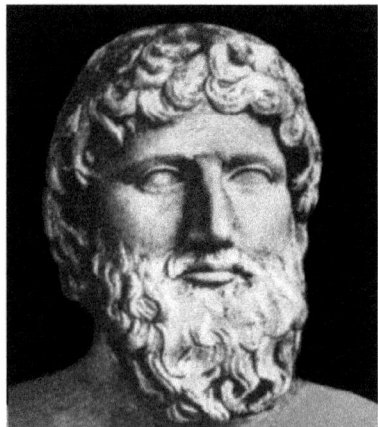

This view of leadership regarded the ability to lead as an inherent quality. It was considered that only particular people had the necessary traits for rule, although even these people required further training to assume the mantle of state rule.[81] In *The Republic* Plato describes how the ruling class are drawn from those

> Until philosophers are kings, or the kings and princes of this world have the spirit and power of philosophy, and political greatness and wisdom meet as one, and those commoner natures who pursue either to the exclusion of the other are compelled to stand aside, cities will never have rest from their evils – nor the human race..
>
> Plato - Republic

that possess the necessary attributes as there are "...some natures who ought to study philosophy and be the leaders in the state; and others who are not born to be philosophers, and are meant to be followers rather than leaders."[82] In order to rule effectively a Guardian was expected to regard the greater good as "...their special concern – the sort of concern that is felt for something so closely bound up with oneself that its interests and fortunes, for good or ill, are held identical to one's own".[83]

Plato proposed that social harmony would result from the citizen's compliance with the rules of justice - as determined by the Guardians. All of these aspects required a form of unspoken compliance – a social contract. [84] The social contract in *The Republic* requires citizens to forego their self-interest for the greater good. Leadership was also conceptualised by Plato as a matter of establishing the bases for the rights and obligations between the state and its citizens – a transactional exchange. [85]

Like Plato, his most famous student, Aristotle (384-322 BCE), also supported leadership traits in his seminal work, *Politics (c.350BCE)*.[86] Aristotle identified specific qualities that need to exist in leaders in order for them to be effective. The most important being the quality of virtue.[87] Aristotle proposed the nobility as the most appropriate class to lead society as they would possess such attributes: "...those who are sprung from better ancestors are likely to be better men, for nobility is excellence of race".[88] This class would continue to produce suitably adept leaders and create a natural distinction between leaders and followers: the concept of aristocracy being immediately apparent. Such views were supported by his prestigious clients, notably the King of Macedonia when he engaged Aristotle to tutor his son Alexander (later to become "the Great"). Leaders w ere seen as a distinct and entitled breed:[89] "...from the hour of their birth, some are marked out for subjection, others for rule..."[90] This presented an important departure from Plato's preferred class of leaders, who derived their status from knowledge, as Aristotle was somewhat sceptical that the philosopher-king persona could exist.[91] What is evident in Aristotle's thinking is the presumption of heredity or even the greater being perception of leadership, whereas Plato advocates environmental conditioning being able to produce better leadership.

Aristotle also considers the attributes of society as a necessary consideration in the type of leadership exercised.[92] His view of the suitability of a particular person, or class, for rule is moderated by the needs of the state[93]. As different states developed different political systems they therefore had different needs for leadership

> Stoic belief [was] that the law of the state should conform with the rational and moral norms embodied in natural laws, for adherence to such rationally formulated law creates a moral bond among citizens.

"for governments differ in kind...we must therefore look at the elements of which the state is composed...".[94] The need to consider context as a factor for good leadership is evident. In only a relatively short period there is clear evidence of a shift from a trait based leadership conception to a trait/contextual one. This observation mirrors the development of trait theory in contemporary leadership research, which moved from a trait-based perspective to a situational one.

To Aristotle the ultimate purpose of social/political leadership was to bring happiness[95] or "good" to society.[96] While this position of serving the "good" of society concurs with the Platonic position it also shifts the rectitude in favour of the ruled as "..political society exists for the sake of noble actions, and not of mere companionship..."[97] In this context a political leader was required to have "...(1)...loyalty to the established constitution (2) the greatest administrative capacity (3) virtue and justice..."[98] Aristotle demonstrates a clear move towards situational dependencies and an understanding of the importance of the role requirements of leadership.

An important philosophical doctrine to emerge in Greece around 300BCE was Stoicism. Originated by Zeno of Citium it espoused a deterministic view of the self; one of rationality and reason over emotion and feelings.[99] Early Stoic philosophy encompassed several areas of philosophical thought but, over time, the ethical aspects became predominant, especially among the Roman stoics.[100]

From a Stoic perspective, leadership was a way of life,[101] based upon a non-materialistic and monistic philosophy. The Stoic leader was considered a sage (*sapiens*) – equanimous, self-controlled, rational and lucid. This type of person would naturally be unperturbed by the tumult of the situation around them, making decisions without passion (*apatheia*), and able to act in the interest of all.

This conception of leadership indicated that leadership was based on character or virtuous conduct *(virtus)*.[102] *Virtus* was governed by natural laws which subordinated emotions and pleasures of the body to the *summum bonum* (supreme ideal) consisting of wisdom (moral insight), courage, self-control and justice (upright dealings).[103]

One such Stoic, Marcus Tullius Cicero (106-43BCE), witnessed and tracked the shift in stoic thinking corresponding with the movement of Rome from a democratic republic to imperial aristocracy. Cicero was a Roman senator and sought initially to become more active in the governance of the Republic but instead left politics and chose to become a philosopher – a wise choice considering that his political opponent was Julius Caesar. He regarded the Roman Republic as an ideal form of political environment in which a particular type of leader would succeed.[104] This ideal is revealed in several of Cicero's most prominent works - *De Oratore (On the Orator)*(55BC),[105] *De Re Publica (On the Republic)* (51BC),[106] and *De Officiis (On Duties)*(44BC). Much in common with the attributes of Plato's philosopher-king,[107] the stoic leader is presented as a pious sage. This type of leader should have the traits of intelligence, persuasiveness and dominance which could be achieved through knowledge of logic, rhetoric and philosophy.[108]

Cicero's philosophy on the role of the civic leader is explored in *De Re Publica*, which parallels Plato's *Republic*,[109] where "Cicero delineates the institutional framework behind his conception of leadership..."[110] Underpinning the constitutional analysis of the Roman Republic are the ethical aspects
of stoicism.[111]

As with the early Greek philosopher's perception of civic leadership being a social good, Cicero also advocates "...the happiness of his fellow citizens is the proper study of the ruler of the commonwealth... for a ruler ought be one who can perfect this"[112] Follower consideration is again given primacy, as is the ethical responsibility of the leader.

Ciceros works display a sentiment of selfless public service in *De Officiis* promoting the ideal that leaders should "further the interests of all".[113] In addition to the former qualities identified in *De Oratore*, Cicero advocates that a leader should possess courtesy, forbearance, circumspection and justice:[114] all stoic qualities.

> For the administration of the government, like the office of a trustee, must be conducted for the benefits of those entrusted to one's care, not of those to whom it is entrusted.
>
> Cicero *De Officiis*

The resultant leader is a sage who serves rather than leads, for it is through service that others are most benefited.

The ethical aspects of leadership were pursued by another significant stoic philosopher to emerge towards the end of the Julian period: Lucius Annaeus Seneca (4bce-65CE). Seneca wrote extensively on the influence of stoic beliefs in *De Clementia* (*On Mercy*)(56 CE) and *De Beneficiis* (*On Benefits*) (63CE). In these works he identifies the "ethical themes within the context of political leadership".[115] His works spiritualised and humanised stoicism when people were looking for greater meaning in their lives.[116] It was unsurprising that the Roman public had lost faith in its leaders given that they were some of the most tyrannical in its history – Caligula, Claudius and Nero.

Seneca promotes stoic thought in *De Beneficiis* where "...the causes of things falls under natural philosophy, arguments under rational, and actions under moral."[117] The coverage of the actions of happiness, virtue, anger, judgement and clemency provides the reader with a perspective of "proper" behaviour according to stoic tradition. Ultimately, the good of the whole transcended the good of the individual.[118] A leader could only operate according to natural laws that elevated the needs of others above their own. These natural laws "entail duties, not rights".[119] A leader must also operate in the context of the situation, choosing the most appropriate position for the circumstance.[120]

Middle age philosophy

The decline of the Roman Empire was attended by the rise of Christianity that became the new dominant social force in western civilisation. One of the most influential philosophers of the new era was Augustine of Hippo (*a.k.a* St Augustine) (354-430CE). Of his many substantial treatises, *De Civitate Dei* (Of the City of God)(*c.*410BCE) is credited with the basis for the establishment of the church system and the relationship between church and state.[121]

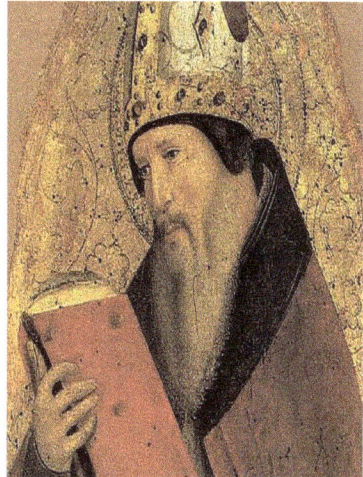

Augustine's philosophy was heavily influence by Plato.[122] He concurred with the Platonic perception that those who rule do so from a sense of obligation to the state, and those that follow from a sense of obedience.[123] However, while Plato proposed that the ability to perceive "forms" (such as truth, beauty and good) differentiated leaders from followers, Augustine proposed that a leader's ability could only come from God.[124] The ecclesiastic structure established a political and social order based on deference to God via the clergy.[125]

A ruler, according to Augustine, who acted in accordance with the "city of God" (God's law) and not the "city of man" would be sanctioned by the Church. The ruler from the city of man was apt to be self-interested and corrupt, while those who rule in accordance with the principles of the "city of God" did so in the interests of others; such individuals were the true and virtuous leaders that we should follow. This was not merely because of their virtuous qualities but because of their focus on followers.[126] The moral philosophy of the Christian faith of Augustine demonstrates the adoption of a distinctly deontological ethic: which would await the arrival of Immanuel Kant for further exposition.

> He should be...slow to punish, ready to pardon; if they apply that punishment as necessary to government and defence of the Republic and not in order to gratify their own enmity...if they compensate with the lenity of mercy and the liberality of benevolence...and if they do all these things not through ardent desire of empty glory, but through love of eternal felicity...
>
> St Augustine *De Civitate Dei*

In the sixth century Pope Gregory I (Gregory the Great) (540-604CE) commissioned a work that would be one of the most important ecclesiastical texts in Europe – *Liber Regulae Pastoralis (c.*590CE*).*[127] Although Pope Gregory is not widely recognised as a philosopher this text's contribution to the development of leadership philosophy cannot be discounted. Initially written as a conduct guide for bishops[128] it provides a detailed account of the behaviour required to lead. Gregory concentrated his attention on the character and behaviours required to lead successfully[129] with a description of the type of virtues necessary.

Gregory commends the clergy to be "pure in thought" and "a leader in action".[130] There are clear overtone's of St Augustine's hand in Gregory's work but Gregory takes Augustine's advice for clerical virtue further in prescribing particular characteristics and behaviours. Importantly, *Liber Regulae Pastoralis* identifies that there needs to be consistency between what one preaches and the way that one acts, as "no one does more harm in the Church than one who has the name and rank of sanctity while he acts perversely".[131] Authenticity in leadership is clearly evident in this advice.[132]

Towards the end of the Middle Ages philosophers began to focus on the importance of reason as an adjunct to faith.[133] One philosopher who focussed on this dichotomy was Thomas Aquinas (1224-1274CE).[134]

Aquinas saw it perfectly reasonable that the socio/political structure be based on the rationality of God.[135] The rationality of the person to whom you served was accepted: God was the most rational, followed by the King/Pope, the Lord of the manor, head of the family and so on.[136] Bearing a strong resemblance with Aristotle's philosophy,[137] he proposed that there was a natural leader and a natural follower which was based on a disparity in intellect and reason. This natural order was rational – the social order was the order of the universe[138] - rule by the most rational.

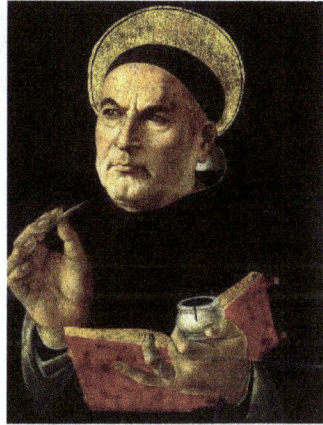

Aquinas' thoughts on leadership are further refined in *On Kingship (On the government of rulers)* (c.1260) which predominantly advocates the responsibilities of leaders.[139] Aquinas proposes that unity is the prime objective of leadership for without it there is chaos. Whether a leader is good or bad is a matter of circumstance. Aquinas presumed natural (good) leaders to be endowed with high intellect but poor rulers the result of wicked followers for "...it is by divine permission that wicked men receive power to rule as punishment for sin...".[140]

> For those who excel in intellect are naturally rulers, whereas those who are less intelligent but strong in body, seem made by nature for service.
>
> Thomas Aquinas
> *Summa Contra Gentiles*

Apart from intellect[141] Aquinas advocated that leaders should also possess wisdom and virtue.[142] Intellect was assumed to be based on reason (a quality derived from God) while wisdom and virtue are derived from the knowledge of, and faith in, God's law. Although rationality was considered a divinely invested quality, Aquinas displays a shift from the views of Aristotle in relation to virtue. Whereas Aristotle proposed that virtue is an inherent trait of good leaders, Aquinas proposed that certain "noble" qualities (similar to virtue) could be acquired.[143] This could be done through the acceptance of God and the teachings of the Church.[144] The devotion to religious prelates [145] thus enabled one to achieve virtue. The importance of this observation identifies the recognition of the development of leadership ability, as opposed to it being considered inherent.

Just as the works of Aquinas had attempted to reconcile Aristotelian philosophy with Christianity, the works of Ptolemy of Lucca (1236-1327) attempted to reconcile Aristotelian politics and government.[146] Largely in the shadow of Aquinas, Ptolemy co-wrote *On the Government of Rulers* (c.1300), often attributed solely to Aquinas.[147] Yet his most significant work, *A short determination of the jurisdiction of the Roman Empire* (c.1301), deals mainly with the internal structure and function of government.[148] With respect to leadership, Ptolemy was an advocate of personal traits tying character to birth and geography.[149] Consistent with Ancient Greek/Roman conceptions Ptolemy advocated the "common good" as being the rationale for good government.[150] It was incumbent upon a leader to transform society and provide the necessary moral and intellectual inspiration to followers to lead better lives, and thereby enhance the common wealth.

This perspective was adopted by Italian physician and scholar Marsilius of Padua (1275-1342). Marsilius was something of an agitator. In his time the Roman Catholic Church still had incredible power over the state. The Pope regularly waged wars to ensure that its dominions were maintained as was the case in the time of Marsilius that saw him produce the treatise *Defensor Pacis (Defender of the Peace)* (1324), which criticised the role of the Pope in territorial acquisition. Marsilius was also fervently in favour of unfettered rule by the people[151] and in this regard he proclaimed that leaders should be accountable to the people.[152] Diverging from the philosophy of Aquinas, Marsilius advocated that leadership was not a matter of religious prelates but the result of behaviours and attributes that contributed to good government. In *Defensor Pacis* he sought to reconcile the conundrum of whether a competent civic ruler should rule over those more entitled through virtue.[153] In other words, should those most qualified to rule a society be drawn from the most capable or the most virtuous? A competent person may have no virtuous qualities, and may even be despotic, yet they may be the most competent person to lead. Such a comment was an affront to the Roman pontiff who naturally viewed that divine mandate had given him the right to rule, and of course that very fact meant he was virtuous. This revolutionary perception of leadership acknowledged the requirements for the skills and abilities of the leader with respect to practical ends, rather than it being based on God given qualities, or the adherence to Church/God's law.[154] This sort of thinking challenged the supremacy of the church and suggested that rulers were entitled to rule not because of a divine mandate but because they possessed the necessary abilities.

This shift in thinking opened the door for a closer analysis of what constituted effective civic leadership. One work that did this better than any other in this period was *Il Principe* (*The Prince*) (1513) written by Niccolo Machiavelli (1469-1527). Machiavelli was an inductionist - his belief was that human being's behaviours are constant and can be predicted.[155] As a result, a leader's behaviour can be gleaned from an understanding of the situation. This principle permeates *The Prince* where Machiavelli demonstrates how a ruler maintains authority in a treacherous environment. *The Prince* clearly identifies the importance of behavioural contingencies[156] where Machiavelli prescribes that leaders should possess chameleon-like qualities to suit the occasion. Rather than

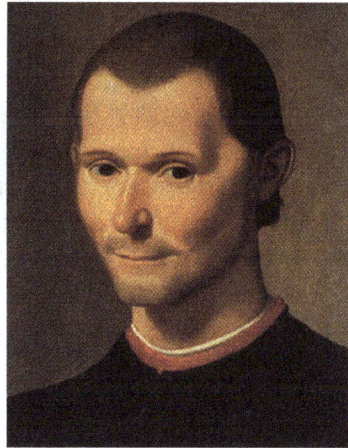

> ...a prince must know how to make good use of the nature of the beast, he should choose from among the beasts the fox and the lion; for the lion cannot defend itself from traps and the fox cannot protect itself from wolves. It is therefore necessary to be a fox in order to recognize the traps and a lion in order to frighten the wolves.
>
> Niccolo Machiavelli *The Prince*

proposing the universality of traits or behaviours, such as intellect or virtuous conduct, Machiavelli proposed that a leader should adapt to the situation.[157] He should appear virtuous[158] yet act in his own interests.

35

Effective leadership resulted from the ability of the leader to interpret the situation,[159] with the end result that a leader could ultimately fail under unfavourable circumstances: "...it is not necessary for the Prince to have all the above-mentioned qualities...should it become necessary ...he will be able and know how to change to the contrary"[160], indicating that a leader should alter their behaviour "according to the ways the winds of fortune and the changeability of affairs require him."[161]

Machiavelli's works[162] also introduced another important attribute of leadership - the focus on power.[163] Machiavelli's proposed that a leader should do whatever is necessary to maintain power.[164] Even though power is self-serving, a ruler must maintain their power as followers (in fact anyone) could not be relied upon. Followers are pejoratively described in general as "miserable creatures"[165] who could not be trusted; hence self-interest is the only justification for conduct. Such conduct has become known as Machiavellian and is seen as an undesirable quality in human nature, notably leadership. The philosophy of the era had swung away from virtue towards legitimate authority based on the acquisition and maintenance of power.

Modern philosophy

Following the theme of power, and in the tradition of the enlightenment, the rationalist philosopher Thomas Hobbes (1588-1679) sought to apply the scientific method to human affairs.[166] Hobbes proposed what could be described as the first social scientific approach to leadership, based upon a holistic observation of mankind in the political context.[167] In this environment man competed against man, and the only way to survive was through power over others.[168] His perspectives on its importance demonstrates a continuation of Machiavellian thinking. Ultimately, Hobbes analysis of the socio-political context sought to find a way of reconciling the constant state of conflict within and between nations.[169] To him people acted purely out of self-interest and it was man's natural tendency to meet his own needs and wants as "...every man has a right to every thing.".[170]

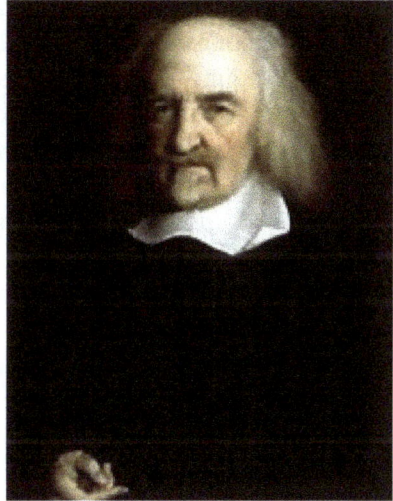

In *Leviathan* (1651) Hobbes postulated that a new political relationship needed to exist, and not one based on the obeisance to King and/or God. Hobbes proposed that the state or commonwealth - in Hobbes terminology "the Leviathan" should assume the role of the moderating force.[171] To co-exist peacefully there needed to be a "contract" between the state and its citizens. This *social* contract would assume all men as equal. They would transfer their rights to harm others to a particular person or group of persons,[172] generally the state, but personified in the sovereign, and that only it had the capacity to enforce justice.[173] In return, the state (the sovereign) owed society protection, and if it could not then society had the right to replace it.[174] The relationship between leaders and followers became one of rights and obligations. The transactional perspective of leadership echoed Platonic notions by placing man back at the centre of self determination.

Not everyone saw the socio-political environment in the same extreme terms as Hobbes. John Locke (1632-1704) took quite a different position on the social contract. Locke advocated a form of liberalist social contract in his *Treatise on Civil Government* (1690). To Locke, people sought to live in peace and it was natural to form societies for the protection of the peace and the maintenance of order.[175] The motive of his social contract was not a fear of anarchy but a desire for peace, where one acted with beneficial self-interest in the sense that no one else was harmed. There were no individual leaders in this conception of society as the parliament served the people in "a state … of equality, wherein all power and jurisdiction is reciprocal, no one hav[ing] more than another."[176]

A similar notion of the social contract was espoused by French philosopher Jean Jacques Rousseau (1712-1778). In his famous treatise, *Le Contrat Social* (1762), Rousseau disagreed with the Hobbesian view of man's bestiality and Locke's perspective of people as selfish and greedy.[177] He also refuted the assertion that reason underpins man's nature.[178] To him, the natural order was not natural at all – it was a social order, a convention – an artificial conception devised by man.[179] Rousseau's social contract is characterised as communitarian.[180] Rather than hand over one's liberty to another class in return for protection Rousseau advocated that "each of us places his person and all power in common under the supreme direction of the *general will*".[181]

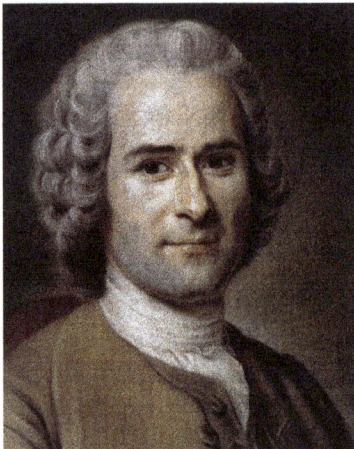

Although not explicit, Rousseau alludes to those that are better able to interpret the general will. Unlike Locke's

Man is born free, yet everywhere he is in chains. Those who believe themselves to be the masters of others cease not to be

38

idealised leaderless state, Rousseau's society necessitates leaders that "feel themselves capable, as it were, of changing human nature, of transforming each individual".[182] The leader must not only be able to understand the needs of the society but be able to elevate it. This transformational nature of the Rousseau social contract occurs in the change that is required for "natural man" to become "social man". Rousseau makes "an explicit appeal to the notion of transformation",[183] and in so doing empowers the polity by instituting a morally binding agreement. This form of social contract augments the transactional nature of previous contractarian dogma[184] and places the state as a function of the whole of society, not just for the benefit of a class or being.[185] *Le Contrat Social* was highly influential in French society of its time. Being some 25 years prior to the French Revolution its concepts played no small part in the disaffection of the people oppressed by the monarchy.

Some regard the next philosopher as perhaps the greatest influence on western thought. German philosopher Immanuel Kant (1724-1804) rejected the notion of natural rights and once again returned to the conception of rationality.[186] In *The Metaphysics and Morals*[187] (1797) Kant proposed that morality is based on reason and that every person is of "equal worth and deserving of equal respect".[188] To behave rationally is to act out of a purpose of universality and consistency.

This type of conduct is described as normative (in the philosophical context of ethics), which obliges one to act for the greater good.[189] A leader could therefore be obliged to act in a certain way out of duty;[190] to follow the course of what "ought to be done".[191] The appeal of acting in the interests of others forces man and society to transcend their selfish needs and act in the interests of all.[192] The result being that the responsibility to others is both cause and effect.

Man possessed reason and free will, but Kant asserted that there was a moral obligation,[193] not a divine directive, to behave correctly. Kant pro-

> Act only according to a maxim by which you can at the same time will that it shall become a general law
>
> Kant *Metaphysic of Morals*

posed that moral conduct is independent of action (the categorical imperative): there should not be an end when considering what is right (the hypothetical imperative). The man who behaves ethically is a man of virtue and acts out of good conscience to behave so. The leader that adheres to such a principle ought to be followed. While Rousseau had advocated a leader-type based around the leader's ability to elevate followers to a different state of intellectual realisation, Kant's leader type achieves this transformational effect as a result of their moral conduct.

The rational conduct aspect of social behaviour ushered in a morally egalitarian notion of leadership and followership.[194] Kant's ethical theory (deontological ethics) is predicated on the basis that only features of actions themselves are relevant to morality - actions are right or wrong independent of their consequences.[195] Rather than leaders justifying their actions on the basis of acting in the interests of others (altruism) the actions themselves are called into question under Kantian ethics. Moreover, while a leader acts in the interests of others, so should all people in a rational society.

This notion was extended by Jeremy Bentham (1748-1832) in *An Introduction to the Principles of Morals and Legislation* (1789) [196] under the principle of utilitarianism. [197] This principle advocated that "the greatest happiness of the greatest number"[198] should be the objective of any action which impacts others. As such, the welfare of all persons must be considered in determining whether a law or action is morally justified. [199]

Bentham proposed that the law is society's moderating force - the extension of the sovereign will (the state).[200] The ultimate purpose of the law must contribute to the overall pleasure or happiness of society.[201] To Bentham, man's actions were driven by the pursuit of pleasure or the avoidance of pain.[202]

Bentham's works followed, and echoed the ideals of, the French revolution. In a similar manner so did the writings of John Stuart Mill (1806-1873), who focussed on the very same aspects that the revolution had achieved – liberty and equality.[203] Mill adopted a liberal, egalitarian approach to social harmony and proposed that the role of government was for the promotion of utility;[204] once again reinforcing the significance of utilitarianism.[205] Mill was to take the ideology first conceptualised by Bentham in an effort to bring about the "quiet revolution" in England: representative government for the bourgeoisie.[206] In *On Liberty* (1859), Mill proposed that the ultimate moral end of society is for the satisfaction of the needs and wants of all members - or in other words, social happiness.[207]

In order to achieve this state, the body politic needed to be included in the governance of society - once again showing an inclusive approach to the role of followers in the decision-making process. Mill proposed that all levels of society needed to be educated so that they may better appreciate and contribute to social improvement.[208] In this way Mill also recognised the importance of follower individuality; a society of diverse individuals which had been developed to their full potential would likely result in a better society overall.[209]

Mill still saw the necessity for strong leadership, which he detailed in his follow-up treatise: *Consideration on Representative Government* (1861). Without prescribing a particular class or person for the leading role, Mill nonetheless advocated that certain individuals were more fitted to lead than others.[210] Such individuals possessed two types of competence – instrumental and moral. The former being "...the ability to discover the best means to certain ends and the means to identify ends that satisfy individuals' interests as they perceive them"[211] and the latter being "...the ability to discern ends that are intrinsically superior for individuals and society"[212]. Utility was not just an end in itself but grounded in moral justification: in a nutshell - the ends justify the means if the ends are morally justified. Consistent with Kant, leadership was a quest to deliver morally acceptable outcomes but from an ethical perspective the consequence and not the action are Mills focus.

The ideal expression of leadership was to be found in practical form in America according to Alexis de Tocqueville in his work *Democracy in America* (1835). To him the American society was the embodiment of equality.[213] Tocqueville saw a distinct difference between the society of Europe, under its fading aristocratic regimes, and the emerging democratic new world of America. Individualism and entrepreneurship marked the new world order where majority rule became the new political force. In such an environment leadership acted to elevate and educate the citizenry.[214]

In a society where the power of its leaders rests on the power of the people Tocqueville saw the leader's role as being one of guiding and transforming them.[215] The elevation of aspirational qualities, and the need to focus on social mores, underpins the nature of contemporary transformational leadership and is brought about through the recognition of the collective power of followers. Unlike previous conceptions of contractual rights and obligations Tocqueville identifies the need for leadership to elevate higher order needs in followers. The leaders that would do this would be drawn from the "higher classes" of society as the lower classes would be less likely to place the interests of the state above their own personal self-interests.[216]

Where the early contractarian perception saw man acting in his own selfish interest for peace or security, Tocqueville proposed that in a stable society man would still act out of self-interest but based on materialism and the desire for prestige.[217] It was a leader's role to understand the nature of

> To educate democracy – if possible to revive its beliefs; to purify its mores; to regulate its impulses; to substitute, little by little, knowledge of affairs of inexperience and understanding of true interests for blind instinct; to adapt government to its time and place; to alter it to fit circumstances and individuals – this is the primary duty imposed on the leaders of society today.
>
> A de Tocqueville *Democracy in America*

this self-interest and so realign base needs with higher order aspirations.[218] Tocqueville describes this in his doctrine of "self-interest properly understood".[219] He acknowledges that people (Americans) still acted in their own interests but in a form which could be described as enlightened self-interest. Similar in nature to altruism, a person will "...sacrifice a portion of their time and wealth for the good of the state"[220] so that one's interests are served by satisfying society's interests. As such, a key task of leadership in America is to teach people to be virtuous.[221] The leader is a person who transforms society by aligning their individual needs with that of the state and society at large.

The effects of the demise of the old order in Europe also influenced the thinking of German philosopher George Freidrich Hegel (1770-1831). Around the time of his writing, Hegel observed that the autocratic *ancien regime* was being replaced by the meritocratic system promoted by the French as a result of the Napoleonic wars.[222] As a result, senior positions in the military were no longer the sole domain of aristocrats.[223] The new regime accorded promotion to men of talent, in several spheres, which paved the way for a complete change in the way in which society functioned. Sharing much in common with the views of Tocqueville, Hegel saw the rise of individual rights and the elevation of the common man as central to an understanding of society.[224]

In *The scientific way of treating natural law* (1803) Hegel investigates moral philosophy and comments on the role of society's leaders, while in the *Phenomenology of spirit* (1807) he touches on the idealised role of leadership, and then refines the relationship between leader and the state in the *Elements of the Philosophy of Right* (1822). He rejects the Hobbesian perspective that society emanates from a desire to resolve conflict, and also challenges Rousseau's perspective that society is a pact for the co-operative production of goods.[225] To Hegel, society is not merely about survival or co-operation but a quest for recognition.[226] Man exists in society for human interaction and seeks recognition for social identity.[227]

As a result Hegel rejected the edifices of previous philosopher's approaches to society and politics as overly complex.[228] In place of such conceptions as a social contract or moral obligations Hegel proposed that society consisted of subsets of different groups that had strong connections between each other.[229] The governance of such a society required a collaborative, participatory approach, reliant upon the involvement of all the "estates".[230] Hegel's approach is one that can be classified as communitarian.[231]

Hegel also proposed that leaders were a special breed.[232] A leader was perceived as being a person with innate abilities.[233] In fact, Hegel saw that leaders had to be almost "hero-like" in order to quell the woes of society - the greater the challenge – the greater the man. The ideal leader is someone who is capable of performing the role of elevating others to a higher state.[234] Hegel clearly adopts a trait based perspective of transformational leadership where the leader, through their innate abilities, raises the consciousness of society. A society's leader (namely the monarch) is a private person who fulfils a social or historical need,[235] a Machiavellian leader who fulfils a Platonic ideal.[236] Such a person carries the spirit of the times[237] as they are able to reflect society's needs and character.[238] It was the leaders responsibility to ensure that the *Sittlichkeit* (morality) of society was maintained, even if it had to be enforced.[239] Divine right was no longer the source of the leader's authority.[240] Hegel also saw the role of conflict in society and politics as essential for the raising of consciousness.[241] Leadership was seen as being able to resolve conflicting information by presenting an acceptable perspective in such a way as to align the views of the polity.

The latter part of the nineteenth century and early twentieth century saw an upsurge in the rights of the working class.[242] The competing needs of industrialists and workers gave rise to new social, political and economic order. One philosopher who turned his attention to this new environment was Adam Smith: widely acknowledged as the progenitor of classical economics through his famous treatise - *An enquiry into the nature and causes of the wealth of nations* (1776). Despite his wide recognition as the father of modern economics Smith's background was as a moral philosopher.[243]

In *The theory of moral sentiments (1759)*[244] Smith commences with the proposition that even though man is inherently driven by self-interest he is also a sensate being who shares the pleasure and pain of his fellow man:[245] "...this correspondence of the sentiments of others with our own appears to be a cause of pleasure, and the want of it a cause of pain...",[246] such that, when we increase another's pleasure, or reduce their pain, we consequently do the same in ourselves. This is achieved through the mechanism of what Smith describes as *sympathy,* a form of compassion towards others.[247] Increasing another person's pleasure or decreasing their suffering leads to greater affection, approval and social good.[248]

Against this backdrop is Smith's much lauded economic opus. This work was a visionary attempt to alter the authoritarian, centralised nature of mercantilism[249] to a society which empowered the lower classes, especially the working class, for Smith's concerns were *primarily* ethical, and the economic system he devised was the *means* to achieve a more moral, ethical, and just social order.[250] Far from just being a treatise on the formation of a capitalist economy, *The Wealth of Nations* is Smith's attempt to reconcile the nature of self-interest with social justice.[251] Smith proposes that the best leaders are moral agents free of vested interests.[252] Church leaders and politicians are censured for being too heavily focussed on self-promotion, with church leaders often "willing to lead a life that often adds hypocrisy to moral shallowness, thus people whose characters are even worse than the people that find politics appealing."[253] Business leaders fare no better as being motivated to "deceive and even to oppress"[254] the public because of their "mean rapacity, their monopolising spirit"[255] and hence are unsuitable to lead society.[256] While Smith prefers to place power in the hands of government, his ideal polity is a form of egalitarian communitarianism which bases itself on the sympathetic connection between all members of society.

> Because human beings are built to attend one another as individuals, and as individuals whose emotions and needs vary greatly in accordance with minute differences in the circumstances, they can best care for one another, monitor and scrutinize one another's behaviour, and lead each other to aspire to standards of propriety and virtue, in small, close-knit communities.
>
> A Smith *The theory of moral sentiments*

The only leader that appears to have the interests of society at heart is the impartial sovereign; [257] one who possesses the qualities which Smith advocates in *A Theory of Moral Sentiments*.[258] It is only when compassion and sympathy for our fellow man are taken into account do we act to increase pleasure and reduce suffering of those around us, and indeed, as leaders, those who follow us.[259] Smith promotes consideration for others and personal interaction: the type of leadership which focuses on followers in an ethical context. This conception of the cognitive affectation and awareness that exists between leaders and followers touches on the principles that underpin emotional intelligence, a theme that would receives significant attention a century later.

Less optimistic about the nature of individuals were the German philosophers Karl Marx (1818-1883) and Friedrich Engels (1820-1895). They viewed the social order basically in terms of a class struggle.[260] Under this conception one's claim to leadership is the consequence of economic necessity and a function of historical context. Just as feudalism had been replaced by capitalism, they advocated that capitalism would in turn be replaced by the natural order of a classless state, as detailed in their *Communist Manifesto* (1848).[261] Their views echoed the communitarian perspectives of Rousseau and Kant that the benefits of society

should be for all rather than a privileged few. Marx saw that the role of the leader was to agitate and enlighten the working class to a higher state of equality and freedom.[262] Leaders would therefore act as change-agents.

With strong similarities to Rousseau's transformative leaders, Marxist leaders would act to enlighten the masses and elevate their awareness. The requirement for leadership was predicated on the assumption that followers were seen as lacking the necessary understanding of a better state of being. Leaders, on the other hand, understood Communist ideals and had the right – and duty – to lead the masses to the new world.[263] Leadership was not just a right, it was an obligation. Leadership thus transcends inherent traits and behaviour, and becomes a duty owed to both the state and mankind.

Men make their history themselves, but not as yet with a collective will according to a collective plan or even in a definite, delimited given society. Their aspirations clash, and for that very reason all such societies are governed by necessity, the complement and form of appearance of which is accident. The necessity which here asserts itself athwart all accident is again ultimate economic necessity. This is where the so called great men come in for treatment. That such and such a man and precisely that man arises at a particular time in a particular country is, of course, pure chance. But cut him out and there will be a demand for a substitute, and this substitute will be found, good or bad, but in the long run he will be found. That Napoleon, just that particular Corsican, should have been the military dictator whom the French Republic, exhausted by its own warfare, had rendered necessary, was chance; but that, if a Napoleon had been lacking, another would have filled the place, if proved by the fact that the man was always found as soon as he became necessary: Caesar, Augustus, Cromwell, etc

F Engels Correspondence with Borgius

The transformative effect of leadership was given further attention by by Freidrich Nietzsche (1844-1900). His concept of the ubermensch (super-man) identifies one who, through sheer personality and will, could over-come all obstacles.[264] This leader type would inspire followership by be-coming an exemplar to others of what human beings were capable of if they overcame the mind-forged manacles of self and society.[265] The leader establishes his position by example for others to emulate and they thereby become leaders themselves.

The dyad of leader and follower was therefore temporary to Nietzsche.[266] Once followers had been elevated then they too would exercise leadership. This concept shares much in common with the Marxist perspective of the role of leaders elevating the proletariat to an enlightened state.

A leader thus possesses an ability to el-evate others through their charismatic effect. We see examples of charismatic leadership in *Thus Spake Zarathustra (1885)* which identifies the emulation and devotion to one with an exemplary characteristic.[267] Nietzsche proposed that such leaders were born to lead, they possessed the traits that make them the ideal person to follow.[268]

> What persuades the living creature to obey and to command and to practise obedience even in com-manding? The will of the weaker persuades it to serve the stronger; ... Overcome, you higher men, the petty virtues, the petty prudences, the sand-grain discretion, the ant-swarm insanity...How much still is possible! ...So *learn* to laugh bey-ond yourselves! Lift up your hearts, you fine dancers, high! higher! And do not forget to laugh well.
>
> F Nietzsche Thus Spake Zarathustra

The requisite traits for such leadership is based on the su-periority of strength; be it intel-ligence, courage, indefatigabil-ity or whatever characteristic other lesser humans do not possess, especially in times of turmoil.

To Nietzsche, man was not equal, and nature was not for-giving. Man's objective is to overcome nature and other men. This Darwinian perspective that only the strong survive gives rise to man's will to power:[269] the drive to overcome and succeed.

Leadership was about achieving this state, a state of superiority over the weak - the overman.[270] In this model followers were simply the result of superior individuals rising above them. Modern leadership perspectives based on power, authority and control share much in common with the Nietzschean conception of leadership. However, his philosophy is highly idiosyncratic and certainly not representative of the norm. Much like Machiavelli, he expresses a specific perspective based on the conditions of the time.

Following in a similar vein to Nietszsche and Marx, the German philosopher Max Weber (1864-1920) observed that self-interest[271] was at the core of human behaviour. Society had become materialistic; with capitalists seeking greater profit at the expense of the reification of workers - while consumers blithely sought to satisfy wants rather than needs.

Webers two seminal works: *The protestant ethic and the spirit of capitalism* (1905) and *Economy and Society* (1922), traverse religious beliefs, economic/ political ideology, social theory and ethics.[272] In these works Weber attempts to reconcile the rational pursuit of economic gain with religious doctrine. One theme that Weber investigates is the phenomena of bureaucracy and the role of rational-legal authority.[273] Weber's investigation of bureaucracy touches on the concepts that underpin modern management and leadership theories, particularly in relation to power/authority.[274] Of interest is the inclusion of charismatic authority where Weber advocates that some leaders will gain authority by virtue of personal attributes.

> The term 'charisma' will be applied to a certain quality of an individual personality by virtue of which he is considered extraordinary and treated as endowed with supernatural, superhuman or at least exceptional powers or qualities.
>
> M Weber Economy and Society

Weber's work also provides valuable insight into political leadership and the machinations of the political system.[275] He identifies the need for strong "hero-like" leadership in a similar manner to Hegel.[276] In order to be an exemplar to followers the concept of charisma is advanced where a person who possesses exceptional powers or qualities[277] is able to exert a form of control over others. The modern conception of charismatic leadership is derived from this philosophy. In an era where both traditional and bureaucratic forms of control are evident in the daily lives of workers and society in general Weber proposed that the charismatic leader is another form of authority. Traits and behaviours are externalised by this conception where it is the follower who largely invokes the authority of the leader.

It is possible to continue to provide philosophical perspectives on leadership from prominent philosophers up to the present day but the foregoing should provide sufficient scope to consider the influence of philosophy on western society's conception of leadership. Generalisations can be made on the different perspectives that philosophers identify. For example, Plato's philosopher king ideal proposes that certain inherent characteristics are required in leaders. This conception is also followed by the early Roman philosophers, notably Cicero. Into the middle ages we see Thomas Aquinas advocating intellect as a natural differentiator between leaders and followers. This aspect is taken even further in the modern era with philosophers such as Hegel and Nietzsche promoting a form of super being as leader. There is clearly a persistent line of thought on the individual characteristics required for leadership.

Personal attributes may be a consistent theme but it should be recognised that the role of the environment around the leader also comes in for consideration. Aristotle views the suitability of the leader as being moderated by the needs of the state. In this conception a leader is only effective under certain conditions: a dictator would not be suited to a democracy and so on. Aquinas adopts similar reasoning and proposes that wicked followers produce wicked leaders, or at the very least deserve them. Parallels could be drawn between corrupt systems producing corrupt leaders. Machiavelli's insight into the role requirements for leaders in an era of rivalry, duplicity and self interest promotes a leader who is able to adapt to the circumstances around them and survive by wit and cunning. This perspective is moderated somewhat by Bentham who views a leaders role in terms of maximising the utility of followers. To do so a leader needs to be aware of follower needs and therefore identifies the need for situational contingencies.

One of the most persistent themes in philosophy is the role of virtue. The early Greek and Roman philosophers identify the conduct of the leader as being instrumental to leadership efficacy. This idea is also followed by philosophers in the middle ages who promote behaviours and conduct necessary to provide guidance to followers. Regardless of the religious connotations the role of morality in a leaders conduct is significant. In the modern era Mills recognised the need for moral competence in leaders. The shift in thinking to an understanding of moral behaviours promotes the view that leaders should act not out of a divine directive but out of what is right. Several philosophers explore the distinctly philosophical question – what is right? Kant, in particular, proposes that one should behave in a way that is desired by others as the norm – the categorical imperative. If we all act in a way that we would wish for everyone to act then there is no need for control – paradoxically there is also no need for leadership. This concept of group or consensus leadership and everyone exercising leadership is very much *en vogue* in the twenty first century hence ultimately restoring the position of acting virtuously and being a good leader.

Chapter 4 - **Napoleon Bonaparte**

A leader is a dealer in hope.[278]
Napoleon Bonaparte

Hope...is the most evil of evils because it prolongs man's torment.[279]
Friedrich Nietzsche

Background

Legend has developed around Napoleon's life, created in part by him. One persistent tale is that of his mother, escaping invading French forces over rocky escarpments while pregnant with Napoleon. Corsica fell in that same year but the spirit of resistance continued. Some authors idealistic-ally claim that Napoleon was influenced by this event and felt the call to arms before he was born.

Corsicans were predominantly of Italian derivation. Corsica itself was ini-tially part of Genoa.[280] It had struggled to maintain its own identity from that famous Italian port when the French laid claim to it in the year of Na-poleon's birth. As a result there was a strong feeling of animus among the Corsicans towards their imperial conquerors. Inherently patriotic, easily offended and vengeful, the Corsicans shared much in common with their Italian cousins on the mainland, but at the same time maintaining a feel-ing of distinct independence.

After Corsica's annexure to France in 1769, a French garrison was placed there. The resistance fighters of Corsica, under Pasquale Paoli, were disbanded and their leader was in exile. During Napoleon's youth he was exposed to high toned, patriotic conversations among the ex-Paolisti.[281] The in-tractable struggle with the French oppressors inflamed the patriot-ism of the country, and in no small part influenced the youth to do something to rectify the in-justice.[282] The Corsican nature,

> The chief satisfaction of these is-landers, when not engaged in war or in hunting, seemed to be that of lying at their ease in the open air, recounting tales of the bravery of their countrymen, and singing songs in honour of the Corsicans and against the Genoese.
>
> J Boswell An account of Corsica: a tour to that Island and Memoirs of Pascal Paoli

and their strong interest in public affairs made the Corsicans born politicians,[283] which meant that they were not only intensely patriotic but cunning in their diplomacy.

Napoleon grew up in a typical close-knit family environment within a traditional, cohesive community. While his start in life is one of legend, his early years were fairly conventional for the time. Born as Napoleone di Buona parte in the town of Ajaccio in 1769, he was one of eight children.[284] Napoleon[285] showed little indication that he would achieve much of note in life, as recalled by one of his closest friends, Fauvelet de Bourienne: "...of all the children...the Emperor was the one from whom future greatness was least to be prognosticated."[286] Napoleon's temperament as a young boy was notably bellicose and he demonstrated pugilistic tendencies towards any aggressors at an early age. While his brothers and sisters would play in a room dedicated to them, Napoleon would beat a drum, wield a sabre of wood, and draw soldiers on the wall ranged in order of battle.[287] He was also known to be wilful, intelligent, self-confident and quick witted, nervous and inattentive to appearance.[288]

His parents claimed a noble lineage yet the reality was more akin to an upper-middle class rural existence.[289] Being of modest means they led an austere way of life. Napoleon's mother was strong willed, industrious and opportunistic.[290] Her influence on Napoleon was far greater than that of any other person, endowing Napoleon with many of the traits that would be instrumental to his later success.[291] The centre of Napoleon's emotional world was his mother;[292] Napoleon freely acknowledged that he owed his success to the character formation by her[293] and later in life described his mother as a "superb woman..of great intelligence".[294] His parents were married by arrangement but both were equally motivated by wealth and prestige; ambition, not l'amour bound them.[295] If Napoleon's father left his son with a dominant impression it was of the importance of improving his social standing. Against this Napoleon developed disgust for his father's capitulation to France and failure to continue the resistance.[296] Napoleon's father (Charles-Marie), a lawyer, held a position of some influence in the town of Ajaccio. He had served with Paoli as his aide-de-camp in resisting the French invasion but, once overcome, threw his lot in with that of the conquerors.[297] Relying on his connections with the local French Governor Comte Marbeuf provided access to the French court of Louise XVI.[298] This opened up financial opportunities for the Buonapartes, but did not provide the means for a life of luxury. Combined with the *petite nobilite* of his background Carlo Buonaparte was able to secure the admission of his two eldest sons, Joseph and Napoleon, to free education.[299] For Napoleon, military school seemed the obvious option.

Napoleon's early preference for the military was also accompanied by a strong drive for achievement. He would object violently when playing games at school if he was on the losing side.[300] Genius, industry and the power of inspiring deep affection were the chief notes of Napoleon's early childhood.[301] It certainly came as no surprise to his siblings that he achieved the heights

> I had been placed by the teacher on the side under the Roman flag, Napoleone, impatient at finding himself under the Carthaginian flag, which was not that of the conqueror, would not rest until he had obtained permission for us to change places.
>
> *Joseph Napoleon*

he did. His younger brother, Lucien, at 17, once ruefully stated with amazing prescience: "...he seems to me to have a strong inclination to be a tyrant, and I believe that he would be one if he were King...".[302]

Napoleon was not to take the throne of France for another 12 years, yet those closest to him identified traits that would prove true soon enough.

In 1778 Napoleon was sent to the "military" school of Brienne in Atun, to the northeast of Paris.

The school was run by the Minims, a Roman Catholic order that promoted humility and religious minimalism.[303] Being Corsican, unable to speak French, and of *petite nobilite* status, Napoleon remained something of an Ishmael at Brienne:[304]

ridiculed by his classmates for his strange accent, unkempt appearance and patriotic fervour, he spent many hours in isolation.[305] Boarding school was a harsh life, one of confinement, with the students rarely able to see their parents. Ironically, religious studies were given short shrift, being limited mainly to saying grace before meals and perfunctory attendance at chapel.[306] Napoleon excelled at mathematics[307] and had a strong interest in history and geography.[308] His other subjects were given only the attention that he felt they deserved, with Latin relegated a waste of time ("why study a dead language"[309] he would remonstrate).

In 1784 Napoleon left Brienne for the École Militaire in Paris – France's elite military school. He achieved entry to the school earlier than normal as a result of completing a three-year course in mathematics – in only one year.[310] His propensity for mathematics was a signal trait in his years at Brienne and fortune was such that it was a prerequisite for entry into the artillery corps (there was no point in assigning an incompetent aristocrat to the command of the artillery corps if they couldn't calculate a trajectory.) This was the one area of the army that recognised and rewarded talent. In the year of his entry, after being away from his family for six years, he learned that his father had died. This made little impact other than to raise Napoleon's ire at his father's ineptitude and the need to locate a suitable replacement to aid his future career.[311]

In contrast to his school days, Napoleon flourished at military college.[312] The École Militaire predominantly focussed on producing officers for the king's army, thereby concentrating on more practical pursuits such as military tactics and the art of warfare. It is interesting to note that in the year of his first attendance the school introduced a course in moral and political philosophy.[313] There are no records of its influence on Napoleon.

In 1785 Napoleon left the École Militaire to join his first regiment at Valence – Régiment de La Fère – as a lieutenant.[314] While stationed at Valence Napoleon took several periods of leave to Corsica where he quickly became involved in local politics and administration. In 1789 the cataclysmic events of the Revolution changed everything. The status of Corsica became arbitrary and Napoleon saw the opportunity to project his political ability on his native countrymen. His intrigues did not last long in Corsica and he soon came into conflict with local identities who saw him as a French sympathiser. A series of local conflicts and some very poor political manoeuvring resulted in the entire Bonaparte family being forced to leave the island in 1793. Napoleon and his family's future now became inextricably linked to France.

In the following years Napoleon rose through the military at a rapid rate owing partly to the dwindling number of aristocrats in the officer corps and partly due to his skills as a strategist and commander. His associations with influential persons in Paris brought him to the attention of the ruling class. In 1795 he quelled an insurgence in Paris (using canon on lightly armed civilians) and was promoted to the rank of Brigadier-General. In 1797 he successfully reclaimed northern Italy from the Austrians in what was regarded militarily as a brilliant campaign, and expanded French influence into Egypt a year later. In 1799, following a successful coup, he rose to political power as part of a Consular triumvirate ruling France.

His political ascendancy complete, Napoleon did not rest on his laurels. Over the next decade and a half the campaigns of the French army of the time (*Le Grande Armée*) have gone down as some of the most brilliant in military history. Napoleon's activity in this period is nothing short of astounding. In 1800 he embarked on the second Italian campaign.[315] The *Grande Armée* engaged in a series of battles with the Austrians and secured northern Italy. In 1802 Napoleon became First Consul with absolute power. That year he also promulgated the *Code Napoléon* as the basis of French law and ultimately a code for conquered territory. In 1803, on returning to Paris, he resumed his plans to invade England. He would later institute the Continental System barring all European ports to English trade. In 1804 he crowned himself Emperor of France. In 1805, as suspicions mounted between other European nations, he proactively marched on Austria and defeated them decisively in brilliant campaigns.

Napoleon at Austerlitz by Baron Pascal

In 1806 Prussia attacked France and *Le Grande Armée* defeated them at Jena-Auerstadt. In 1808 Napoleon commenced the Peninsula Campaign and invaded Spain in order to keep the English from gaining a continental foothold. In 1809 he resumed conflict with the Austrians after they invaded Bavaria: Austria being decimated at the battle of Wagram. France was effectively in possession of most of Europe at that point. In 1812 Napoleon marched the largest army the world had seen to cow the Russian Emperor for breaking the Continental Blockade. *Le Grande Armée* was almost annihilated in retreat. In 1813 the Continental powers seized the opportunity to attack France. In 1814 Napoleon was defeated at Leipzig and deposed to the isle of Elba. In 1815 he returned to France to mount another campaign against the Continental powers and was defeated at the penultimate battle of Waterloo. In 1816 he was again forced to abdicate and was exiled to St Helena where he was incarcerated until his death in 1821.

Napoleon is widely regarded as one of the most accomplished military leaders in history. His determination and tenacity were formidable. Time and again his army took on superior forces and decisively defeated them. Yet his position was not always ideal, nor did he always have a technological or material advantage. Napoleon's timing and strategic ability were often the differentiating factor in his campaigns. Many commentators have detailed the attributes which made the French army of the time feared throughout Europe, but the one factor that all are agreed upon is the ability of its leader.[316]

Napoleon's restoration of the monarchy may have been a bare-faced attempt to disguise dictatorship but he nonetheless introduced reforms that have endured to this day: a common law system, the Bank of France, the court system, centralised government, national schooling, religious freedom, and so many more fundamental social and political changes that seem commonplace today.[317] Napoleon also sought to standardise the Continent under a common governance, currency and set of laws (albeit French). Such things would not materialise for another two centuries with the European Union.

Ultimately, the monarchies of Europe could not allow the principles of the Revolution, or Napoleon's rule, to stand. After a fateful expedition to Moscow, and deteriorating conditions in Spain, the allies eventually brought about his downfall. Imprisoned on the Isle of St Helena, bereft of family or friends, he died at the age of 52. His military success and social reforms have become the most enduring aspects of his leadership and indeed, one has a hard time naming another modern political leader who is more identified with an entire people, both in his lifetime, and especially afterward, than Napoleon.[318]

Influences

Napoleon was the second of seven children but was only really acquainted with his older brother, Joseph, and his younger sister, Maria Anna, in the time before he went to boarding school (Brienne). He was thus the middle of three children for most of his early youth. His next sibling was Lucciano (Lucien) who was six years younger and would have been only three by the time Napoleon left for Brienne. Napoleon was therefore nearer in age to his older brother. His sister died at the age of five, when Napoleon was seven. As such he had little involvement with his sister and would have felt a strong need to compete with his older brother. In fact the age of his sister may have motivated him to act as carer for her rather than compete. Alternatively, Napoleon may have been taught to despise[319] his younger sister as she would be seen as no equal companion to him.[320] The gap between him and his older brother being so close would have compelled him to equal if not better him. This may have instilled in him an intense competitiveness and need for recognition: so were laid, firm and immutable, the foundations of their adult characters: the elder one easy-going, indolent, courteous; the younger active, aggressive and rude.[321]

It is clear from the accounts of Napoleon during his youth that there were frequent attacks by him on his elder brother. This situation necessitated his mother sending him to a local girl's school to learn some manners and civility.[322] Unfortunately, this recourse simply left him open to ridicule by the local children, which merely incensed him further into fits of rage and attacks.[323]

Apart from his parents and brother, one of the earliest figures that featured in his life was Pasquale Paoli. Paoli led the Corsican resistance movement against France and was the country's unofficial head of state prior to French occupation.[324] Napoleon revered him for his dedication to the liberation of his homeland and for his bravery against overwhelming odds.[325] Napoleon exhibited many of the same personal attributes as Paoli later in life and was significantly affected by both Paoli's legend and his character.[326] Combined with the fact that Napoleon felt contempt for his father's capitulation to the French, Paoli became a surrogate father figure.[327]

Napoleon's schooling had a variable influence on him. At Brienne he was different from the other, primarily French, students, and so, treated differently. This caused him to seek isolation and perceive himself as different. He was arrogant in his belief that Corsica was a superior nation and relished the compliments by writers, such as Rousseau, of the exceptionality of the culture. Such accolades contributed to his self-perception of difference and superiority.

When commissioned as an Officer in the French army, he initially had mixed emotions. He was still a Corsican at heart but now served the king who had subjugated his countrymen. This reticence manifested in his initial lacklustre commitment to the army where he spent far more time on furlough in Corsica than in service; to the point where he was expelled from the army, and subsequently reinstated.[328] In his first four years of service he spent half of it on leave. Even though he demonstrated an enthusiasm for his particular training as an artillery officer, it is not entirely clear whether he did so for reasons of service or personal benefit. His attitude changed dramatically with his first military engagement at Toulon (1793), which proved to both him and his superiors that he was not only capable in his craft but a superior officer. By this time, occurring shortly after the French revolution and his family's banishment from Corsica, he knew that his destiny was inextricably linked to the nation of France. As such his devotion to France and his profession became the single focus of his life. Napoleon's self-image was one of extreme self-confidence. In his first real command in a campaign[329] he stated to one of his officers, Colonel Auguste Marmont: "They haven't seen anything yet...In our time, no one has the slightest conception of what is great. It is up to me to give them an example".[330] He wanted to be a great man and he knew that such men possessed great qualities. His focus was on the creation of that image.

The great man syndrome

Napoleon's isolation from his schoolmates forced him to escape in books. His favourites included Macpherson's *The Works of Ossian* (1765) and Vertot's *Histoire des Chevaliers de Malte (History of the Knights of Malta)* (1565), which he learned by heart. These works glorified great deeds and heroism. He was also absorbed by the great men of Plutarch's *Lives* (c.1CE), Polybius's *Histories* (146BCE) and Arrianus's *Anabasis Alexandri (Campaigns of Alexander the Great* (c.90CE). The military campaigns of Plutarch fascinated him, in particular those of Leonidas, Dion, Curtius, Decius, Cato and Brutus. Every boy has heroes but Napoleon's were the great military leaders of ancient Greece, Rome and Macedonia. Plutarch's accounts portray military leaders in an almost superhuman way. Napoleon admired Brutus and Caesar equally, but he did not draw the careful moral or political lines between them that the Romans drew. What mattered was that both were *viri illustres*: great men. The effect of these accounts on Napoleon was profound and he was to say later in life in his maxims: "Read and re-read the Campaigns of Alexander, Hannibal, Caesar, Gustavus Aldolphus, Turenne, Eugene and Frederick; take them for your model, that is the only way of becoming a great captain…". His model was to become one of these people and he did not conceal it: "His whole soul was devoted to the profession of arms, and he began to be conscious that he was born to impose his will on others", as recounted by Bourienne, Napoleon's closest school friend, who would note Napoleon's preoccupation with delusions of grandeur in his memoirs. This extended into later life when Napoleon stated to Pope Pius VII at Fontainebleau: "My business is to succeed. I make my Iliad in actions, every day."

Social/political philosophy

Napoleon's early years on Corsica were without much formal schooling. He was nine when he was sent to the military school at Brienne in 1778. Much of his early social and political development occurred as a result of the material he came into contact within this institution. While he was initially interested in the historical accounts of great leaders through the works of notable historians such as Plutarch and Arrian,[331] the works of the philosopher Rousseau were of more significance to the development of his worldview.[332]

Rousseau had written *Du contrat social* (*The Social Contract*) (1769), in the year of Napoleon's birth. In this work he advocated Corsica as the ideal city-state in the foreword to this work,[333] identifying it as the "ideal laboratory for political experiment" [334]and prophetically stated that "this little island will some day astonish Europe".[335] Napoleon overtly admired the support that Rousseau expressed for Corsica[336] and would extol his sentiments to his fellow schoolmates. To a large extent he used Rousseau's work as a vindication of Corsica's suppression by France.

Following his commission (1785), in the year of his first posting, Napoleon took leave from the regiment and returned to his home in Corsica, after not having seen his family for five years.[337] Arriving at his home with more books than clothes, he proceeded to devour works by authors such as Plutarch, Plato, Cicero, Cornelius Nepos, Livy, Tacitus, Montaigne, Machiavelli, Montesquieu, McPherson, Raynal and, of course, Rousseau.[338] As a portent of things to come, he also read Duclos's *Memoirs of Louis the XIV*, Barrow's *History of England* and Marigny's *History of the Arabs*.[339]

His teen years identify him as an extreme idealist but at the same time highly intelligent, at once passionate, yet calculating. He read widely and made notes on a range of subjects, from the history of Corsica and patriotism, to religion and suicide.[340] The latter being prompted by a particularly popular book at the time, Goethe's *The Sorrows of Young Werther* (1787).[341] Napoleon read this book on no fewer than five occasions and it is claimed to have been highly influential on his worldview.[342] It was seen as promoting individualism, violence and irrationality: concepts not dissimilar to what occurred during the Revolution. The idealistic conceptions in this book left its mark in more ways than one.[343] It also reinforced his solipsistic nature, a feeling of being separate and independent of others.

The influence of Goethe's work and those of Rousseau manifested in a contempt for France and jingoistic fervour for his homeland. In one of his letters, about Paoli and Corsica, he writes in 1786:

the people are always wrong in revolting against their Sovereign. Divine laws forbid it. What have Divine laws to do with human affairs? But do you perceive the absurdity of this general rule which Divine laws make that you must never shake off the yoke even of an usurper? So an assassin, clever enough to seize the throne after having assassinated the legitimate Prince, is at once protected by Divine laws, and all the time if he had failed he would have been condemned to lose his criminal head on the scaffold. ..the pact by which a people establishes a sovereign authority in any body politic is not a contract – that is, the people can at will take back the sovereignty which it has given. Men in a state of nature do not form a Government. To establish that it is necessary that each individual should consent to the change. The act constituting this convention is necessarily a reciprocal contract.[344]

He continues at length but ends with the words: "It is not the same with the relations that may be held with neighbouring peoples."[345] Clearly the requirement for internal social order of one's own country differs from the system required for other countries. This is clear sign of Napoleon's attitude towards the rest of Europe, and an indication of his own view of governance: one set of rules for the leader and another set for everyone else. To a large extent this was central to Napoleon's character. He could advocate the most reasonable position but contradictorily maintain that there were specific exemptions, particularly in relation to himself.

The works of his youth show a clear understanding of the principles of the social contract, the role of natural laws and ambivalence towards royal authority. The latter is prominently revealed in his *Dissertation sur l'autorite royale (Dissertation on Royal Authority)* where he candidly states: "there are very few kings who haven't deserved to be dethroned".[346] This was an extremely dangerous sentiment to commit to paper in a country infused with revolutionary fervour where repressive authoritarianism could have resulted in him being tried for treason.[347] Around this time he no longer felt as a subject to Louis XVI.[348]

> The contradictions in Napoleon's thoughts and behaviours persisted long after he had jettisoned Corsica and all its works, so it may be that Napoleon's "traditional" manifestations – the hatred of anarchy, the fear of the mob, the strong family feelings – simply meant that his heart was with the *ancien regime* even if his brain was with the Revolution. The deepest obstacle to Napoleon as a man of the Revolution always remained his profound pessimism about human perfectability and his conviction that human beings were fundamentally worthless.
>
> F McLynn *Napoleon*

Napoleon abhorred the monarchy, in fact all aristocrats, in part due to the invasion of his homeland by a country led by a monarch, and in part due to his treatment at Brienne at the hands of the sons of aristocrats. He viewed monarchy as a usurpation of society's sovereignty (consistent with Rousseau). His early views appear to be indicative of someone contemptuous of monarchy, with the monarch viewed as not being entitled to their position, as it is only based on birth rather than achievement. He advocates in *Dissertation sur l'autorite royale* that "the goal of government is to lend a strong hand to the weak against the strong, permitting each person to taste sweet tranquillity, to find himself on the road to happiness."[349] This sentiment reflects Rousseau's work and shows signs of Napoleon's interest in the role of politics in society, with a strong sense of social justice.

But this is deceptive. Napoleon was not interested in an egalitarian nation at all. Rose indicates that Napoleon's view of equality shows no confidence in the integrity of the motives either of an individual, class, or people [350] and it was his personal pique and vanity that made him opposed to kings and nobles and privileges, not concern for the oppressed.[351] In fact Napoleon feared the oppressed as an unruly mob that could disturb the peace. Contradictorily, he both supported the stability of the monarchy but also despised it.

After an almost two-year absence from his regiment in Corsica he then returned to it, now based in Auxonne, in 1788.[352] Here he led an ascetic existence where his mind began to range and his ideas crystallize. Free from a hidebound curriculum and occasionally mediocre instruction, the born autodidact came into his own.[353] It is primarily in this period that we see the development of Napoleon's more mature social and political worldview.

Napoleon's fascination with constitutional aspects and affairs of the state were developed early in his self-tuition.[354] His ideas on governance matured to the extent that when his corps was asked to compose a constitution he volunteered for the assignment and compiled a 4500-word treatise on how the Calotte[355] should conduct itself.[356] What was actually required was somewhat far less lofty but it nonetheless indicated a clear aptitude in this arena. The document was a blueprint for strong leadership[357] yet was also fundamentally a derivation of the works he had studied, such as Plato's *Republic*.[358] His concern for constitutional matters was twofold: on the one hand it had become of national concern[359] in how the country would be governed after the deposition of the monarchy, while on the other hand he saw it as a skill for the success of a conqueror.

Napoleon also used his time at Auxonne to consume a wide array of material. He wrote extensively and filled over 36 notebooks with his observations:[360] Auxonne may be said to have been his university, the period of youth devoted entirely to the acquisition of knowledge which, in his case, was to remain in his mind as a store, ever fresh, ever crystal.[361] Among the works read in this period were Raynal's *Histoire philosophique des établissements et du commerce des Européens dans les deux Indes (Philosophical and political history and institutions of European trade in India)* (1770), Montesquieu's *Esprit des Lois (Spirit of the Law)*(1748), Machiavelli's *Istorie Fiorentine (The History of Florence)* (1520–1525) and *Il Principe (The Prince)* (1532), Filangieri's *Scienza della legislatione (The Science of Legislation)* (1780-85) and Adam Smith's *Wealth of Nations* (1776).[362] Each book has distinct social, political and moral leanings. Napoleon's own works at this time reflected much of what he had absorbed, demonstrating his own beliefs, his critique of religion, church-state relations and his feelings about Corsica.[363]

Napoleon was particularly attracted to Raynal's book because it spoke of the Corsican struggle for liberty and revolutionary tendencies: these ideas correspond with Napoleon's own wishes and made a deeper impression on him than even Rousseau's teachings, of which he was already sceptical, and which he denounced as the ravings of an idealist.[364] Clearly, Napoleon's views were beginning to shift. Raynal's work proposed challenging the status quo - a view gaining momentum across France at that time.

Next to make an impact was Montesquieu's *Spirit of the Laws,* which equipped him with a fundamental understanding and appreciation of the need for strong government, and the various forms it could take. This was particularly relevant in a time when the deposed regime would need to be replaced with a new form of governance. While England had adopted a constitutional monarchy, Napoleon's initial views on the best form of government, like those of his countrymen, were not clear. Democracy appeared to perpetuate chaos and allowed strong factions to hold the country to ransom; monarchy was simply not tolerable, as the aristocracy could not be allowed to gain control and continue the suppression of the common man; despotism seemed dangerous and would simply replace the *ancien regime* with a new oppressor. The dilemma that faced the nation was: how would they be governed? This dilemma prompted intense interest in obtaining more information on the most ideal constitution for the new French republic.[365]

In September 1789 Napoleon returned to Corsica on leave again. By then the Revolution had effectively swept away the aristocracy and in its place laid the foundations for the rise of ambitious men. Napoleon was no stranger to this and while on leave he began to dabble in Corsican politics and to seek military command in the local militia.[366] He still felt himself to be more Corsican than French, with little demonstrated commitment to either his regiment or France. In common with his older brother, Joseph (who was by then a lawyer) he would have a passion for "the nation" and "equality before the law", and a taste for "the political", that is, the expectation that being active in the public arena was natural and desirable.[367]

Napoleon demonstrates his coalescing views on social and political philosophy in a response to an essay competition run by the Academy of Lyons in 1791. The essay required applicants to respond to the following question: "What are the most important truths and feelings to instil into men for their happiness?" The question reflected the concerns of the time. Consistent with the trend towards utilitarian and communitarian thinking of the time, the Academy was obviously curious about what the public thought. Napoleon was well placed to respond, having made himself familiar with a range of social philosophy perspectives.

His essay runs to 40 pages and is an invaluable source for Napoleon's views at such a young age.[368] Its basic tenet is that morality is a function of freedom, although this is nothing more than a *rechauffe* of Rousseau and Raynal.[369] As such, Napoleon demonstrates a respect for Rousseau (notwithstanding considerable divergence of view)[370] and an understanding of the crude materialism of the school of Raynal.[371] In this regard Napoleon proposes, somewhat cyncically, that "the only one who does find happiness is the man who is ambitious for the general welfare, who uses his strength and energy to conquer ambition instead of being conquered by it, who strives to rise solely that he may promote the happiness of others."[372] The statement does not ring true of someone who was known as being pathologically ambitious and self-centred. His essay response expresses idealistic overtones, a repressed need for recognition and psychological contradiction. Napoleon observes that while all men are born with unequal means they still have equal rights[373] but he then goes on to express that one can only enjoy one's wealth if one is strong.[374] His essay demonstrates a desire for equality but a revelation that the polity must be controlled by a greater 'being'.

He subsequently writes *Dialogue on Love,* in which he continues to display Rousseauesque sentiments. However, by this time the young Lieutenant had already outgrown the Genevan's philosophy.[375] He would mark his copy of Rousseau's *Discours sur l'origine et les fondements de l'inégalité parmi les hommes* (*Discourse on the Origin and Basis of Inequality Among Men*) (1754) - "I do not believe this",[376] revealing an already independent view of human relationships.[377] Rousseau's philosophy becomes relegated to idealism while his reading of Montesquieu becomes more of a practical discourse in administration.

The next most significant philosophical influence on Napoleon's worldview comes through the works of Machiavelli. Machiavelli combined the social and political with the military. The Machiavellian Prince quickly became his model. As a result Napoleon's military maxims are a synthesis of Machiavelli's *Art of War*. The similarities between the two are not mere coincidence, as Napoleon was generally known for his adaption of principles and techniques advocated by others. While Machiavelli had theorised on the best forms of government, administration and waging war, Napoleon was determined to put the concepts into practice. This, too, was not unusual, as other French military leaders, such as Marshall Gouvion-Saint-Cyr who esteemed the writings of Machiavelli, had also employed Machiavelli's advice.[378] Napoleon not only adapted the military aspects of Machiavelli but was aware of the political implications as well but recognised the close relationship between military and political tactics.[379] He was an also an admirer of Rome and saw in it the formula for success for any city-state, something which would enable France to project its force throughout Europe as Rome had done.[380] Long an admirer of Rome and the achievements of great men like Julius Caesar, the ideology of Machiavelli eventually supplant Napoleon's idealistic notions as Machiavelli contends that the strongest possible instrument of expansionism is the well-ordered force of the citizen-soldier who will be fighting for their own honour and glory.[381] This was Napoleon's view of post-Revolutionary France. Machiavelli also proposes that the ideal statesman is a capable general who possesses the requisite attribute of *virtù*. This is not the virtue proposed by Plato. Machiavellian *virtù* is a military quality denoting masculine and aggressive conduct [382] which includes characteristics such as boldness, bravery, resolution and decisiveness[383] and not the qualities proposed by the Roman Stoics. These are not only the characteristics of Napoleon but those of post-revolutionary France. Napoleon harnessed post-revolutionary fervour and gave it direction. Combined with the insight of Machiavelli, Napoleon was on a mission: one that relied on military dominance and political control – the two being inextricably linked.

Although Napoleon initially shared the egalitarian views of Rousseau, this was primarily in relation to his patriotism towards Corsica. It suited him at the time to seek support from anyone who advocated the superiority and liberation of his homeland. Over time his views shifted from the idealistic conception of brotherhood to a more practical appreciation of politics as a means of social control, as proposed by Montesquieu and Raynall. In part, his alienation from Corsica caused him to jettison much of his earlier feelings of patriotism and community – his mission was to become individualised where the French army was his vehicle.

Napoleon's worldview presents as being based on self-interest. Thomas Hobbes wrote: "Man in nature knows no other law than self-interest: take care of himself, destroy enemies; these were his daily jobs".[384] Such views accorded with Napoleon's perceptions as displayed in an essay written in 1785: "the natural spirit of man is the wish to dominate";[385] and in his maxims: "In the eyes of founders of great empires, men are not men, but instruments".[386] It is evident that Napoleon's true character shows through in these statements, in effect Napoleon echoing Machiavelli. By 1890 Napoleon's personality was formed in all essentials; there would be no decisive change in attitudes until 1792 and probably no fundamental shift in worldview until 1795 when he first tasted real power.[387]

It is difficult to determine whether Napoleon had a preferred mode of government in mind from his readings. Clearly his later actions in becoming a member of the triumvirate that ruled France after the revolution indicated a leaning towards a despotic form of rule. As his power increased, he then transformed that to monarchy. As such, in complete contradiction with his renunciation of the monarchy, Napoleon adopted the system that best suited his own purposes, rather than adopting a system that was best suited to the needs of the polity. To be fair, democracy had only just been instituted in America so it would seem that Napoleon was also simply adopting a system that was accepted in Europe. Nonetheless, the move from triumvirate to first consul to monarch would tend to suggest a desire for absolute rule.

Even though some of his views of government echo sentiments from political works (such as Montesquieu) they show signs of missing the point of political liberty. To wit, one of his maxims states: "At bottom the name and form of the government is but little moment provided that justice is rendered to all the citizens that they are equal before the law, and the state is well governed."[388] Although there is a clear grasp of the importance of equality and government efficacy in this maxim, Montesquieu in fact advocated that there are fundamental principles that underpin every form of government that should not be ignored, or at least ignored to the peril of the constitution. Napoleon seems to fall into this trap, justifying dictatorship if there is equality among the masses (reflecting a comment he made in 1803 to a similar extent: "I have come to realise that men are not born to be free").[389] This again reveals a schism between what Napoleon found suited himself and others, regardless of its effect.

Napoleon's skewed conception of equality is substantiated by another conflict in his maxims: "Every government should not view men but as a whole",[390] against "a ruler, at bottom, must be a soldier; a horse is not ruled without boots and spurs."[391] Although Plato advocated that the ruling class should be derived from the military due to the inherent civic devotion resulting from such service, Napoleon takes this further when he states in yet another maxim: "Constitutional States have no springs, the action of the government is too trammelled; this is which makes them inferior in their struggles with powerful and absolute neighbours. A dictatorship might help them, but the ram is at the door of the Capitol before they are ready."[392]

Again, the pragmatism of Machiavelli is evident. The clear justification of Napoleon's absolutist attitude is evident and is reinforced in the following statement: "absolute power has no need of a lie; it is silent. Responsible government, obliged to speak, acts and lies shamelessly".[393] It would therefore seem that Napoleon adopted little of the moral basis of *The spirit of the laws*. His view of government is based on order; by whatever means is effective and justifiable.[394]

Clearly, Napoleon had little real ideological appreciation of Montesquieu's work and adopted the works of Machiavelli as his *vade mecum*. The latter providing him with the justification for self-serving ambition and strong rule. The progression in the development of his social and political views is of interest in the way it parallels the influences to which he was exposed: it began with a need for the honour and restoration of his homeland, through to a need to understand the most efficacious form of government following the revolution, and finally the means that justified his actions in seeking ultimate power.

Moral/religious philosophy

Rousseau's work *The Social Contract* had more of an effect on Napoleon from a religious perspective than through its social philosophy. Rousseau believed in a "civil religion", one the state had created rather than one that had been imposed on it, which is a direct rejection of Roman Catholicism. He loathed Catholicism for forming a middle layer between the citizen and society.[395] Rousseau (like Machiavelli and Voltaire) believed that Christianity emasculated the polity.[396] Moreover, Christianity represented a divisive force which threatened the legitimacy and efficacy of the state.[397] These views impressed young Napoleon, who was at the time of reading them growing contemptuous of the religious hypocrisy at Brienne.

The influence of Rousseau on Napoleon in his teen years was clearly strong. In 1785, aged 16, Napoleon became so agitated by a criticism of *The Social Contract* by a Swiss priest named Roustan that he wrote an essay in response. Roustan had written *A defence of Christianity considered from its political aspect, with a reply in particular to the eighth chapter of the fourth volume of The Social Contract.*[398] Napoleon responded:

> *Is the Christian religion good for the political conditions of the state? Rousseau has so little doubt on the subject that he says: "The third" (the Roman Catholic religion) "is so evidently bad that it is a waste of time to amuse oneself in demonstrating it." Whatever breaks up the social unity is bad...Christianity forbids men to obey every command opposed to its own laws, every unjust command, were it to even emanate from the people. It is therefore against the first article of the social part, the basis of all government, for it substitutes its own particular approval for the general will which constitutes sovereignty...The inconvenience of this resistance made by the Gospel is so severe in a Christian State that it destroys completely the unity of the state, for the ministers of laws and the ministers of religion are not the same persons.*[399]

Napoleon criticises the divisiveness of religion and the inability of a government to effectively govern in a nation whose people are split between an allegiance to God and to government.[400] Christianity is blamed for the ills of society rather than recognised as providing society with moral direction. His views are vehemently secular and echo the sentiments of Rousseau completely. They also reflect Voltaire's declamation on religion ("wipe out the infamy"),[401] to which Napoleon subscribed on reading *Essai sur les moers et l'esprit des nations (On the spirit and customs of the nation)* (1756).[402]

Following the Revolution, France attempted to abolish all vestiges of the Church.[403] This was not simply because of an anti-Christian or irreligious sentiment, but because the Church was in fact a form of Italian aristocracy.[404] Revolutionary France even attempted to displace the Gregorian calendar in order to do away with adhering to the Italian system.[405] This was yet another attempt to establish a secular state and put France's standing religions out of business.[406]

Napoleon, like many of his countrymen of the time, showed little regard for religious observance. Although his parents were of Italian decent (and so generally assumed to be devoutly Roman Catholic), there is little, if any, reference to his mother or father paying any real attention to religious doctrine, save but to perform their expected attendances at Church.[407] Despite Napoleon devouring numerous texts on a vast array of subject matter, none had any religious content eshewing moral doctrine.

His years at Brienne exposed him to a perfunctory role of religion and scant theological doctrine. The Minims who ran Brienne placed little emphasis on theology, other than to cover the events in the Bible. Brienne was also known for its rampant homosexuality and immorality[408] and Napoleon saw little evidence of the moderating influence of religion, or any role model to admire. By the end of his schooling he had effectively lost his faith.[409]

Napoleon's alienation from the church was based on three elements: (i) the hypocritical force-feeding of rote learned religious doctrine[410] at Brienne, which served no more than to inure him to its content, (ii) his reading of Rousseau, who believed in a civil religion that was the ideology of the state, and the loathing of Catholicism for forming a middle layer between the citizen and society,[411] and (iii) the bigotry of his school masters who held that the ancient Greeks and Romans were obviously condemned to hell for not being Christians.[412] To Napoleon this was simply absurd. How could anyone be condemned to hell if the religion did not even exist at the time? This attitude remained with him for life and is reflected in a statement made while on St Helena – "I would believe in the Christian religion if it existed from the beginning of time. Then Socrates would be dammed, and Plato, and the Mohammedans".[413] But it didn't and so, Napoleon would contend, it makes no sense to condemn the innocent. Besides – what sort of religion advocates condemning people?

Napoleon may have been irreligious but he nonetheless saw political benefit in religion. While his views on Christianity do not evince a grain of interest in religious beliefs or doctrine[414] he still saw it as a useful political weapon. This is revealed in a comment made to his brother Lucien in a personal correspondence: "Skilful conquerors have not got entangled with priests, now they can both contain them and use them".[415] Napoleon thus views the Church merely as performing a role for swaying public opinion. Religion was therefore an opiate on which a ruler could rely regarding religion as a political emollient, useful to administer in times of excitement -the priest holding in reserve a spiritual sedative.[416]

Napoleon's concerns about religion rests upon the presumption that Christianity both removes the power of self-determination from society, and inhibits effective government.[417] His awareness of the might of Rome and subsequent reading of Rousseau identified that the ideal state was that of pre-Christian Rome,[418] and Rome declined the moment that Christianity emerged.[419] Roman society's allegiance was henceforth split between God and the state when Christianity entered the social mix. From that point on religion was the cause of civil dissent, division and war – not unity.

One story of Napoleon seeking to establish the Jewish state supports the position of him possessing a cynical view of religion in general.

> In support of religious emancipation Napoleon issued an edict to convoke the Sanhedrin of the Jewish community to be held in Paris. For this he received wide acclaim. On the agenda was the formation of the Jewish state.
>
> Napoleon's uncle, Cardinal Fesch, warned him that the Bible foretells of the end of the world (the apocalypse) when the Jews are recognised as constituting a nation. Napoleon dismissed the advice. Noticing that his uncle was serious, Napoleon entered into a private conference with him and returned to announce the dissolution of the Sanhedrin. Napoleon's concern was not so much for the superstitions of the Bible but for the impact of it on public opinion, and the resultant effect on taxation revenue and stock prices.
>
> F McGlynn *Napoleon*

Around the turn of the century it was a cornerstone of equality in the eyes of the new republic that all peoples should be entitled to practice their faith openly and without persecution. Napoleon adhered to this principle of emancipation of any oppressed religious group as he moved across Europe. For this he received wide acclaim, in particular from the Jewish communities,[420] yet he did so only as a political necessity (his views on St Helena reflecting his actual views: "the Jews are an ugly race, cowardly and cruel."[421] His own statements on religion are generally contradictory and inconsistent. One of his maxims on Catholicism states: "Without the Bible, we are marching in the darkness.

The Catholic religion is the only one which gives man safe knowledge as to his beginning and last end."[422] In another he states: "to ask how far religion is necessary for the State, is to ask when to tap a sufferer from dropsy".[423] He wrote to his priest at Brienne: "Without religion, no happiness, no success is possible".[424] Yet he never once expressed the same opinion to his family or close friends. In fact, he stated the exact opposite on St Helena when he pronounced that: "Jesus should have been hanged like scores of other fanatics who posed as the Prophet or the Messiah."[425] Consistent with his view of religion being a social sedative he would support it when necessary to further his own ends. For example, when addressing the people of Erfurt in 1808 he publicly stated:

> *Sirs, philosophers torment themselves by creating systems. In vain will they find a better than that of Christianity which, by reconciling man to himself, assures both public order and quiet to the States.*[426]

Yet on another occasion he demonstrated his true intent:

> *By becoming a Catholic I have ended the Vendean War, by becoming a Moslem I gained a footing in Egypt; by becoming an Ultramontane I won over public opinion in Italy. If I governed Jews I would rebuild the temple of Solomon...*[427]

Napoleon was effectively a pragmatist who did what was necessary to gain and retain power. He would say that his "policy consists in governing men as the greatest number wish to be governed. That, I think, is the way of recognizing the sovereignty of the people."[428] Religion and morality formed no significant part in his rule, other than for political control. One of his early biographers notes: "I confess I can find in his early writings, his letters, and his more intimate confessions, few if any signs of genuine religious feelings, still less of conviction."[429]

Ultimately, Napoleon was irreligious despite any statements to the contrary. After all, he was, at core, a chameleon. He would do what was necessary to facilitate his goal, or appease whoever was necessary in order to succeed. Religion was never important to him personally, but merely a system that he had to be aware of in order to achieve his social and political ends. Morality, too, seems to receive scant attention with his views on religion failing to recognise any moral underpinning.

Leadership approach
The Corsican nature plays an important role in the development of Napoleon's character. The spirit of conquest and glory formed a strong driving

force for achievement. Both his parents had this drive to achieve social standing. His father sought out and maintained influential contacts while his mother maintained an image of elegant sufficiency when reality resembled frugality.

Initially, Napoleon's conception of leadership was acquired from the influence of Paoli.[430] Napoleon revered the Great Man image which Paoli presented. He was also influenced by the impact of certain figures who were able to assist the family: Governor Marbeuf being important in this regard. People of position had power and the ability to make his family's life easier. Achieving a powerful position obviously seemed to bring status and comfort.

In relation to morality, it is clear from his education that he had little or no knowledge of moral philosophy. There is no evidence of him reading anything of note with any real focus on morality. In relation to religious philo-

> He was telling us that, being before Toulon, where he commanded the artillery, one of his officers was visited by his wife, to whom he had been but a short time married, and whom he tenderly loved. A few days after, orders were given for another attack upon the town, in which this officer was to be engaged. His wife came to General Bonaparte, and with tears entreated him to dispense with her husband's services that day. The General was inexorable, as he himself told us, with a sort of savage exaltation. The moment for the attack arrived, and the officer, though a very brave man, as Bonaparte self-assured us, felt a presentiment of his approaching death. He turned pale and trembled. He was stationed beside the General, and during an interval when the firing from the town was very heavy, Bonaparte called out to him, "Take care, there is a shell coming!" The officer, instead of moving to one side, stooped down, and was literally severed in two. Bonaparte laughed loudly while he described the event with horrible minuteness.
>
> F de Bourienne *Memoirs of Napoleon*

sophy, Napoleon had limited tolerance for religion and his religious education at school was perfunctory at best. There is little evidence that there was any influence from theology. It is quite apparent that social and political sources were of significant influence. These consisted of primarily of works by Rousseau, Montesquieu, Raynall, Machiavelli and Voltaire. These sources gave him an understanding of the relationship between the polity and the state, the role of the church, and an understanding of the necessity for order. Yet despite the breadth of his erudition, his understanding at the time was largely superficial.[431] In particular, there is evidence to suggest that his reading of some works was somewhat superficial. He lacked interest in anything that did not suit his way of thinking.[432] This can be gleaned from the notes that he left which demonstrate a very selective approach to knowledge formation. For example, in relation to the Republic he evidently read only a few pages and makes brief and somewhat superficial notations from the work that do not reflect the extent of its depth.

Undoubtedly, Napoleon was gifted, but he was not that gifted. He did manage to pass a three-year course in mathematics in one year, but then he was at a school full of aristocrats whose lives were predetermined, and so he may not have had much competition. His classmates would have had little more concern for schooling than was necessary to maintain their own ego or social status; it was not as if any of the sons of aristocrats were going to miss out on a placement at military college or future staff roles. Napoleon, on the other hand, was not of their class and could not rely on the wealth of his family. If he failed, he went back to Corsica. Also, he did not initially understand French so mathematics would have been the only subject that seemed comprehensible; numbers became a way of expressing and distinguishing himself. The first time he was actually rated relative to his peers was at the *École Militaire* where he finished 42 out of 58 in his class: hardly outstanding.[433]

From a leadership perspective, Napoleon seems to be the quintessential charismatic leader.[434] He is often depicted as having magnetic control over others. The conception of men following him unquestioningly across Europe has become part of the pantheon of his legend. So, if Napoleon was an example of charismatic leadership, then what was the source of his charisma? Tracing his early life it would seem that he had very few, if any, friends on Corsica. At least, he wrote of no one and spoke of no one. At Brienne he developed enemies more readily than friends and only had one person (Fauvelet de Bourienne) whom he could confide in. [435] At the *École Militaire* we see nothing but contempt for his fellow officers, with the only person willing to support and stand by him being Alexandre Des Mazis[436] (who finished 56 out of 58 in the same class as Napoleon). We hardly see a picture here of someone with a natural magnetism.

Napoleon does not demonstrate a desire to engage followers. In fact, he appeared to go out of his way to shock and belittle his audience.

There was a distinct distance between him and others – as if they were objects. Notably, on the island of St Helena he would state to Gourgaud: "I care only for people who are useful to me – and only so long as they are useful."[437] He was known to be unpredictable, rude and arrogant towards even his friends, such as when he became first consul when he ceased to address his close friends in the style of familiar equality.[438] This behaviour is certainly consistent with that of his early relationships – or lack of them. His people skills with his court verged on being childish. He would pinch, push and trip people, throw himself on the floor in tantrums, throw water and objects at people, abuse them, refuse to talk to some and make his attendants stand for long hours while he played chess.[439] Contrary to the popular perception of him this behaviour extended to his military command. There were certainly few endearing qualities in the manner in which he treated people. His relationships with women were worse, despite the myth of his all-consuming romance with Josephine. She, in fact, was known to cuckold him from the day they commenced their relationship. There was certainly little or no fidelity on either side. He was notorious for his affairs with prominent women of the time, and when in power he gave no positions of any importance to any women. He was well known for his contemptuous encounters with Madame de Stael, a prominent feminist and socialite of the time. [440] On St Helena he stated: "..in reality they are nothing more than machines for producing children" [441] and inferred that they should be "subordinate" [442] to men. Although his attitude towards women was fundamentally chauvinistic he probably was no different from the men of his era, although his misogyny transcended the norm.

Could his charisma have extended from his military success? He strongly believed (correctly so) that "nothing succeeds like success". [443] His military genius is unquestioned and in this regard his abilities are an important part of his "gifts". It is easy to say that soldiers revered him and saw him as magnetic – most subalterns naturally see senior officers this way, especially if they are successful and behave in a confident and dynamic manner. But his success was also a fabrication through the effective use of propaganda. If a battle was really a defeat, he would report it as a victory. He would change numbers and details to suit the image he required. People needed a hero and a vindication of the Revolution. They also wanted stability and he was going to provide it. He had a grandiose view of himself and the world which commenced quite early in his life and remained prominent: "In our time nobody has had a grander conception than mine, and it's my example that must point the way." [444] This would seem to suggest that he was seeking to establish an image for the purpose of fulfilling a grand vision. He would portray a particular image in order to dominate others rather than elicit their followership. Dominance and grandiosity are seminal traits of narcissism.

The sociological influences that acted on him manifested in the perception of the state as a medium and politics as a tool for achieving control. This is, in fact, what resulted. People were exploited by him in order to achieve status and control. Image was important – even essential. His conception of government started out as being a force for the strong to help the weak (when he and Corsica were in need of it), but ended up being the force that ensured that dissenters did not disturb the peace.

What we see is a picture of a morally vacuous person with no religious interest yet possessing a strong interest in political control and social order. Napoleon identified with the Great Man image and he cultivated this im-

Napoleon crossing the Alps – fact v fiction

age, projecting his superiority through propaganda.[445] On the behavioural front, there is a typically autocratic leadership style with a strong focus on task orientation and little regard for consideration of others. His military success was primarily responsible for his role as a leader in both his profession and later as civic ruler.

The fact that his rule was achieved through a military coup provides little indication of the people's desire for his inherent abilities. There was no real evidence of any particular gift that motivates others, except his natural flair for command and military strategy, which could account for his charisma. Firsthand accounts comment on his magnetic effect on others, but in the main this resembles dominance inculcating fear, rather than being motivational. Dominance may be an attribute of a military commander and dictator but it is not an attribute of a leader who desires or naturally attracts followers. To a large extent Napoleon had few loyal followers: whenever he was absent from court on campaign there was unrest, usurpation and contempt for his rule or his partner or heir. He did not appear to have any great control over either his court or the people.

It would seem that Napoleon was the right man at the right time in the right place and knew what was required in order to be successful. He was able to deliver results and carry the revolutionary ideals of France to the rest of Europe: a warrior who continued the struggle against the oppressive *ancien regime* and institutions. There was no real need for either moral or religious sensibilities required during this period – just someone who enabled the ideals of the revolution. It was a period of social and political upheaval where the social contract of Rousseau need only conform to the practicality of Montesquieu. Even though the writings of Rousseau were distinctly transformational in their appeal, Napoleon rejects them as "idealistic" and prefers to mimic the approach advocated by Machiavelli to the point of formulating his maxims around his philosophy.

The greatest influence on him appears to be the work of Machiavelli. This is consistent with his narcissistic nature and low-quality relationship with others. As a political leader he knew only too well the relationship between martial and political systems, for it was military success that paved the way to political success, and it was his political success that allowed him to continue his military campaigns. His leadership was solely based on the positional power he achieved through military success. This was built on a manipulative approach in dealing with others and making the most of opportunities that arose. Paraphrasing *The Prince* he said: "I am a fox and sometimes a lion. The whole of government is when to be the one or the other:"[446] Napoleon was effectively the Machiavellian Prince in practice. He would adapt to the circumstances and adapt the circumstances to suit his needs.[447] Power was essential for this, in any form, so long as he was able to control others. Political and social theory provided him with the tools to achieve control. He acknowledged that upheaval enabled him to take the throne and it was only though waging war that he would be able to maintain his personal power and control: "I can only keep myself here by force...my empire is destroyed if I cease to be terrifying."[448]

From a social scientific perspective Napoleon meets most of the criteria of narcissistic leadership. His character and attitudes demonstrate grandiosity, lack of empathy towards others, extreme arrogance manifesting as hubris, a lacking of a true moral compass, a strong need for power and control, inflexibility, bursts of rage, high concern for appearance and position, a superiority complex, and finally, a paranoid obsession over the intent of others.

Yet Napoleon's leadership approach appears to differ from how posterity has classified him. He is widely identified as charismatic or transformational,[449] and while these classifications are relevant to certain aspects of his leadership they do not adequately explain his actual approach. This would more closely resemble a hybrid of the individual, adaptive and functional approaches, perhaps most closely aligned with narcissistic leadership. Napoleon sought to be a great man and projected an image of dominance, intelligence and superiority. He had an acute situational awareness and adaptability while providing an image of how a leader should be portrayed. Overall his approach was predominantly individualised, emanating from a strong belief in personal attributes and the need for power and control.

Despite this pejorative leadership ascription, Napoleon is nonetheless widely acknowledged as one of the greatest military commanders in history. His military successes were certainly outstanding, but these must be balanced against his failures, which were also legendary in their devastating effect. As a military commander his personal attributes are those praised in military commanders and promoted as essential: drive, determination, courage and so on. But if we are to evaluate Napoleon from a leadership perspective of his ability to influence followers, then what emerges is an image more closely resembling coercion and control, self-gratification and self-promotion. He was certainly an iconic military commander but the greatness of his leadership lacks the essential element of a concern for followers or moral intent. He may have performed great deeds but as a good, normatively good, leader he does not meet the standard. One would not describe his leadership as ethical, or indeed his personality. His background demonstrates that the manner in which he led is entirely consistent with the influences that acted upon him.

Chapter 5 - **George Washington**

Few men have virtue to withstand the highest bidder.[450]
George Washington

All men, or most men, wish what is noble but choose what is profitable...[451]
Aristotle

Background

Life on the American frontier involved many privations. George, the fourth in line of his father's two marriages, and first of five to his mother, was born into a relatively simple environment in 1732. The early life of George Washington is remarkable by contrast to what he achieved. Born into a rural family in the state of Virginia, his life was not dissimilar to the many immigrants who called America their home: a simple but difficult life in the new world.

George Washington's family was a hybrid of his father's two marriages. Augustine Washington lost his first wife after 15 years of marriage, which bore him three children. He then wed Mary Ball some three years after the death of his first wife, predominantly to care for the children.[452] Augustine had independent means, with land and an interest in an iron mine.[453] He held prominent civic roles as Burgess and Sheriff in the county (a role also held by his father).[454] Despite his prominent civic roles, he had no ties with the bourgeoisie of Virginia.[455] There is little or no documentary evidence available with respect to the relationship between Augustine and his children.[456] The one story of young George chopping down a cherry tree and not being able to lie to his father is apocryphal.[457]

Augustine's second wife, Mary, gave birth to her first child, George, on 22 February 1732. Despite being her first born, George effectively became the middle child of the extended family – the youngest to his three step-siblings and eldest to his direct siblings (Mary was to bear another five surviving children). His mother was known to be stern and controlling, typical of the hardy, rural folk that made a success of an austere lifestyle.[458] Friends of young George would recount later that Mary Washington was kind and courteous but a strong disciplinarian.[459] Other accounts describe her as narrow, begrudging and unimaginative.[460] She ran the family, farm and business, for most of her life by herself, so was obviously a formidable woman.[461] In her twilight years her eldest son Augustine (junior) offered to take care of her, to which she simply replied that she could take care of herself.[462]

In 1743, George, aged 11, lost his father.[463] His mother was 35 at the time and then left in charge of a family of eight children. If anything, George's eldest stepbrother, Lawrence, 14 years senior, became a surrogate father.[464] Lawrence would provide not only a role model of character, but became highly influential in young George's desire to enter the military.[465] Martial interests were also fostered by visits from Lawrence's comrades who would recall stories of military campaigns.[466] Significantly, Lawrence inculcated a desire for social standing and the benefits of wealth.[467]

Even though Virginia was one of the more advanced cities of colonial America, the educational system was still predominantly based around rural schools. Higher education could only really be obtained from abroad. Both of Washington's older stepbrothers were schooled in London, but not George.[468] His education centred around the local county school, which focussed on the basics of arithmetic, geometry, and English.[469] Anecdotal evidence indicates George as being interested in penmanship, "ciphering", and mathematics.[470]

In 1747, aged 15, George embarked on a career as a surveyor. His fine penmanship, attention to detail[471] and desire to be outdoors made this a natural choice. An appointment was facilitated by his family connections with the Fairfaxes. Lord Fairfax had been granted royal consent to lands in the Ohio Country which needed to be surveyed. This desirable role went to George partly as a result of the marriage of his brother, Lawrence, to Lord Fairfax's grand-daughter. To discharge his duty as a surveyor, it was not uncommon to travel on horse and foot over mountains and watercourses, camping out in a hostile environment.[472] In 1751 George's efforts and skill in surveying earned him the respect of Colonel Fairfax[473] who suggested that he might join the Virginian militia.[474] A commission as one of four Adjutant-Generals for the area comprising Virginia would entitle him to the rank of Major.[475] At an early age he became familiar with the importance of status.[476]

Later the following year, in 1752, George's brother Lawrence died. His brother's estate was largely passed on (directly and indirectly) to George. In addition, his brother's death also vacated the northern district militia command.[477] Naturally, George sought this role and, combined with his influential contacts, was granted command of the militia of the northern Ohio country. Around this time, tensions had been mounting between Britain and France in relation to the border area of Virginia and the Ohio country.[478] Both countries laid claim to the same land – conflict was inevitable .

In 1754, Washington was given the mission to lead a force in carrying a despatch to the French informing them that they were on British land. The request on the French to withdraw was rebuked. Later that year Washington was promoted to Colonel and was charged with enforcing the claim against the French. The battle of Great Meadows (1754)[479] ensued, which saw Washington capitulate to the French, leaving behind a fort and artillery.[480] Despite this failure, Washington and his officers and men received wide acclaim for their efforts.[481] It was at that time that Washington resolved that military life was his calling.[482]

The following year, 1755, he found himself part of a British force to again seek the ejection of the French. The British and Virginian forces were entirely routed in what became known as the Monongahela Massacre. Once again, Washington received wide acclaim for his participation in this failed campaign.[483] Ironically, he was subsequently promoted to Commander-in-Chief of the Virginian forces.[484]

In 1758 he led the Virginian forces with a British contingent to again oust the French from the borderlands.[485] On that occasion, the fort was taken without contest after its abandonment by the French.[486] Washington subsequently retired his commission to tend to his personal interests and farm at Mount Vernon.[487]

It is said that Washington's higher education came on the battlefields of the Ohio country.[488] He demonstrated bravery and indefatigability which was noted by fellow officers and soldiers.[489] Washington also seemed to enjoy tremendous personal luck. He was never wounded in battle, although came very close,[490] and always seemed to come out of any difficult situation unscathed, both physically and politically. This was all the more amazing because death seemed to track every step of the early colonialists. He was readily promoted, partly because of his connections, but in the main because his superior officers died in battle.[491] His promotions simply placed him in more senior roles that provided wider social focus on him. When defeat came, as in the Monongahela Massacre, he emerged as a hero for simply surviving. This somehow generated an aura of bravery and selflessness that accompanied him throughout his career. After all, the militia was a volunteer brigade placing itself in harm's way to protect society. Whether they won or lost they emerged as heroes.

In 1759 Washington married the widow Martha Custis.[492] Martha had independent means and brought with her substantial wealth. This independence enabled Washington to seek election to the political position of Burgess in Frederick County, which he achieved.[493] Both his father and grandfather had held similar roles.[494] He spent the following two decades in local politics while focussing on increasing his landholdings and wealth from his farming and investments.[495]

During the 1760s, relations with Britain deteriorated as it attempted to levy greater financial imposts on the American colonies.[496] Although the colonies were bound to Britain there was a growing feeling that the imposts were unnecessarily burdensome and without connection to the benefit to local citizens. The colonies were more like nation states, as they developed so, too, did their autonomy with the people developing an identity independent of British control. While colonial society had acquired a puritanical, royalist character from Britain,[497] the people still harboured ideals of being citizens in their own land.[498] The American colonies had initially peacefully co-existed as part of the British Empire, yet the growing perception of Britain was one of elitism and rapacity.

In 1765 the British Parliament passed the *Duties in American Colonies Act*.[499] Widely opposed in the colonies as an unfair form of taxation, it was repealed in the following year. Further Acts were passed by the British Parliament, imposing taxes on a range of products, which met with equal resistance.[500] By 1769 the colonies had largely reached consensus that the only way to oppose the intervention of Britain was to cease importing her goods.[501] Ultimately, the momentum surrounding the issue of taxation resulted in a call for secession. At the First Continental Congress in 1774, the colonies resolved to seek independence from Britain, thus precipitating the American War of Independence.

Although Washington professed a desire to remain in retirement, his actions betrayed his protestations when he attended the Congress in full military uniform.[502]

When it came time to elect someone to lead the new colonial army against the British, there were few contenders for the role who had the notoriety of Washington. His political connections were influential enough to encourage the Second Continental Congress (1775) to nominate retired Colonel George Washington to the position of General of the Republican Army.[503] The subsequent war against Britain dragged on for the next six years. In that time Washington's military exploits were hardly outstanding.

First Continental Congress

Most battles with the British were lost and much of the eventual success of the colonial army only came after the involvement of foreign nations, notably the former foe France. Despite his lack of military genius, his most notable attributes were tenacity, perseverance and the power to command respect and admiration.[504] The War of Independence, as it became known, concluded in 1781 with the capitulation of the remaining British forces at Yorktown.[505] Although Washington was encouraged by his officer corps to become the new king of America, he instead resigned his commission and returned to his farm and personal interests.[506]

In 1788 Washington was elected to chair the Confederation Congress to determine the form of government the new nation would take.[507] With the decision to adopt a democratic government, the recommendation for the first President was advanced. Washington was proposed and accepted without contest. Despite his reluctance to undertake such an auspicious role, his unanimous nomination arose out of the recognition of the selflessness with which he had provided service to the independence of the nation.[508]

Influences

The familial position of Washington gave him a unique status among his siblings. He was the youngest of his step-siblings, making him a new and exciting addition to the family, but at the same time he was the eldest of his direct siblings. His younger brother was two and a half years junior but his oldest step-brothers were 12 and 14 years senior.[509] As a result, he was neither competitive with his eldest brothers nor complacent about his natural superiority as the eldest of his siblings. He would have enjoyed natural superiority over his younger brother, yet always been aware of his inadequacy with respect to his older brothers. He was noted to be satisfied with his position in the family but envious of none.[510] His position in family would generally inculcate a lack of ambition, aloofness, and a supercilious disregard for others -[511] yet it did not.

If anything he had a dual role to fill in his family. It was necessary for him to both assert himself in the presence of his elder step-brothers, and to maintain the role as head of his immediate siblings. This desire for recognition from his elder step-brothers and sisters, and need to command respect from his younger siblings, would have left an indelible impression. His mother's recognition of him as the head of the rival family to the reigning family was fostered.[512] In some respects George was being groomed by his mother to take over from a regime that had held sway but would one day no longer be the dominant power – a somewhat auspicious predestination.

By the age of five, George's brothers had left home to attend school in England. From an early age he was therefore the oldest male sibling in the family. Six years later his father died, leaving him the oldest male and imposing a high degree of responsibility on him to manage the household.[513]

At school he enjoyed a natural superiority to his classmates by virtue of his height and athleticism. Stories of his ability to throw a stone across the Rappahannock River,[514] run long distances and possessing superior equestrian skills[515] are commonplace. His height advantage over fellow students bestowed on him a sort of authority. Like most young boys he would play war games but he would almost invariably be the one in command.[516] When there were schoolyard disputes, the other boys would defer to his judgement, acknowledging his honesty and fairness in the resolution of disagreements.[517] Unfortunately, there is little reliable evidence of his personal opinions and observations from these years on which to make any reliable analysis.[518]

His greatest early influence came from his mother. Of note was her insistence for obedience from her children.[519] From this, Washington derived the belief that "it is only by obeying that we learn to command".[520] As a consequence, he attributed the foundation of his fortune and fame[521] to his mother. Even though she was renowned for being independent and self-sufficient some biographers have challenged the nature of his relationship finding his attitude to her somewhat indifferent.[522]

Despite the loss of his father at an early age, several figures of note provided guidance. Foremost was his brother Lawrence, to whom we attribute influencing Washington's entry into the military. Lawrence stood in *loco parentis*[523] to George, and for the enlargement of George's mind and the polishing of his manners, Lawrence was an almost ideal elder brother.[524] It is undoubtable that his brother's marriage into the Fairfax family, and the trappings of wealth that attended this union, would have impressed George.

At sixteen, George formed a relationship with an Adjutant Muse who had been introduced to him by his brother.[525] Muse served with Lawrence and provided young George with military stories, books and training in tactics.[526] Although not a formal military education, it nonetheless maintained his interest in martial affairs. Additionally, Colonel William Fairfax (Lawrence's father-in-law) and Lord Thomas Fairfax (William's father) both recognised and fostered the importance of military training, while also inculcating a need for proper behaviour befitting an officer and gentleman.[527]

Washington's involvement in the Virginian militia brought a sense of importance and social standing which was to become central to his conception of self.[528] He was acutely aware that social status was important and so he went about cultivating contacts with local dignitaries and persons of good repute.[529] His quest for ever-higher rank was, in his mind, the main way to achieve social status.[530]

Status and recognition were of central importance to Washington and this in turn drove his ambition. His brother's marriage to Anne Fairfax presented a picture of what could be achieved and so set a model for aspiration.[531] Washington's ambition also stemmed in part from his involvement in the military and the notoriety attached to his commissions.[532] His early exploits as a young officer saw him rise in prominence and the esteem of both fellow soldiers and countrymen. He declared: "the chief part of my happiness" is the "esteem and notice" of the country.[533] Freeman's comprehensive biography on Washington notes that "the perfection of Washington's character was marred by...his ambition..".[534] By his late twenties the emerging pattern of his behaviour was one of bottomless ambition and near obsession with self control".[535]

Washington was also highly opportunistic, being regarded by commentators as one who took what history offered.[536] His acquisition of land was a passion that sometimes came into conflict with others. In one instance, his regiment was bestowed a tract of land and Washington ensured that the better parts went to himself.[537] He also married a wealthy widow who increased his social standing and wealth. Similarly, his movement through the military was marked by constant manoeuvring on a political level to obtain higher command.

What remains is a picture of a person with a strong sense of self and a recognition of the need to maintain that image through civic duty. His desire for status and recognition goes hand-in-hand with a desire for land holdings and title. Though his ambition was great, his stoic disposition tempered this, and stopped him from being perceived as rapacious. While his need to achieve the standards set by his brother drove his outward behaviour, his inward conscience was heavily influenced by his mother. This dichotomy between the superficiality of appearance and the circumspection of conscience is a unique aspect of Washington's character.

> The consideration that human happiness and moral duty are inseparably connected, will always contrive to prompt me to promote the progress of the former by inculcating the practice of the latter.
>
> George Washington

Social/political philosophy

The social and political philosophical influences in Washington's early life are limited. The only real social philosophy was that of Roman republicanism.[538] Early colonialists were ardent in their views of a new order – a better and more democratic republic.[539] Rome stood as a perfect example of a successful nation state: the Romans captured the American imagination because they had done what the Americans hoped to do – sustain an extensive republic over the course of the next century.[540] Even though America had not reached the point of secession from the British Empire during Washington's youth, there was still a sense of independence and destiny among colonialists.

The other work that underpinned the social philosophy of the time was the Bible.[541] Although not strictly a work of social philosophy, it nonetheless provided the fabric for man's relationship with his fellow man and also the role of man in relation to the state and the state to God.[542] As a result, Washington's views were centred on the higher-order values in life: order, security, societal happiness.[543]

Several of his proclamations as President contained direct references to scripture in this regard.[544] In a nutshell, the attitudes that Washington took into his social and political life were an extension of his Christian morality.

Even though Washington had no formal training or erudition in any notable social or political doctrine, he was always quick to address his deficiencies. His views on government and society later in life concur with elements of the early formation of his worldview. For example, in relation to government he stated later in life that the goal of government is the "aggregate happiness of society", [545] which accorded with his early Christian and civic attitude. It also reflected the philosophical influences in England during the late eighteenth century, such as the works of Rousseau and Bentham. Moreover, his attitude towards a utilitarian ethic was based on moral foundations. This is further reflected in "his adherence to Enlightenment definitions of happiness as public happiness, founded in reason, as a human responsibility rather than mere personal enjoyment, ultimately as fulfilment of a moral responsibility to the nation".[546]

This position reflects his early religious and moral perspective that maintained a strong belief that the rights of every man were sacrosanct. His attitude towards political power and the role of society is aptly described in one of his "maxims" with the humility with which Washington demonstrated throughout his life.

Washington advocated that good government was one that served the people for "it is substantially true, that virtue and morality is a necessary spring of popular government."[547] Although Washington was to read many books in his later life before making this comment, his views on the role of politics and society remained fundamentally unchanged.

With no identifiable social or political influence in his early life, it can only be surmised that his conceptions of politics and society were derived principally from moral and religious sources.

Moral/religious philosophy

If there was a dearth of social and political philosophy in the early life of Washington, the opposite can be said of moral and religious philosophy. As with many of his countrymen, he was born and raised in the Christian faith and tradition. He had a strict upbringing, where an emphasis was placed on proper behaviour. The combined effects of his disciplined upbringing and the moral education and religious doctrine to which he was exposed provide the backdrop for understanding the character of Washington.

We know that Washington was baptised as a Christian in the Episcopalian Church.[548] His mother read the Bible to him at home and was strict in her adherence to a Christian lifestyle,[549] as were most Virginians of the time. [550] He attended Church regularly throughout his life,[551] although Freeman states: "...of religion, there was at Ferry Farm an acceptance or belief

> As, under the smiles of Heaven, America is indebted for freedom and independence, rather to the joint exertions of the citizens of several states than the conduct of the commander-in-chief, so is she indebted, for their support, rather to a continuation of those exertions, than to the prudence and ability manifested in the exercise of the powers delegated to the President of the United States.
>
> George Washington

in God and a compliance with the ritual of the Church, but no special zeal or active faith".[552] This makes it difficult to determine Washington's true attitude to religion. His equanimous persona obscures where he stood on religious matters and this can only be gleaned from anecdotal evidence. Some scholars have referred to him as a "lukewarm Episcopalian", [553] saying that he never took communion and would talk about Destiny or Providence rather than God. They also point to the fact that he was a Mason and therefore fundamentally deistic.[554] Some authors maintain that he did not carry his faith with anything more than the required obeisance of the era.[555] Each of these claims needs to be examined further to determine their contribution to Washington's worldview.

On the one hand, there is a body of evidence that asserts Washington was religiously devout. On the other, Washington is regarded as being agnostic. The support for Washington's religiousness is based on several first-hand accounts.[556] A contemporary of Washington, John Marshall, noted: "Without making ostentatious professions of religion, he was a sincere believer in the Christian faith, and a truly devout man."[557] This is reflected in several anecdotes from his life: his actions in counselling his soldiers on the adherence to Christian mores and praying in the battlefield;[558] the inclusion of biblical and religious references in his correspondence;[559] his encouragement for the Indian nation to adopt Christianity;[560] his daily practice of praying while in the office of President and reading from the Bible;[561] the fact that he is reputed to have owned over 150 religious works at the time of his death.[562] His view on religion is no less demonstrated than in his own affirmation that: "religion is as necessary to reason as reason is to religion."[563] These facts do not paint a picture of a "lukewarm" follower of a faith. The evidence seems to support the claim that he was, in fact, a deeply religious person. However, the Christian religion was not the only influence on his attitudes. Other moral philosophy featured prominently throughout his early years. For example, at around 15,[564] he was known to have transcribed a document titled *Youth's Behaviour*. This was in fact an abridged translation of the *Rules of civility and decent behaviour in company and conversation*[565] written by Francis Hawkins (1640).[566] The significance of the influence of these rules on Washington remains controversial. Several biographers have indicated that they form the keystone

of Washington's personality, for example Harrison says: "The last of these useful maxims became the guiding star of Washington's whole career: 'Labour to keep alive in your breast that little spark of celestial fire called conscience'."[567] Such comments attribute great significance to the impact of the rules whereas others have indicated that the transcription of these rules may have been no more than an "exercise in penmanship".[568] Nonetheless, Washington undoubtedly read these "rules" and would have spent some time on them, even if it was only a transcription exercise. The *Rules of civility* are, in their way, a volume on moral philosophy whose assimilation are accentuated at every point in Washington's public and private life.[569] Moreover, they taught that "there was little difference between moral qualities and social ones; they explained that one lived one's life among others, and that, to be successful in society, one must be polite, modest, pleasing, and attentive to others; one must strive to win their confidence and respect."[570]

These qualities describe Washington with more than a passing similarity, and some authors have indicated that this formed the basis of his social interaction.[571] He was noted for having "an acute sense of responsibility to others combined with a desire to win their respect...".[572] Washington's focus on morality is supported by other sources his mother consulted in the rearing of her children. Paulding cites the work of Sir Matthew Hale,[573] *Contemplations, Moral and Divine (1676),* which focuses on good character and moral behaviour. It contains lessons of "piety, morality and wisdom". [574] Paulding goes on to describe Hale as a "sage" and his book as being "filled with lessons of virtue and wisdom".[575] The actual book that was read to Washington by his mother still exists at Mount Vernon, with passages underlined and signs of extensive use. There is no doubt as to the moral effect this work would have had on Washington.

In his late teens, Washington was provided with a copy of Seneca's *Morals* by Colonel William Fairfax.[576] He also provided a copy of *An English compendium of the principal Dialogues of Seneca the Younger*.[577] Reading such literature was not unusual for the time, as many people of the upper class saw the Roman republic a model for their new society.[578] The influence of Seneca's works would have provided Washington with a model for personal conduct.

The contents of *Morals* is almost an exact description of Washington's persona. Several references seem to underpin Washington's conduct, supporting the identification of him as the American Cincinnatus.

> Honours, monuments, and all the works of vanity and ambition are demolished and destroyed over time, but the reputation of wisdom is venerable to posterity.
>
> A good man is happy within himself, and independent upon fortune, kind to his friend, temperate to his enemy, religiously just, indefatigably laborious, and he discharges all duties with a constancy and congruity of actions.
>
> For what does it profit us to know the true value of things if we are transported by our passions? Or, to master our appetites, without understanding the when, the what, the how, and other circumstances of our proceedings?
>
> Seneca *Morals*

This philosophy is reflected in many of Washington's actions on the issue of his reputation and conduct. Examples abound demonstrating this, such as not accepting payment for his command of the revolutionary forces, resigning his commission after successfully leading the victory of the War of

Independence, and his insistence that the new republic establish a noble moral character.

The message of Seneca's *Morals* would be important in tempering the ambition of any young man, and would invariably leave an indelible impression on the need to be circumspect in idealistic aspirations. It would seem that it did, indeed, have such an effect on Washington as he quoted from *Morals* all his life.[579] The *Morals* provided a guide for behaviour (in the stoic tradition) and an insight into what mattered in life.[580]

Washington and his family viewed civic service as a tradition. This is consistent with stoicism, which advocated that civic life is an obligation.[581] It is thus entirely consistent with the literature and philosophy in Washington's life that the adherence to civic duty was seen as an obligation. Whether it was in the capacity of joining the army, or a political role, the motivation was not so much of personal advancement but of personal responsibility.

Christianity derives much of its philosophy from stoicism and early variants adhere to the same principles. It is widely acknowledged that the family consulted the Bible, as the book from Washington's youth is still on display at Mount Vernon. However, biographical accounts of his early life do not acknowledge it as playing a major role in his early education. Moreover, any "religious instruction as George received was of a sort to turn his mind towards conduct rather than towards creed."[582] This aspect is also apparent, as many personal contacts identified Washington more through his deeds than his words.

> A good moral character is the first essential in a man. It is therefore highly important to endeavour not only to be learned but virtuous.
>
> Washington

By the time Washington came of age he joined the Fredericksburg chapter of Freemasons.[583] This was partly another form of social networking and partly a statement of moral uprightness.[584] The Freemasons of colonial America were primarily a society of Christian males who were concerned with the moral integrity of the nation.[585] Moral uprightness and an untarnished reputation were entrance requirements. This would have had immediate resonance with Washington and would have tied in with his upbringing. While Freemasonry in our time has become something of a secret society, in Washington's time it was predominantly a Christian organisation.[586]

The Masons also promoted similar attributes to the stoic ideals which embodied virtue and the regulation of desires and passions; again reflected in Washington's personality. In other words, it was a society that Washington himself was able to use to validate his approach to life.

Washington's morality was at the core of his being. He stated that "".[587] From an early age he placed significant emphasis on good character[588] having been inculcated with courtesy and politeness[589] from his exposure to high society. One of his closest peers, Thomas Jefferson, commented: his integrity was most pure, his injustice the most inflexible I have ever known, no motives of interest or consanguinity, of friendship or hatred, being able to bias his decisions...[590]

To Washington, Christianity provided the rationale for a righteous code of conduct. This was not just a matter of personal propriety but the basis of a sound society. In a letter to the infamous Colonel Benedict Arnold, written in 1775 before the traitor defected, Washington wrote in relation to the manner in which Arnold should conduct himself against opponents "I also give it in Charge to you to avoid all Disrespect to or Contempt of the Religion of the Country and its Ceremonies. Prudence, Policy and a true Christian spirit, will lead us to look with compassion upon their Errors without insulting them..."[591]

The importance of Christianity in this quote is undeniable, but he goes on to say "While we are contending for our own Liberty we should be very cautious of Violating the rights of Conscience in others, ever considering that God alone is the judge of the Hearts of men, and to Him only in this case, they are answerable."[592]

The religious overtones and significance of God is evident, although the line "...only in this case..." is curious. While some would contend that Washington, and his attendants (most likely to have written the notes), would have also had one eye on posterity, the fact remains that he would have had to authorise the correspondence and support it.

Far from being the perfunctory Christian, Washington shows signs of being a religious and highly moral person. His early years reveal significant influences from both moral and religious texts, which are reflected in his personality and his speeches. His personal characteristics are also a reflection of the stoic tradition. The influence of moral and religious doctrine is almost exclusive, as there are little or no other influences of any significance that can be said to have played a major role in the development of his worldview.

Leadership approach

In George Washington we have a person with little formal education and scant erudition in many areas in which he would succeed.[593] The main driving force in his early years was the acquisition of land (wealth) and social standing. This motivation was acquired from both his father and elder brother and seemed something of a family trait. Yet the family was not wealthy. He experienced a modest life with his widowed mother, and then saw a more affluent world in his exposure to life at Belvoir with the Fairfax family. His father and grandfather both held prominent social positions as Burgess, Justices of the Peace and Sheriffs, so there was both a desire to succeed financially and socially.[594] His brother also held a senior appointment in the Virginia militia and married into an influential Virginian family, giving him both social standing and access to influential people. It was not surprising that Washington would seek to emulate the role models to which he had been exposed. It was also customary at the time to marry equal to or higher than your class. This was also a family trait that Washington followed.

The wealthy role models and influences in his life might tend to produce in a person self-aggrandizement and avarice. While it is true that Washington's early years demonstrate a driving ambition[595] and a desire for personal gain, there are also strong signs to indicate that his attitudes were tempered by significant moral sources.

We know that his mother insisted on him being pious and reverent, and his association with the Fairfax's brought him into contact with stoic philosophy and "proper" behaviour. Even though he could have developed a superficial and idolatry lifestyle the opposite in fact ensued.

From a leadership perspective Washington's desire for positional power suggests a clear desire for legitimate authority. While he understood the importance of position, he also recognised that the power he derived was for the benefit of others. This demonstrates a focus on socialised rather than personalised power. Position gave Washington the ability to perform duties that he perceived were primarily for the greater good.

It is safe to say that the main influences in his early life were derived from moral sources. Moral and religious philosophy predominate in his early life, with a continuum from Roman moral philosophy through to contemporary etiquette of his era: from Seneca's *Morals* to Hawkin's *Youth's Behaviour* and Hale's *Contemplations*. While the "Rules" in *Youth's Behaviour* are based on outward behaviour, *Morals* is about the "inner peace and rectitude"[596] which one should maintain. In the middle, we have the moderating influence of the Bible which seems to have only played an initial role supporting a code of conduct. Washington's latter involvement with Freemasonry also supports the morality in the Bible rather than elements of faith.[597] The overall indication is clearly the development of normative behaviour towards others – consideration and respect.

Morality formed the cornerstone of Washington's character. Statements such as: "morals were the way he governed himself",[598] are commonplace among biographical accounts. The correlation between religious and moral philosophies and his character is self-evident. It is more than coincidental that the stoic personality traits of Washington bear strong resemblance to the influences he was exposed at an early age. The focus on virtue and happiness, the personal traits of temperance and tolerance, are all directly out of the stoic conception of a sage.

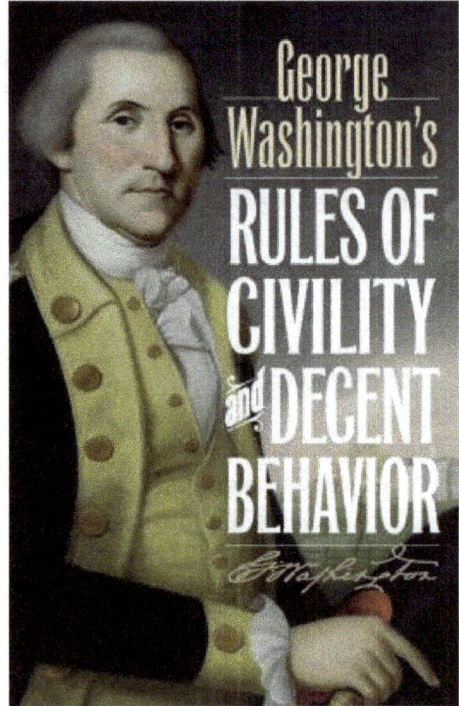

George Washington's RULES OF CIVILITY and DECENT BEHAVIOR

The Rules have now adopted Washington as their creator

The morality demonstrated by Washington is reflected in how he conducted himself, both in actions and words. From his earliest days in absorbing rules of etiquette, and being fashioned for proper behaviour, through to adulthood, where he continued to buy "...handbooks of politeness",[599] is a consistent theme in his life. His farewell address as President proposes that "religion and morality are indispensable supports",[600] as a final statement of the important role these elements play. His actions matched his words. As a salient example: when his officer corps proposed that he should become king at the end of the war, rather than thank them he stridently rebuked the suggestion and warned that such talk would undermine what he and the army had fought for – a civil republic. [601] Weeks later, he wrote: "We now have a national character to establish and it is of the utmost importance to stamp favourable impressions on it".[602] Becoming a self-imposed monarch would not achieve a favourable impression in his mind, and in typical form he resigned his commission and returned to civic life.

The effect of this attitude on others was significant. His selflessness and dedication to the cause of independence led to the unanimous call for him to become the first President of the nation. As with his appointment to Commander-in-Chief of the revolutionary army, he projected an equivocal attitude, expressing unworthiness for the appointment. The fact remains that this reluctant hero's behaviour, based on proper conduct, had a resounding impact on those around him.

Washington recognised the importance of courtesy and politeness in personal relationships.[603] These are manifestations of normative behaviour, such behaviour being an essential ingredient of politics (especially of that time), as "courtesy meant behaviour appropriate to a court" such as the quality of "chivalry which comes from the *chevalier* – a knight".[604] "Politeness is the first form of politics – the way men behave in polite society is related to how they order society".[605] "With an acute sense of responsibility to others combined with a desire to win their respect..."[606] Washington demonstrated that building and maintaining relationships with others was central to his success. He would say in his later years: "Be courteous to all, but intimate with few; and let those few be well tried, before you give them your confidence",[607] a sentiment almost directly taken from *Youth's Behaviour.*

Washington has prompted numerous books on his leadership style and abilities. He is glorified as the founding father of the nation and accorded the respect of his countrymen throughout the ages. Somehow, though, he remains enigmatic to the American public – cold, aloof, unpersonable.[608] Such a persona does not resonate with modern audiences.[609] It also seems that his leadership style was not based on any particularly outstanding quality. He was no orator, no great military commander or even widely popular in social circles.

Most leadership literature around Washington tends to focus on his behaviour as the key basis of his leadership. This is supported by several statements both by himself and others. He said that behaviour is underpinned by character: "in every nomination to office, I have endeavoured as far as my own knowledge extended, or information could be obtained, to make fitness of character my primary object."[610] If asked, "what is the single most crucial quality of a great leader he would reply – Character".[611]

Washington's leadership approach has distinctly ethical elements. His behaviour demonstrates high levels of consideration for others and participatory and collaborative leadership skills[612] with a strong moral overtone. Virtue appears to be a central quality of his behaviour and underpins his relationship with others. There is no real evidence of high-quality personal relationships but his attitude towards others is perceived as having a moral dimension. His behaviour is fundamentally normative, with the aim of acting as a model of leadership. His normative behaviour and his dedication to public service is perceived by followers as having a distinctly socialised focus. The social scientific theory of ethical leadership most closely aligns with the functional elements of his leadership approach. "Ethical leadership is the demonstration of normatively appropriate conduct through personal actions and interpersonal relationships."[613] This form of leadership is often characterised in terms of the conduct and character of the leader - the former concerned with the means and ends of leadership, while the latter being about the internal attributes of the leader. On both accounts Washington conforms with ethical leadership in that his core values drove both his conduct and his actions. While other social scientific theories may also have relevant elements his leadership approach emanated from the manner in which he behaved towards followers and the intent of his actions.

Chapter 6 - **Charles de Gaulle**

Training for war is, first and foremost, training in leadership, and it is literally true, for armies as well as for nations, that where the leadership is good, the rest will follow. [614]
Charles de Gaulle

And any Guardian who survives these continuous trials in childhood, youth, and manhood unscathed, shall be given authority in the state. [615]
Plato

Background

The era in which Charles de Gaulle was born has gone down in history as one characterised by European nationalism. European nations sought to maintain their empires and prestige in an environment of suspicion and detente. France had been struggling with its two implacable opponents for hundreds of years – England and Prussia. Many French saw their county's prestige and reputation as a matter of national pride. This was no less felt by the de Gaulle family who had a long history of resistance and patriotism, dating back to the battle of Agincourt (1415). [616] Despite France losing that battle, a family ancestor, Sieur Jehan de Gaulle, [617] fought defiantly against the English and when offered the option to either serve in the army of King Henry V of England or choose exile and forfeit his estates, he chose the latter. From that time, honour, patriotism and pride became the family creed.

Charles André Joseph Marie de Gaulle was born in northern France, Lille, bordering Belgium, in 1890. He was the third child, second son, of four boys and a girl. [618] His parents both came from prominent French families dating back over five centuries. [619] The family's predecessors had been lawyers, writers, historians and academics, mainly from the bourgeoisie. [620] Around the time of the Revolution of 1789, his parents' families were part of the *petite nobilite* and lost much during the Reign of the Terror. [621] His parents and grandparents were ardent monarchists, Catholics and patriots. [622]

They blamed much of the demise of France and the resulting diminution in their social status on the Revolution. To this single event they attributed the social maladies of France: the rise of individualism, the shift to republicanism and the secularisation of religion (even by 1905 outright disestablishmentarianism). [623] The 1870 War (Franco-Prussian War) under the heir of the Revolution's champion, Napoleon, had then added a spirit of revanchism, and even an element of pacifism and denial in the French nation. [624] To a proud family these were anathema to the national character.

Charles's father, Henri, was an historian and academic. He had a strong sense of social justice and an ardent commitment to both France and the local community. He was able to support the family on his modest income yet still managed to travel around France with them.[625] His connection with his son Charles was particularly strong, demonstrated by Charles later describing the many fond memories of his father in his memoirs.[626]

Charles's mother, Jeanne, reared her six children in what can only be described as typical for the time. Some biographers say that his mother's passionate and sensitive nature was passed on to her son.[627] Charles acknowledges his mother's "passion" for France in his memoirs.[628] Despite this, some biographers indicate that his childhood relationship with her was somewhat tempestuous and disrespectful.[629]

As a child Charles had a pugnacious temperament. He was known to be the bully of the family, with an independent and surly nature.[630] In games with his brothers and friends, he would invariably be on the side of France, usually the General of the French forces. In the tradition of the kings of France who pronounced "*J'etat, c'est moi*", he would say to his brothers "You Xavier, are Austria. Jacques is Prussia. Pierre is Italy. Of course, *I am France*".[631] He was acutely aware that de Gaulle simply meant "of France" and he and the rest of the family took that seriously.

The de Gaulles were a strict Catholic family who valued education. Charles was initially taught by the Christian brothers and then the Jesuits.[632] Academically he was average.[633] With an independent nature, de Gaulle took interest in only what appealed to him, dismissing everything else as "absurd".[634] His central interests at school were literature and philosophy.[635] This was inspired by his father, who was a professor of history, mathematics and philosophy.[636] His father became the headmaster of the school Charles attended towards the end of his schooling – the Jesuit College of Immaculate Conception.[637] More than anyone else, his father fostered Charles's interest in the arts.[638]

Some authors have also noted the culture of northern France having more patriotic influence on the attitudes and behaviour of its inhabitants.[639] The region where de Gaulle grew up was at the crossroads where invasions

occurred for over half a millennia. The northerners were somewhat elitist, and considered the southerners less cultured. A sense of contemptuous disdain was characteristic of the inhabitants of the north – the typical Gallic aloofness and arrogance of which de Gaulle was a typical example.

By the time de Gaulle was 10 years old the 1870 War was still fresh in the national conscience.[640] In the age of the *Belle Époque,*[641] the loss to Germany was seen as a blot on France's reputation. France had relinquished the regions of Alsace and Lorraine to Kaiser Wilhelm I of Prussia, exposing the regions west of the Rhine to further incursions. This was no less felt by the de Gaulles: "an anxious concern about the fate of our country came as second nature to my three brothers, my sister, and myself".[642] De Gaulle's father had fought in that war under Napoleon III.[643] He would recount stories of the glory days of previous rulers of France from Charlemagne to Napoleon;[644] the greatness of the latter still foremost in the minds of the army. To many Frenchmen, and the army in particular, revenge for the defeat of 1870 was just a matter of time.

As a boy, de Gaulle took exception to the contretemps that France faced during his youth.[645] The country's loss of honour in the previous war, her receding dominion in the world, her political instability and her ignominy from foreign intrigues all featured prominently in current affairs.[646] He prayed that he would one day do "something great"[647] to restore France to her previous glory. He later recounted in his memoirs that as an adolescent: "the fate of France, whether as a subject of history, or the stake in public life, interested me above everything."[648] This sense of public devotion was a driving force in both his later decision to join the army and his dedication to public service in general.

At the turn of the century, France was going through a revival of secularisation, and the Jesuit schools of France were subsequently closed down.[649] Charles was attending a Jesuit school where his father was principal at the time of the school's closure and so was subsequently shipped off to Belgium to complete his education.[650] Towards the end of his schooling in that country, he decided that he would join the French army. In an amazing transformation, his grades improved significantly to meet the standard of entry to Saint-Cyr military school.[651] By the end of 1904 he had achieved his aim.

Even though there was no early indication that Charles would enter the military, the conditions were all present for it to seem likely: his father had been a soldier and there was a strong sense of identity between them in relation to national honour.[652] His earliest family experiences reinforced the importance of national prestige, as his father would recall the glory days of France on their visits to places such as *Les Invalides* and *L'Arc de Triomphe*.[653] By age 15 Charles had developed a firm desire to join the army and lead it to some future glorious victory.[654] With a deeply patriotic family, and growing concerns about the safety of France, Charles's decision to enter Saint-Cyr military school was met approvingly by his parents. In 1905 he became entrant 119 of 221 (800 applied).[655]

Saint-Cyr was the prestigious military training school established by Napoleon Bonaparte. A young man could not but be inspired by the statue of the great commander at its gates. The school turned out the future officers of the French army, trained to high levels of military expertise and *élan*. However, de Gaulle was not popular there. He had few friends and was mostly ridiculed for his height and awkward looks.[656] What was emerging during this period was the persona of a loner.

In 1911 de Gaulle graduated as Second Lieutenant from Saint-Cyr – thirteenth in his class.[657] His performance at Saint-Cyr saw him develop into what his superiors regarded as an "excellent officer".[658] For his first posting he was able to select the 33rd Infantry Regiment, commanded by General Pètain (later to head the Vichy Government under German occupation in World War II). He could have chosen the more prestigious cavalry but instead chose the infantry, because it was "more military".[659]

At the same time, matters in Europe were deteriorating. Kaiser Wilhelm II had made even more threatening moves towards France and it was clear that Europe was once again on the brink of war. A tenuous peace ensued as both countries readied themselves for confrontation.

The Prussian states had unified after the War of 1870, creating the German nation. This, and growing nationalism during the early part of the twentieth century, provoked neighbouring countries to form a system of alliances across Europe. The situation was such that if two countries went to war then all countries were committed. When Germany attacked Belgium in 1914, France was immediately brought into the conflict.

De Gaulle's 33rd Regiment was called into service to defend France's border and to come to the aid of its Belgian ally.[660] In his regiment's first engagement, he was wounded and hospitalised.[661] He rejoined the regiment for the early phase of the Battle of Verdun but was wounded from a bayonet and subsequently captured.[662]

De Gaulle was presumed dead by the army after his encounter at Fort Douaumont near Verdun.[663] He was entered into the Legion of Honour for the bravery displayed in charging the German onslaught with his men.[664] He would be relegated *persona non grata* as a prisoner of war under German control for the remainder of World War I. But his internment did not sit well with a man of destiny. He repeatedly attempted to escape (no less than five times) and was imprisoned at higher levels of security over the years.[665] If there was a medal for persistence, then de Gaulle would certainly have been a candidate. Stories differ about whether the attempts were acts of defiance or survival. His internment nonetheless gave him the opportunity to coalesce his thoughts. He also remained active in pursuing the affairs of France and gave military appraisal seminars to his fellow prisoners from the news that reached the camps.[666] He may have been a captive, but at least from his perspective he was still active in the affairs of the state.

On his release in 1918, de Gaulle returned to his former regiment.[667] The allies had prevailed, and France dictated harsh peace terms designed to cripple the German state. Initially serving for a brief period in Poland with the 4th Division of the Polish *chasseurs,*[668] Captain de Gaulle received a post to instruct at Saint-Cyr, and then subsequently entered *L'Ecole Supérieur de Guerre* (War College).[669] At this time "he began to realize the gifts of intellect and leadership that he had always felt within himself, and his superiority over his fellow officers stood out for all to see."[670]

His career followed a fairly bureaucratic path during the ensuing years, with his promotion to Major in 1927 taking rather longer than expected.[671] By then de Gaulle was notorious for his emotive lectures and writings on the role of the army and its function in warfare. To the army he was nothing short of a gadfly, often criticising its defensive policy towards

Germany and its reluctance to rearm. He won no friends in high command.[672]

With de Gaulle's promotion to Major came command of the Army of the Rhine (19th Infantry - *Battaillon de chasseurs à pied* (BCP)) from 1927-1929.[673] This was followed with a two-year posting to the Middle East.[674] By 1932 his knowledge and reputation on strategy gained him a position at the *Conseil Supérieur de la Défense Nationale*.[675] Still an ardent opponent of French strategy, he continued to agitate for change. By then he was a firm believer in the pre-emptive force of the modern tank.[676] In 1937 he was promoted to full Colonel and given command of a tank regiment to prove his theories.[677]

Two years later France was again at war on her own soil. Germany had once again invaded Belgium and surged across the French borders in waves of tank divisions. Initially de Gaulle's opposing division achieved some success in repelling the German onslaught. As a result de Gaulle was

promoted in the field to General.[678] However, France was falling around him, and in a last-ditch effort by the French military, de Gaulle was recalled to take the position of Under Secretary of Defence in 1940 to formulate a final strategy for survival. These efforts came too late and France crumbled under the German onslaught and capitulated. De Gaulle and his family departed the country for London. He would spend the remainder of the war years as a sort of leader in exile, taking it upon himself the *de facto* role of resistance leader against the Vichy regime.[679]

General de Gaulle was the voice of Free France during the war years and the reformer of his country in the years after. He did not achieve any great military successes during his career, (the halcyon days of French military supremacy had long passed). Instead he acted as an agitator by demonstrating the flawed strategy of the government as the lone voice of dissent. As with his persistence to escape internment in World War I, his rebelliousness against the establishment was eventually recognised as an expression of patriotism. This independent cause to support his countrymen while in exile was his only means of opposing the oppressors. De Gaulle may have been outnumbered and outmanoeuvred but he never gave up.

By the end of the war de Gaulle attempted to create a political party and take control, but it was not to succeed. His famous return to France from exile as the country's defiant champion did not materialise into civic leadership, at that time. He then spent the years 1945-1957 in a form of political stasis. Yet he still raged against the political dissention in France under the Fourth Republic, until 1958 when he was called to commence the Fifth Republic.[680] He was inaugurated as President in that year and remained in political control of the country until 1962, and then again from 1965-1969. As President he saw and introduced some of his country's most significant foreign and domestic policies, and of course, the restoration of his country's honour in Europe and on the world stage.

Influences

De Gaulle was effectively the middle child of the family. He had an elder brother and sister and two younger brothers. With elder siblings he would have needed to assert his position, but at the same time be aware of the intricacies in dealing with a male and a female. His brother and sister were only a little older, two and one year older respectively. The proximity in age of his slightly elder sister may have made her more of a peer than an older sibling. His next sibling, a brother, arrived three years after he was born, placing Charles in the exact middle of two brothers – one to revere and one to mentor.

Young Charles's pugnacious and competitive nature has been cited by both his mother and sister.[681] He was known to dominate both his older and younger brothers from an early age.[682] He took war games rather seriously (to the point of beating his younger brother on one occasion for failing to swallow a secret message).[683] This competitiveness and need to assert himself could be related to his uncertain position in the family, with a need to contend with the strong paternal bonds already established with his elder siblings, while at the same time competing for attention with two new arrivals.

Both parents feature prominently in de Gaulle's early life. There does not appear to be anything but an ideal relationship with both of them. His *War Memoirs* exhibit an adulation of his parents.[684] His father was something of a hero to young Charles. He had fought in the 1870 War and relayed stories of his encounters defending France. His father also recounted the previous glories of France; the reign of the Bourbons, Bonapartes and the empire. His father's status as a professor and headmaster at the school Charles attended would have provided him with a model of authority. It is notable that de Gaulle later says of his father that he "was filled with a feeling for the dignity, the worth of France. Through him I discovered her history."[685] An early interest in philosophy was of importance to him and his siblings being provided by their father: from "Racine and Moliere" to "Victor Hugo and Edmond Rostand".[686]

The families of Charles's parents not only lived close by, but also spent holidays together.[687] Inside this close-knit realm was perhaps the next most important influence in his life, Josephine Maillot, his maternal grandmother.[688] She was a writer and wrote several novels in a "high moral tone" [689] in addition to serious biographical works such as the life of Daniel O'Connell, *The Liberator of Ireland*.[690] Young Charles read this, which detailed the life of a reactionary struggling against the established regime for Catholic emancipation. It demonstrated to de Gaulle that one man can have an effect when confronted with injustice. Further family influence came from the work of his uncle, also named Charles, who wrote *The Celts of the nineteenth century: an appeal to the living representative of the Celtic race (1865)*.[691] It sought to re-establish the Celt's social bonds which had atrophied. The overwhelming lesson in the book is one of struggle and the need to maintain one's heritage if it is not to vanish.[692] Both the above works identify the importance of national identity. De Gaulle also absorbed numerous philosophical works by Pascal, Socrates, Cicero, St Augustine, Chateaubriand, Corneille, Goethe, Descartes, Kant, Heine, Hegel, Charles Maurras, Henri Bergson, Péguy, Maurice Barrès, Marquis Rene de la Tours du Pin, Ernest Pischari, Niccolo Machiavelli and Nietzsche.[693] His coverage of poets exceeded the school curriculum and consisted of Lucretius, Virgil, Racine, Corneille, Rostand, Péguy, Goethe, Heine, Vigny and Déroulèdes.[694] Where his education differed from his peers was in the exposure to additional history, philosophy and poetry. In relation to history de Gaulle became acutely aware of the campaigns of Caesar, Hannibal, Turenne, Flaubert and Napoleon. His nature was to absorb disparate works of varied content, no doubt supported by his philosopher father and literary family. To this an overall awareness of current affairs was added. It was shared and fostered by a patriotic family who took a keen interest in the socio-political matters of the time.[695]

Socially, there does not appear to be any notable issues with school colleagues. His height gave him a natural superiority but also tended to single him out as different. As with his brothers, he attempted to assert his authority over others and projected an air of command that seemed innate.[696] After his entry to Saint-Cyr Military Academy he met the next most influential person in his early life – Philippe Pétain.[697] Pétain was known as the hero of Verdun yet was unpopular with the military hierarchy for his intransigent and dogmatic views. There was an immediate attraction to this outsider which de Gaulle was to later acknowledge as the most significant leadership influence in his life: "My first colonel – Pétain – taught the art and meaning of command"[698] and "from him I learned the principles of leadership".[699] It is not unusual for a new recruit to consider their first military commander with reverence, but the similarities between Pétain and de Gaulle are striking. In many ways de Gaulle modelled his leadership style on Pétain's. A profile of Pétain is illustrative: he maintained a distance from his sub-ordinates and was considered cold and aloof; he was extremely knowledgeable on matters military; he rebelled against accepted military doctrine; he maintained an image of excellence; he was self assured and despised mediocrity; and above all, he was a patriot and revered the role of the army.[700] The same could be said of de Gaulle.[701]

Man of destiny

De Gaulles decision to enter the military came as a result of seeing the play *L'Aiglon;* the story of the tragic life of Napoleon's son. *L'Aiglon* was the nickname for Napoleon Bonaparte's son and is literally translated as "the eaglet". He was also known as Napoleon II, and after the defeat of France at Waterloo he spent his life with his mother, Marie Louise, an Austrian princess. Marie Louise had been forced to flee France following Waterloo and Napoleons subsequent abdication. Although Napoleon II should have been the emperor of the French he grew up as the Duke of Reichstadt. Raised in the Austrian tradition, he is portrayed in the play as living in a gilded cage, kept from his true destiny and tormented by the greatness of his father and his own inferiority as a sickly aimless aristocrat. He died at only 20 years old - having achieved nothing.

Such a fate horrified de Gaulle. After seeing this play, at only ten years of age, he pronounced to his family that he had decided to join the army when he was old enough. By age 15 he was already fashioning himself as a French commander by imitating past officers and composing essays on how he would save France in a conflict with Germany. By the time he was ready to leave school his grades had improved mainly to satisfy entry to the military academy. His conduct during his years of service showed no signs of diminishing his spirit to be the voice of free France. Despite repeated setbacks in his career de Gaulle persisted to establish himself as one of the key figures in restoring and maintaining Frances status and pride.

Social/political philosophy

The main source of de Gaulle's social and political views emanated from his family. They were conservative, religious and nationalistic.[702] As a boy he pronounced that his "interest in life consisted in one day rendering some signal service and that I would have the occasion to do so".[703] This was a lofty aim for a young boy and may be directly related to the influence of his nationalistic parents. To understand de Gaulle, it is critical to understand the family in which he grew up. His family shared a central concern – the welfare of France. This was the touchstone on which de Gaulle's   views
developed.

His parent's political influence was complemented by other notable individuals such as Charles Maurras.[704] He was a friend of his father's, and would meet with him at the family home.[705] Maurras was a member of *L'Action Française* (a political counter-revolutionary movement and publication of the time, which sprung out of the intrigues of the Dreyfuss affair which divided French citizens).[706] For conservative Frenchmen *L'Action*

Française was the staple reading of the time.[707] It began circulation in 1898 and operated as the voice of nationalistic France through most of de Gaulle's youth.[708] The views expressed in *L'Action Française* were predominantly nationalistic, monarchist and counter-revolutionary.[709] The periodical advocated that all citizens owed an obligation to the state and the restoration of the monarchy was one of its central tenets. Maurras proposed the concept of "integral nationalism"[710] which involved the creation of an ordered society based on strong leadership. His two principal theories were "politics first" and "France, France only".[711] These views suited the de Gaulle family's conservatism, which could be labelled Social Catholicism,[712] a doctrine that greatly influenced like-minded French families.[713] "De Gaulle's distinction between *la nation profonde* and the regime is reminiscent of Maurras's between the *"pays reel"* and the *"pays legal"* – between, as he saw it, the "reality" of the nation and the "legal" Republic artificially imposed on it. De Gaulle's ideas of carving up Germany in the late 1940s were entirely in *L'Action Française* tradition."[714] Above all de Gaulle's debt to Maurras is clear in his emphasis on the need for a strong executive authority. De Gaulle's presidency, and the rationale for it, was in a sense a democratized and republicanized version of Maurras's monarch. The principles in *L'Action Française* acted to coalesce de Gaulle's political views as Social Catholicism based on social and moral principles. "It is probably in the tradition of Social Catholicism that de Gaulle's social thought should be situated."[715]

It was claimed de Gaulle was "fascinated" by Maurras;[716] so much so that some writers have coined his influence as the Maurrassisme of de Gaulle.[717] This influence lasted de Gaulle's entire career.

The similarity between the de Gaulle family's opinions and those of Maurras are more than coincidental. They, too, blamed most of the decline in France's "grandeur" (a term that de Gaulle favoured and used in his speeches at the military colleges and in his writing) on the revolution of 1789. Maurras did not agree that there was a social contract between state and polity and regarded the views of writers like Rousseau as contributing to the decline of France.[718] Maurras developed social and political thought that helped establish right-wing theory in France.[719] De Gaulle maintained a lifelong relationship with Maurras.[720]

Another influential conservative reactionary of the time was Maurice Barrès, novelist and later resistance fighter. He, too, was well known to the de Gaulle's and also a member of *L'Action Française*.[721] Along with Maurras he promoted a form of ethnic nationalism,[722] which was at the heart of revanchism.[723] De Gaulle "...was attracted by Maurras's insistence on the need for a strong state, but otherwise he seems to have felt a greater affinity for the ecumenical nationalism of Barrès."[724] Barrès, too, rejected the notion of the social contract as "imbecilic because it is a dialectical construction about an abstract man"[725] – dismissing Rousseau's contract as idealistic. To him there was no general will of the people but a pre-existing national character.[726] As such, he opposed the French Revolution as an act of rampant individualism, and the apposite view of the state being more important than its individuals. Barrès advocated that the state is grounded in the soil, its history, its traditions and its inheritance.[727] These views left an indelible impression on young de Gaulle and found expression in later works, most notably *Le fil de l'épee (The Edge of the Sword)* (1932) and *La France et son armée (France and her army)* (1938).

Both Maurras and Barrès promoted a monarchistic political model that relied on strong independent leadership. This perspective was consistent with that of Hegel who proposed the qualities of leadership based on character and an ability to overcome adversity. Hegel also inspired the notion of heroic leadership - a man of history would be required in a time of crisis. De Gaulle was aware of Hegelian thought[728] and felt that he was destined to fulfil some signal role that these perspectives would have only entrenched.

Another person of relevance to the development of de Gaulle's social and political views was Henri Bergson.[729] De Gaulle himself acknowledges his influence in *The Edge of the Sword*.[730] Bergson was a contemporary philosopher in the liberalist tradition who also influenced Maurras and the famous French poet Péguy.[731] Bergson's philosophy is based on the "holy trinity of decisive qualities: instinct, intuition and intelligence".[732] His appeal to de Gaulle has also been attributed to his "readiness to accept the spiritual side of life, and his pragmatism".[733] From Bergson de Gaulle derived his belief in intuition, instinct and intelligence:[734] "It is Bergson, also, who has shown that the only way in which the human mind can make direct contact with reality is by intuition",[735] as "the leader, like the artist, must have an inborn propensity which can be strengthened by the exercise of his craft."[736]

The diversity of philosophical influences is mirrored by the poetry de Gaulle consumed. One of his favourites was the nationalistic poet Charles Péguy.[737] De Gaulle opens his book *France and her army* with the Péguy quotation: *"mere, voyez vos fils, qui se sont tant battus!"*[738] The passion of Péguy and the appeal of nationalism are immediately apparent. Most of Péguy's writings were in the form of poetic verse laden with social and political overtones. This is evident in de Gaulle's own writing from an early age, as in his essay: *Une mauvaise rencontre (An unfortunate meeting)*.[739] The subject of this small piece seems simple enough – a traveller is confronted with a gentleman rogue who proceeds to fleece him of all his possessions in a decorous manner. The moral of the story is that the powerful can do what they want to the weak as long as they follow accepted conventions.[740] Péguy's writings on the inappropriate use of power within an established framework are clearly reflected in de Gaulle's thought.

Péguy became the inspiration of World War II French resistance fighters.[741] His works most likely aroused a sense of defiance in de Gaulle, as at heart de Gaulle was a *resistant*.[742] His writings were a departure from the hatred-inspired nationalism of Barrès and shifted de Gaulle's thinking over to a more socialistic/communitarian view.[743] This presented a more humane view of the role of the citizen in society, one based on selflessness, defiance, patriotism and bravery. Péguy was a strong supporter of the army and giving oneself for one's country.[744] Such views undoubtedly left an indelible impression on a young man focussed on restoring the national honour.

De Gaulle's social perspective continued to moderate, with his exposure to other works. Towards the end of his schooling his father made him read François-René de la Tours du Pin's *Vers un ordre social Chretien (Towards a Christian social order)* (1907) and *Aphorismes de politique social (Aphorisms of social policy)* (1909).[745] Du Pin advocated "the harmony of the social body"[746] which implied a break with "the liberalism and individualism of 1789, which were responsible for the class struggle".[747] Du Pin also advocated Social Catholicism and was a member of *L'Action Française*.[748] His republican ideals and Catholic allegiance found immediate receptivity among de Gaulle's parents who were both republicans and devoutly Catholic.

> When faced with the challenge of events, the man of character has recourse to himself. His instinctive response is to leave his mark on action, to take responsibility for it, to make it *his own business*... We say of a statesman, a soldier, or a man in business who conceives rightly, that he has a 'sense of reality', that he has a 'gift' or that he is in possession of 'vision' or 'flair'.
>
> C de Gaulle *Le fil de l'epee*

It is clearly evident that the works de Gaulle consumed promoted a need for strong leadership in order to change the status quo.[749]The importance of strong leadership was reinforced by his appreciation of the political philosophy of Nietzsche. Nietzsche described a leader as a man of action[750] and possessing a "gift"[751] which de Gaulle describes in similar terms of a "man of character"[752] that possesses a "gift".[753]

De Gaulles conception of leadership was an amalgam of concepts, which is are also reflected in another work: *La discorde chez l'ennemi* (*The enemy's house divided*). This is succinctly describes in Robert Eden's translation of the same in these terms:

> *The enemy's house divided* is a philosophically fundamental book for understanding de Gaulle. It reveals the extent to which de Gaulle's statesmanship was a deliberate and carefully premeditated response to Nietszshe's influence over men of action and over educated opinion. The foundations of de Gaulle's understanding of military and political action was his sustained reflection on the significance of Nietzsche's philosophical influence for political life, for serious citizenship and statesmanship...Insofar as Nietzsche's philosophy of action is the great alternative to which de Gaulle opposed his own thought, it is the touchstone of de Gaulle's thought...[754]

De Gaulle's perspective of strong leadership is also tempered by the need for moral conscience. Social justice and order are common themes in many of the works and would undoubtedly be core to Social Catholicism. Ultimately, the need for leadership was to better the nation of France and her people: "the search for national unity was to be a constant theme of his life".[755]

Moral/religious philosophy

De Gaulle attended Catholic and Jesuit schools throughout his youth and obtained a Christian education taught in the Catholic tradition of the time.[756] This form of religious education concentrated on theological doctrine from the New Testament that was expected to be learnt to a high standard. Inherent in these stories is Christian morality which is based around man's relationship with others. What is of interest is the extent and manner to which Catholic doctrine influenced such a nationalistic individual as de Gaulle.

It has been identified that the de Gaulle family adhered to a philosophical perspective that integrated social and political philosophy – Social Catholicism. De Gaulle's worldview does not seem to make a clear distinction between the philosophies. It could be said that he was equally influenced by both the moral and temporal aspects of religion and that he developed a system that tried to blend those in order to develop a better nation. Although he had been exposed to Catholic ideology,[757] it would appear that he shifted his allegiance from God to the state.[758] "France appears on almost every page of his writing, God almost never."[759]

De Gaulle was well aware of the teachings of the Bible but he only credited them with a simplistic morality. Combined with the moral philosophies of Montaigne, Pascale, Lucrece and Saint Augustine[760] (with which he was aware) seemed to direct his attention to the moral elements of religion rather than the spiritual. In *The Edge of the Sword* he demonstrates a leaning towards the pragmatic through statements such as: "The perfection preached in the Gospels never yet built up an empire."[761] To de Gaulle action rather than values were the key to leadership because it was more important to "...satisfy the secret desires of men's hearts..."[762] and "capture their imagination"[763] than to preach. When de Gaulle talks in terms of "...all leaders of men, whether political figures, prophets, or soldiers, all those that can get the best out of others, have always identified themselves with high ideals...",[764] his concept of "high ideals" are more akin to goals and aspirations than morals. However, he also states: "to be obeyed, the man in command must today rely less on his rank than on his own values".[765] This reference to values is what he describes as character.

The "man of character"[766] is clearly portrayed in *The Edge of the Sword*. To de Gaulle, character is a moral quality. In order for an army to be effective he opines that it must have a sound moral base which is to be found in its leadership. Its leaders must have an "ideal" which he describes as a "moral revival".[767] The qualities required in such a leader include acceptance of responsibility, an ability to make decisions and the exercise of will (determination).[768] The leader is a lone decision-maker – aloof, energetic, autonomous and arrogant. The latter being supported by de Gaulle's stipulation that a leader must remain apart from his followers in order to establish a mystique, as "there is no authority without prestige" and "no prestige unless he keeps his distance".[769] He goes on to quote Cicero in *The Edge of the Sword*: "judge all conduct in the light of the best examples available"[770] in further support of the need for exemplary conduct. As such, de Gaulle's ideal leader is one who acts from sound moral principles.[771] He is not explicit as to what these are but it is evident that the honour and reputation of the nation are paramount.

A man of character did not simply emerge in the humanist sense but was created and formed through exposure to education and moral direction. Behind Alexander (the Great) there was Aristotle, he would proclaim.[772] Yet de Gaulle's self-concept was somewhat arrogantly conceived as moral superiority. The basis for this seems to lie in his dedication to the nation's grandeur and the self-justified belief that this was the highest moral purpose.

Leadership approach

De Gaulle's leadership approach is heavily influenced by both the family environment in which he was raised and the literature to which he was exposed. His youth exposed him to a range of social and political doctrines. He was not overtly religious but he was certainly exposed to Christianity at school and home. At an early age it would seem that his country, the state, had become his *raison d'être* with social and political philosophy his touchstone.

> Nothing great is ever achieved without the passion which is to be found in the man of character... nothing great will ever be achieved without great men, and men are only great if they are determined to be so.
>
> C de Gaulle *Le fil de l'epee*

Recounting the chronology of his character development bears some explication for its link to his worldview. At age six he was always the leader of the French army in war games against his brothers. At age 10 he had decided to become a soldier after being disturbed by the broken image of Napoleon Bonaparte's son in *L'Aiglon*. At age 15 he wrote a school essay where he, General de Gaulle, saved France from a war with Prussia,[773] and also pretended to be a famous past hero, General Faidherbe,[774] in a practical joke on his family.[775] Even his environment was influential: his first family home, where his father recounted the grandeur of imperial France, was near the palace of Versailles; his next home was near *L'École Militaire,* where tales of Napoleon and the *Grande Armée* would be regular topics of conversation; his final childhood home was near *Les Invalides,* again used to invoke images of past glories.[776] These facts he recounted in his *Memoirs as:* "...the symbols of our glory...the conquered battle flags quivering in the vault of the *Invalides*"[777] were ever present in his mind. The concepts of greatness and heroism are recurring themes in de

Gaulle's life. These concepts are also present in the works he consumed, such as those of Hegel, where most likely derived his "heroic notion of leadership".[778]

The notion of being a saviour was instilled from an early age, such that by age 19,[779] while at military college, he was writing heroic notations in books, such as:[780] "In a camp, surprised by a night attack, when everyone fights alone against the enemy, no one asks the rank of him who first raises the flag and gives the first call to rally..",[781] to statements in his books such as: "when crisis comes it is him they follow".[782]

At school de Gaulle did not appear to have many friends and was something of a loner. This continued into military college where he did not enjoy any great camaraderie among fellow cadets.[783] As an officer he remained aloof and distant from peers,[784] preferring solitude to interaction.[785] The focus always seemed to be on himself and his ideals. Such an attitude could be cultural, as it is similar to the solipsistic nature of young Napoleon and, like Napoleon, de Gaulle only sought attention when it meant furthering his reputation or agenda. A case in point is when he was made Under Secretary of Defence in World War II, where his first action was to call a press conference to have his picture taken and make a public statement – even as the Germans were rolling towards Paris.[786]

Lacouture quotes Paul de Villelume in an illuminating encounter on the day of de Gaulle's appointment:

> De Gaulle came into my office. The first thing he did was to tell me how happy he was to have me under his orders. I instantly told him that I was in no way subordinate to him.

To Paul Reynaud,[787] Baudouin and I painted the liveliest, most disturbing picture of his new colleague's boundless ambition.

> "But what more can he want?"
> "Your place, Monsieur le President." [788]

De Gaulle's attention always seemed slightly different to the allies

De Gaulle is frequently described as arrogant, aloof, contemptuous, image conscious, stubborn, authoritarian and egocentric.[789] He lacked warmth and was only capable of inspiring loyalty in a few.[790] He had little interest in women.[791] He claimed to be a man of the people and a patriot, yet re-marked that "the French are cattle".[792] In politics he didn't care what your political allegiance as long as you were useful.[793] His style was distinctly authoritarian: "It is the task of the political leader to dominate opinion: that of the monarchs of the council, of the people, since it is from these that they draw their authority."[794] He was certainly not egalitarian, main-taining a set of rules for himself and a set for others: he was contemptu-ous of politicians and their involvement in military affairs yet this never applied to himself.[795] He described other politicians disparagingly as achieving their goals through "trickery and calculation".[796] He rarely aligned himself with political parties or other people unless absolutely ne-cessary. He seemed to have had few close followers. For example, when he left for London after Paris fell he did so without a retinue.[797] Churchill ad-mired him for his resoluteness but he aggravated Roosevelt to the point of distraction. Roosevelt observed that de Gaulle: "could create power for himself with nothing but his own rectitude, intelligence, personality and sense of destiny".[798]

De Gaulle's leadership does not identify with any single leadership approach. On one hand his approach could be described as conforming to an individualistic approach based around his self belief. In his writing he goes to lengths to identify particular leadership traits that he prescribed as necessary: decisiveness, responsibility, determination,[799] intelligence and intuition.[800] He also believed that only great men achieve great things and that a successful leader possesses a certain *je n'est ce quoi*: an indefinable element which he sought to manufacture.

> Men, in their hearts, can no more do without being controlled than they can live without food, drink and sleep. As political animals they feel the need for organisation, that is to say an established order and for leaders.
>
> C de Gaulle *Le fil de l'epee*

On the other hand he also displays quite and adaptive approach to leadership. To him every situation was unique and one adapted to it accordingly. He was contemptuous of "systems" and standard protocols. He cited Napoleon as a master of the contingent, when he summed up a commander's success as based on the ability to: (1) grasp the situation, (2) adapt to it, and then, (3) turn it to his advantage.[801] The latter was achieved through the possession of power. But de Gaulle's conception of power differs from Napoleon's.

This confluence of purpose and desire result in the pragmatic realisation of the need for power. The picture emerges of de Gaulle as a person driven by a need for power to achieve his mission. This presents a conundrum with de Gaulle – was he an ardent, selfless patriot or a constitutional megalomaniac?

While his rhetoric and youthful ardour tend to portray the former, other commentators have noted the latter.[802] While one has noted that "there is but one theme in the life of Charles de Gaulle, and that is power,"[803] another notes that de Gaulle's motivations were about "the effective use of means, and not about ends."[804]

It is true that only in a position of power can one achieve great things, but the dilemma with de Gaulle is whether it was power for power's sake or for the good of the nation. De Gaulle said: "However egocentric it might seem to the rest of the world, it was a matter of simple historical necessity to become the State."[805] This seems to be the case as "his every act and every word are designed to carry out his single minded purpose to restore France to greatness, without which, according to him, she is not France."[806] This is consistent with his character from an early age. De Gaulle took it as his personal mission to restore the grandeur of France. If power was what was needed to do so, then that is what he would pursue. He was never clandestine in its pursuit and even his lectures at military college made it well known. In political office he was known to be secretive and used surprise as a weapon to achieve his objectives.[807] His dealings with others could be described as narcissistic and Machiavellian. His adaptive approach relies heavily on the need for positional power to augment task and follower contingencies.

It was well known that in office he sought complete control, to the point that the Fifth Republic has been described as a thinly disguised dictatorship.[808] Whenever de Gaulle could not dominate the situation he would simply resign – initially in 1944 and then again in 1969.[809] It was obvious to him that the political leader derived his authority from public opinion – legitimate authority. However, once he had that authority, then de Gaulle saw it as an absolute right. By corollary, a military officer's authority is also based on legitimate authority, yet it does not require the support of the public: an attitude that de Gaulle takes into political life. The logical extension, to him, seemed to be that if one had legitimate authority, then they were entitled to lead (rule) un-

> What, above all else, we look for in a leader is the power to dominate events, to leave his mark on them, and to assume responsibility for his actions... For the soldier there is always yet some higher rank to attain, some recognition to be gained... Even when he has it in his grasp, he can never be completely open in his dealings for he must still be concerned to please, to know how to convince prince or parliament, how to gratify popular passions and soothe the anxieties of vested interests.
>
> C de Gaulle *Le Fil de l'epee*

fettered. While legitimate authority provided the means for the exercise of power, it was character and ability that he saw as differentiating a mere official from a leader.

We also observe de Gaulle as the visionary needing to project a particular image based on a leader's "prestige", vision,[810] and exemplary conduct.[811] De Gaulle's conception of the need for "prestige" in a leader is consistent with Weber's notion of charismatic authority.[812] In *The Edge of the Sword* de Gaulle stated: "the main spring of command is now to be found in the personal prestige of the leader",[813] which he describes as "...a matter of feeling, suggestion, and impression, and it depends primarily on the possession of an elementary gift, a natural aptitude that defies analysis"[814] where "an essential element of leadership...creates a spirit of confidence in those under him" with the leader able to "imprint his personality on them" such that he can "make their wills part and parcel of his own, and so inspire [followers] that they will look upon the task assigned to them as something of their own choosing".[815] The de Gaullean leader conception, then, is similar to what Nietzsche and Weber identify as the *ubermensch*, but "we should not confuse his idea of grandeur with Nietzsche's idea of the superman".[816] De Gaulle's "grandeur" was a state of existence for the nation and not for a person.[817] If anything, grandeur in a leader foments hubris – the basis, as he saw it in *The enemy's house divided*, of the German state's leadership failure. Even though de Gaulle promotes and even tries to manufacture his own prestige he views this as a functional quality where "at crucial times in history, when political structures are weak, unstable or transitional, the intelligent and well prepared leader can maximise his use of symbolism and manipulative resources in order to shape the course of events".[818]

De Gaulle displays all the elements of a visionary leader. Such leaders are change agents with an idealised conception of a future state.[819] One model of visionary leadership presents these type of leaders as possessing high levels of self-confidence and cognitive capabilities combined with a strong power orientation.[820] These leaders seek grand transformation in line with their vision. De Gaulle projected an image of a leader that possessed such a vision, and of a person of high intellect, drive and self-confidence. Power was essential for him to achieve his mission and he accepted the responsibility of ensuring that his mission was achieved. De Gaulle also places a high degree of importance on individual capabilities and competence, a need to adapt to situational contingencies, and the need to project a particular image. These elements all conform to the visionary model of leadership.

In terms of leadership De Gaulle has been described as a "typological half-breed"[821] and this would seem to be an accurate observation. The identification of personal attributes, vision, nobility of purpose, power and control, all tend to provide a multi-dimensional conception. His writings evince a development from elements of the individualistic approach consistent with the leadership notions of the age in which he lived where he sought to be a model to others and project an image of "prestige" that was perceived as a trait,[822] through to a recognition for the need for adapting to situational contingencies and the acute need for positional power.[823] All of these elements present a complex perspective of a person focussed on the objective to deliver a positive outcome for those he led. From his resistance in the war through his Presidency his primary concern was for *La France*. His idealised notions of this being formed very early in his life and the influences which acted upon him reinforcing the notion of the common good. This virtuous recognition of the welfare of followers and the primacy of the state contributed to him being the great leader which resulted.

Chapter 7 - **Dwight D Eisenhower**

The one quality that can be learned by studious reflection and practice is leadership.[824]
Dwight D Eisenhower

The only virtue special to the ruler is practical wisdom.[825]
Aristotle

Background

Dwight David Eisenhower was born David Dwight Eisenhower in 1890 in Denison, Texas.[826] He was the middle son of six brothers,[827] with two older and three younger. Both his parents were from devout religious families. Both were proud and ambitious[828] but lacked the means for advancement, tied down rearing six boisterous sons. Their predecessors had immigrated to America from Germany and were predominantly of rural origin. The rural tradition continued until his father, also David Eisenhower, commenced a retailing business.[829] It failed, and the family moved to the town of Abilene, Kansas, where they lived modestly.[830]

His father married Ida Elizabeth Stover before the relocation to Abilene. She was caring and friendly, leaving a greater impression on her sons[831] than the father, who was reserved and hard working:[832] "She supplied the driving energy which he lacked".[833] In the German tradition, the father was the authoritarian figure and the mother the nurturer.[834]

The mid-west Bible-belt environment in which Eisenhower grew up is credited as being the most important influence in his early life.[835] His hometown of Abilene had only recently emerged from the cowboy town image of Wild Bill Hickok[836] to become a rural community of 4000 people living in relative isolation on the Kansas Great Plains. A basic existence confronted the townsfolk, with little more than farming and the retailers that supported them.

The most remarkable aspect of Eisenhower's early life is that it is unremarkable[837] with only commonplace anecdotes about the trials and tribulations of growing up in a country town. Even though researchers have directed significant attention to his early life they have not been able to uncover anything noteworthy in relation to leadership qualities.[838] He expressed no desire for a military or political career, or any career, in his youth.[839] His interest in military history was no more or less than many other boys, and he certainly did not display a desire to emulate any particular leader at the time.[840]

The chief concerns for the Eisenhower family centred around their devotion[841] and livelihood.[842] His family were followers of the River Brethren,[843] a Christian sect that adhered strictly to the Bible's teachings. Everyone in his hometown, where there was a strong sense of community, was Christian.[844] To make ends meet he and his brothers worked from an early age at all manner of odd jobs[845] and sold the family produce door-to-door in order to raise extra cash.[846] Their father was the sole breadwinner who worked for a modest wage as a maintenance engineer at a local creamery operated by the River Brethren Church.[847] Clothes and shoes were a luxury, as was space in a small home with a family of eight.

Growing up in a small community on the wrong side of the tracks (literally) imposed a feeling of inferiority in the Eisenhower boys.[848] When taunted, the brothers, Edgar and Dwight, usually settled the matter with their fists. These two sons were known to be the local "toughs", with both boys taking pride in their pugilistic image.[849] Dwight had an exceptionally bad temper[850] and would often fight with his elder brother simply to see if he could succeed. Confidence, self-reliance and physical ability were the hallmarks of the elder Eisenhower boys.[851]

At school Dwight's grades were average. He directed most of his energies towards sport, in which he was also somewhat average but nonetheless enthusiastic.[852] By the time he left school he had no idea what he wanted to do in life.[853] He simply continued on at the local creamery with his father.[854] Despite what looked like a predestined existence, his parents inculcated a strong need for an education in all their sons in order to encourage them to do more with their lives.[855] This was understandable, as both parents had attended college, which was quite unusual at that time, and valued education.[856] As a result the two Eisenhower brothers, Dwight and Edgar, formed a pact to alternate between working in the creamery and attending a nearby university.[857] Apart from that, Eisenhower had little more ambition than to stay in his hometown of Abilene. By 20, Eisenhower had settled in to small-town life. When an old friend from his early school days returned to town and informed him that he was seeking entry to military college this seemed to jolt him from complacency,[858] as it presented an opportunity to obtain a free education. Eisenhower was successful in the entrance examination but being over the age for entry to Annapolis he settled for West Point.

At West Point his results were predominantly average but he maintained a liking for sport; football was the overwhelming focus of his life.[859] His football career did not last long after sustaining a significant knee injury.[860] He then continued to be associated with the sport in a coaching capacity.[861] His skills in coaching a junior college team were notable and demonstrated an obvious predisposition for leadership.[862]

Eisenhower showed an aptitude for the military while at West Point, but nothing more than would equip anyone to be a competent officer. Mostly contemptuous of his superiors, he maintained an aura of quiet confidence coasting through the system. On the occasion of injuring his knee, he was told that he may be discharged from the army as unfit.[863] The discharge did not eventuate and by the time he graduated, in 1915, Europe was in the grip of the Great War.

Dwight's classmates imagined that military duty in the Great War would present them with opportunity.[864] Not Eisenhower, he planned to go as far as possible away from the theatre of war – to the Philippines.[865] This, too, did not eventuate, so he accepted his fate to join an army training camp at Fort Sam, Houston, Texas.[866] When asked to train the camp's football team he initially refused but relented when the request came from the camp commander. Ironically, his achievements in football and aptitude for coaching were more important to his future attainment of a high army position than any other attribute.[867]

Eisenhower joined the infantry predominantly because his knee injury precluded the cavalry. When the cavalry transmogrified into the armoured corps, this option opened to him. He was committed to the new tank technology and pursued a training role in support.[868] In 1917 he received notice that he would command a tank battalion in France.[869] By the time his orders finally came through the war had ended. Military command in the Great War did not eventuate.

Eisenhower spent the intervening years between World War I and II in a growing military bureaucracy. Promotions were "excruciatingly slow".[870] During this period he began taking the army far more seriously as a career. He continued to be assigned to training roles and performed well in them. Noted by his superiors for his ability to motivate and organise, his responsibilities for command grew.[871] By this time he was completely dedicated to the tank as being a crucial part of the army's arsenal (aided no less by fellow West Point graduate, George S Patton). In a meeting with General Fox Connor the two young officers impressed their views so adroitly that Eisenhower found himself assigned to Connor's staff as Executive Officer in 1920.[872]

It is at that point that Eisenhower's life reads like a who's who for organisational success. General Connor was a career soldier and knew how the organisation worked. He also had a keen interest in military history and impressed Eisenhower with his knowledge and commitment. This left an indelible impression on a young officer. Of greater import were the contacts that Connor had within the army's senior command. Eisenhower's attention to detail and commitment so much impressed Connor that he was rewarded with a recommendation to attend the Command and General Staff School in 1925.[873] Eisenhower threw himself into the course and finished top of his class.[874]

This paved the way for an assignment to the War Department under General Pershing,[875] another highly influential person in the military establishment. Eisenhower again won over his superior with an insightful account of US military involvement in France during the Great War. This undertaking was achieved with the assistance of his younger brother, Milton, who was by now a journalist in Washington.[876] The assignment was not only fortuitous because of its effect on the head of the War Department (earning Eisenhower a commendation), but because it gave him first-hand knowledge of the French theatre of operations that would be instrumental in the next war.

Eisenhower was then assigned as Chief of Staff to General Douglas MacArthur.[877] MacArthur was another highly influential senior officer in the military hierarchy, and Eisenhower's association with him opened doors. Although not the easiest posting of his career, MacArthur praised Eisenhower, referring to him as "...the best officer in the Army".[878] This sort of praise did not go unnoticed.

In 1939 Eisenhower was 49, and a Lieutenant Colonel.[879] Europe was again at war and America looked on. The following year, after the bombing of Pearl Harbour, the US committed to a war in the Pacific. Eisenhower was requested by General Marshall to be his Chief of Staff in the War Plans Division to oversee operations in the Philippines/East Asia region.[880] Marshall was then the most senior officer in the army and by far the most influential. Yet again Eisenhower impressed Marshall, who also regarded him as a superior officer.[881]

The following year the US committed to the war in Europe. Marshall chose to assign his best officer, that is, Eisenhower, and by the end of 1942 Eisenhower was in Britain as the US Forces Commander. He continued to impress all whom he met and demonstrated a natural flair for public relations.[882] His contacts in Britain included Admiral Lord Mountbatten and Air Marshall Sir John Cunningham who immediately took a liking to him.[883] Churchill also developed an immediate bond and confided in him Britain's dire need for American assistance. He was then assigned the role of Commander in Chief of the allied forces in Europe and charged with overseeing the war effort to defeat Germany and liberate Europe.

In 1944 Eisenhower was given the task that only two other military commanders in history had been able to successfully achieve – the crossing of the English Channel to defeat an entrenched foe. Julius Caesar had achieved it in 55bce and then, almost exactly 1000 years later, William the Conqueror. No one had yet crossed the channel to conquer the continent.

The subsequent success in this endeavour all but ended the war and brought an era of peace and prosperity to America that was unparalleled. Eisenhower returned to his homeland as one of its greatest heroes. Determined to ensure that the peace remained, he ardently supported the United Nations and served as head of the North Atlantic Treaty Organisation (NATO).

Eisenhower prior to D day rallying the troops

In 1950, while in France, the Democratic Party of America nominated Eisenhower to run for President. After some persuasion he accepted the nomination and was subsequently elected as the country's 34th President. He successfully contested a second term, which saw him presiding over a conflict that involved the country in the Korean War. In 1958 he retired as President and re-entered society, proud to be a citizen again.[884]

Influences

The most significant influences on Eisenhower during his youth were his family and community.[885] The family could trace its origins back to the sixteenth century, to the Rhineland region of Germany.[886] For several generations the family[887] remained devout followers of the teaching of Menno Simmons.[888] Simmons started a relatively obscure religious sect whose followers were known as Mennonites, an offshoot of the Anabaptist movement.[889] Like many other protestant religions of the time, the Anabaptists were persecuted during the Reformation as followers of Protestantism broke away from Roman Catholicism due to the corruption that had become endemic in the Papal system. At that time the ruler of the Holy Roman Empire, Charles I, sought to mercilessly crush the Reformation sects.[890]

The Eisenhauers eventually became part of the Brethren in Christ[891] and in the eighteenth century they fled Germany, and religious persecution during the 30 years war, to Switzerland, then Holland. After continued persecution, they fled to America (where, ironically, the Holy Roman Empire did not extend).[892] Dwight's paternal grandfather was a devout follower, as was his great grandmother. The migrating family settled in the Pennsylvania region and formed the River Brethren,[893] a dissident Protestant sect, also part of the Mennonites.[894] Two of the sons, Dwight's grandfather included, became preachers: "Like the Quakers they stood for peace, amity, and decency in human relationships, in the brotherhood of God."[895] Dwight's grandfather, Jacob, then moved the family and his ministry to Kansas where David, Dwight's father, was born and raised. By then they were known as the "Eisenhowers". Coincidentally, the background of Dwight's mother was "remarkably similar".[896] Her family also fled Germany under religious persecution and were also in the Mennonite movement.[897] Like the Eisenhowers, his mother's family (Stovers) were also farmers. As a result, the Eisenhower household was devoutly religious and adhered to the virtues of "sobriety, thrift, strict moral standards and hard work."[898]

The community and their parents were significant influences in all the Eisenhower boys' lives.[899] Their religious devotion formed the backbone of Dwight's interaction with others.[900] His father was pious and strict,[901] his mother nurturing and tolerant, with "her teaching based on such homely precepts as the virtue of the initiative and the fact that the essence of life was a struggle."[902]

Dwight was flanked by his two older brothers: Arthur (four years older) and Edgar (one year older), and three younger brothers: Roy (two years younger), Earl (eight years younger) and Milton (nine years younger).[903] He was closest in age to Edgar with whom he spent most of his time. His competition for attention with his older brother was constant, as if he was competing for the next highest place in the family, but he demonstrated respect for his elder brother Edgar. The three eldest brothers were required to assist with chores and earn money. The youngest brothers were separated from the three older ones by several years, thus establishing a division of seniority in the family.

Sporting pursuits featured highly in Dwight's youth. He and Edgar,[904] (the family's "natural athlete" – "strong and agile")[905] were fiercely competitive,[906] as both boys were physically the same size for most of his youth.[907]

Dwight naturally emulated his older brother Edgar and sought to compete on an equal footing.[908] His perception of self was so bound up with sport that on one occasion, when faced with the option of losing his leg or dying (after suffering blood poisoning), he told his parents that he would rather die.[909] Later in his youth, after suffering a knee injury that ended his sporting career, he was thrown into deep depression: expressed in his memoirs thus - "...life seemed to have little meaning; a need to excel was almost gone."[910] A strong desire to succeed and a need to physically excel existed from an early age.

The competitive struggle between Dwight and Edgar dominated his early childhood.[911] The two fought regularly, with Dwight generally faring worse off. Dwight saw himself as Edgar's equal, being only one year younger. On one occasion, when Edgar was allowed to go trick-or-treat at Halloween, Dwight was told to stay home and went into a fit of rage, pounding his fists into a tree until they bled.[912] When roused from the fit he was not aware of the fact that his fists had started to bleed.[913] Yet the bond between them was strong: on the occasion when Dwight developed an infection in his leg, he contracted with Edgar to prevent the doctor from taking him to hospital to remove his leg if he was to lose consciousness.[914] Despite the doctor's protestations, Edgar remained true to his promise and prevented the doctor from evacuating his brother.[915]

Dwight's youngest brothers, Earl and Milton, [916] posed no threat to his position in the family, being several years younger. His next brother,[917] Roy, was two years younger and Dwight enjoyed a natural advantage in size over him. Interestingly, Roy became a bit of a loner, caught in the gap between his older and younger brothers.[918] The two youngest brothers were not athletic and were quite different to the older ones, being less rambunctious and more inclined to study and the arts.[919] As a case study in sibling differences, the brothers demonstrate a remarkable consistency between birth order and character formation.[920]

Dwight was therefore compelled to be competitive, independent, confident and resourceful. He recounted in a speech opening the Eisenhower Museum that his parents had taught him and his brothers the "...simple virtues – integrity, courage, self-confidence and an unshakeable belief in the Bible".[921] This was a result of the family's belief in "honesty, self-reliance, integrity, fear of God and ambition".[922] Dwight recounted that his mother told her sons that they could either "sink or swim, survive or perish"[923] – inculcating strong self-reliance. Eisenhower recalled that she was

"...by far the greatest personal influence in our lives."[924] Many years later he recalled "her serenity, her open smile, her gentleness with all and her tolerance of their ways, despite an inflexible loyalty to her religious convictions and her strict pattern of personal conduct."[925] Eisenhower could have almost been making this statement about himself.

The Eisenhower family was predominantly male and this also had an effect on his attitude. Eisenhower always said that he was more comfortable in the presence of men "with whom he empathised and really understood"[926] than with women. While growing up he was notoriously shy around girls of his own age.[927] His birth position would indicate someone who knew that he was not the most senior or the most junior but still had a need to prove himself. He would be able to observe the strengths and weaknesses of his brothers while reflecting on his own.

At school Eisenhower was an average student.[928] His main interests were in history and geometry.[929] In his autobiography he also recounts his interest in ancient history and a keen interest in the military campaigns of the Greeks and Romans.[930] Hannibal appears to be his favourite, not only for his military prowess but because he was the "underdog".[931] It would appear that his success must have been significant for the victory to have been so faithfully recorded.[932] Eisenhower also favoured Frederick the Great, Napoleon and Gustavus Adolphus.[933] His American heroes included Sherman, Lee and Washington.[934] Washington represented the qualities he admired: "...stamina and patience in adversity...indomitable courage, daring and a capacity for self-sacrifice".[935] It is of interest that he identified the latter.

At school his primary focus remained on sport with his "chief asset... his will to win."[936] It was in this pursuit that he discovered, and others noticed, his leadership ability. When he and other classmates established the Abilene High School Athletics Association, he was elected its president.[937] His ability for organising and motivating others in groups was observed by classmates and teachers alike.[938] Ironically, he shied away from other social groups and chose not to join community social clubs, possibly because of his social status.[939]

The lessons Eisenhower derived from his sporting involvement left an indelible impression. So much so that later in life he noted them as the key attributes of effective leadership when he stated that in relation to football, or any contest, "...victory comes through hard — almost slavish —

work, team play, self confidence, and an enthusiasm that amounts to dedication."[940]

As an adolescent there were few other major personal influences in his life apart from his parents and close family. His father's brothers were both preachers, which compounded the religiosity of his home life. He mentions in his autobiography a man named Bob Davis who he describes as a "philosopher" and "teacher".[941] However, the extent of Davis's erudition seems to have only included hunting, fishing and poker. This interaction further strengthened Eisenhower's self-reliance. By the time Dwight left school "he was socially mature, for he had grown-up with the constant realisation that other members of the family were as important as he. As a younger son, he did not feel compelled to be a pacesetter; nor did he have a number of older brothers that he would feel impelled to emulate to exceed. He was aggressive and confident, but he was also cautious in never underestimating his opposition."[942]

After school Eisenhower commenced working at the local creamery in Abilene with his father.[943] He had worked there for most of his teenage years on a part-time basis.[944] Through a fortuitous reunion with an old friend, Everett (Swede) Hazlett, he learnt of the benefit of a free education in the military.[945] Eisenhower began lobbying prominent local business people and the state's Senator for entry to military college.[946] Successful in gaining the local Senator's recommendation, he sat the entrance exam and was entitled to admission. Eisenhower had no great desire to enter the military but for the education it offered.[947] Entry to West Point would normally have been a godsend to a family like the Eisenhowers but instead it was met with consternation. Their religious belief system, now Jehovah Witnesses, obliged them to be pacifistic conscientious objectors,[948] who abhorred war and killing.[949] "Like the Quakers they stood for peace, amity, and decency in human relationship, in the brotherhood of God".[950] His mother, in particular, "..loathed war with a sense of spiritual outrage; it was to her the ultimate wickedness".[951] Despite his obligation to adhere to these beliefs, the desire and benefit of personal advancement prevailed and he was permitted to attend. Their confidence in him was such that "his basic character was set when he arrived at West Point"[952] and that would place him in good stead for his future.

Eisenhower's time at West Point did not reveal any particular outstanding quality.[953] He showed little by way of any great burning desire for knowledge, if anything the opposite, as most of his free time was dedicated to

sport.[954] His overall academic standing at that institution was above average but without much significance.[955] His first-year ranking of 57 from 212
classmates was similar to his final year ranking of 61 from 168.[956] West
Point did not provide a liberal education,[957] as it mainly concentrated on
technical aspects for military engagements. There was little or no exposure to philosophy or the arts.[958]

What emerges then is that Eisenhower appears to be something of a
drifter in his youth. Despite the encouragement of his parents to seize opportunity and the self-reliance that the environment of his birth inculcated, he had no real desire for any particular career. He had an interest in
some academic areas but no real desire to really understand the significance of what he learnt or any idea of what he wanted to do later in life.
There were no signs that he would become a military leader, nor a civic
leader, in his youth. He demonstrated some aptitude for organisational
ability and motivating others, but nothing out of the ordinary. His parents
and community were the main elements that influenced him on a personal level. It is the influences from his family that we see the main
factors that determined his worldview.

Social/political philosophy

Three fundamental influences acted on Eisenhower in his youth: religion,
family and community,[959] whose effect was "...explicable in terms of influence which operated on him during his earliest years".[960] Each of the
brothers were subject to the same influences which have been proposed
as being the basis for the notable achievements of his family (Arthur became a prominent banker; Edgar established a law firm; Roy became a
pharmacist; Earl an engineer; Milton the president of a university.)[961] The
Eisenhower boys were taught "the virtues of self reliance and self denial.
Intemperance of any kind...was considered an act of impiety – and any
kind of vainglory or extravagance was considered an act of intemperance."[962]

The values of the society formed the central part of Eisenhower's social
views. He had travelled no further than a few hundred kilometres away
from his hometown of Abilene while growing up, and had not been outside the states of Kansas or Texas before travelling to West Point. There
does not appear to be any real interest in the outside world except the
casual curiosity that he had for adventure.[963] Social and political matters
played little or no role in his early development other than the influence
that came from his community.

Few, if any, works Eisenhower read could be regarded as social or political philosophy. Similarly, he never wrote anything of importance in his youth or even early adulthood. Politics was rarely discussed in the household.[964] Social matters were confined to the town and there is no evidence of any national sentiment in the family. Only in his later years do his speeches and writings give us any clues of his thoughts and influences. The Bible seems to be the primary source of any pedagogy in his early years. The only other books he read in his youth, or early adulthood, seem to consist of novels such as *Pilgrim's Progress*, *The White Company*, or *A Connecticut Yankee at King Arthur's Court*.[965]

At West Point his education was not supplemented with any political or social content. The curriculum itself shed little light on social or political affairs. If anything it was apolitical and distinctly conservative.[966] English, European history and language studies "were the only concessions the curriculum made to the humanities".[967] West Point imbued in its cadets a

> The conventional view – the consensus of his first half dozen biographers – is that young Eisenhower's superior character was tempered within the circle of his family; what would lift him so far above the average was the "religious teachings of his parents", the "strict family discipline", and the "stern instructions in the need for hard work and thrift". Unimpeachable doctrines, like these, which have come to be described, rather pejoratively as old-fashioned, are, to be sure, indispensable to the rearing of any future hero, but it can scarcely be argued that they were the exclusive property of the Eisenhower family. One must look further.
>
> Lyons *Eisenhower*

belief in the "inevitability of violence in the relations between states and a lack of concern with the social and political consequences of warfare."[968] As such, his later education was purely militaristic with little or no social/ political awareness.

His nascent understanding of the world outside the US came at West Point. In taking the oath of allegiance he would recount later "A feeling came over me that the expression "United States of America" would now and henceforth mean something different than it ever had before...From here on in it would be the nation I would be serving, not myself."[969]

Although this was written in his twilight years, it is not uncommon for anyone taking the oath to have similar feelings. Eisenhower seemed to look at West Point as abstract, something outside himself. Studious classmates who feared demerits and craved higher scores were contemptible to him.[970] There is no evidence that he sought to understand anything of political or social consequence at West Point. The only evidence of any significance is in relation to a heightened national pride, but little more can be prognosticated from his time there.

Moral/religious philosophy

The wisdom imparted by his parents, particularly his mother, had a profound effect on all the Eisenhower boys.[971] Eisenhower talks of her instilling in him the notion that they should not do the right thing for fear of punishment but because it was the right thing to do. This sentiment closely aligns with Kantian ethics. In his memoirs he recounts the significant effect of the advice of his mother in controlling his anger as one of "the most important of my life".[972] His mother was highly moralistic with a strong sense of justice. In his memoirs Eisenhower raises his mother's attempt to learn law in the hope that she would one day find the business partner that ruined her husband and bring him to justice.[973] There is no other real philosophical influence on him, as he admits in his memoirs: "...I could read about scholars and philosophers but they seldom loomed so large in my mind as warriors and monarchs."[974]

Eisenhower and his brothers were all exposed to a strict religious education. From an early age the Bible was central.[975] The family read it together each night and his parents recited verses from it as a form of moral training.[976] They sang, they praised, and they read the Bible. On the surface then it would appear that religion was the main influence in his life.

Looking further into Eisenhower's youth identifies some interesting moral contradictions. An example of this is his entry into West Point. The friend who encouraged him to join was from a much wealth-

I believe fanatically in the American form of democracy...a system that recognises and protects the rights of the individual and that ascribes to the individual a dignity accruing to him because of his creation in the image of a supreme being and which rests upon the conviction that only through a system of free enterprise can this type of democracy be preserved.

D Eisenhower (letter to S Hazlet)

ier background and did not need the benefit of a free education in the military to obtain a degree.[977] This presented an interesting conundrum for Eisenhower – joining the military would give him a free college education but it would violate his parent's morality as pacifists and conscientious objectors. Yet he seemed to ignore their moral code and joined anyway. Additionally, when writing to the local Senator to request his patronage (this was essential for recommendation to sit the exam), he lied in his correspondence about his age.[978] Personal advancement clearly outweighed moral propriety.

Eisenhower's time at West Point indicates little adherence to religious practice. He attended the usual religious services but there is no account of him continuing to read the Bible or lecturing his fellow students on its teachings. There is no record of him adopting a pious attitude at all – in fact quite the opposite:[979] "Eisenhower was not a traditional religionist. Indeed for one raised in an explicitly Christian family and environment, he cared little for ritual, ceremony or religious observances."[980] After West Point his attendances at church were, at best, "sporadic".[981]

> For Eisenhower, the superstructure that allowed for and supported all human choice – moral, ethical, political, religious, economic – was the constitutional Republic and the peculiar form of democracy that it had spawned.
>
> Medhurst *Eisenhower*

While these occurrences may seem inconsequential, they need to be considered in light of other incidents in his life. On one occasion during World War II, a group of journalists asked him what he would do to win the war. Eisenhower replied that he would "lie, cheat and steal to beat the Hun".[982] While such a statement in wartime may not be immoral (considering that war is itself an immoral act), it demonstrates that "Eisenhower [had] a situationist, not a relativistic, ethic".[983] He would do what was necessary in the circumstances to achieve his goal. The means may be negotiable but the ends are not negotiable in Eisenhower's ethics: "The defense of the country and its values, founded upon Judeo-Christian

> There is a direct relationship between any form of free government and a deeply felt religious faith...an essential foundation stone of free government is this sincere religious faith.
>
> D Eisenhower Letter to General Lorenzen

presuppositions, was to Eisenhower, a mission of sacred, almost religious, nature."[984] he clue to Eisenhower's morality is bound up in the state.

Even though he had no formal training or erudition in social or political philosophy, he developed a belief in the value of the state (Republic). From the moment he swore the oath of allegiance, where the term "United States of America" meant something "completely different",[985] to his command in World War II, Eisenhower's "locus of value" became the Republic.[986] To him the Church and state were inextricably linked.

Patriotism became Eisenhower's *raison d'être*. Once he had accepted the responsibility of his position in the military, he accepted the responsibility of serving the country and protecting the system that embodied his moral code. What we see is something of a transformation during his early adult years, from purposeless youth to ardent proponent of the state. Eisenhower's family, community and religious indoctrination provide the base on which he constructs a worldview that holds up his community (the country) as his standard of value.

What we see in Eisenhower is a person with a strict religious education resulting in an adult who was able to discern the moral lessons of that education and apply it to the circumstances. His behaviour was not pious or condescending, he did not hold his beliefs in a sanctimonious manner, yet they influenced his behaviour in a way that ensured that his approach to society was essentially a moral one.

Leadership approach
The first signs we see of Eisenhower demonstrating leadership could be said to be his role as president of the Abilene Athletics Association. Here we see an ability to motivate and organise others: "At this task he proved himself to be a true leader."[987] It seems that he had natural people skills and an ability to motivate. The Athletics Association is an interesting example, as he was not very engaged in any other social groups during his youth and this would clearly demonstrate that his interest was motivated by his focus on sport rather than any interest in group activities *per se*.

At West Point Eisenhower continued his interest in sport under the guise of obtaining a free college education. There was no burning desire for military leadership and, in fact, he states in his autobiography that he would constantly ask himself, "what am I doing here?".[988] On one occasion he even threatened to leave that institution after suffering a serious knee injury which ended his sporting career.[989] When it was realised that he would not be able to participate in sport at the level desired, and facing the dilemma of not being able to graduate, he simply accepted his fate and chose instead to leave West Point and disappear to Argentina.[990] This scenario did not eventuate, but it demonstrates that he was hardly the obsessive leader with a desire for command. Paradoxically though, his supervisors at West Point noted that he was "born to command".[991] So while he may have had no burning desire for leadership, others were able to identify it in him.

Eisenhower's perspective on society and the development of his morality emanated from both his family and community. His strict, moralistic parents imposed the requirement to read the Bible and live by its precepts. Their only ideology appears to be their religion.[992] He would say later of his community that it "...eliminated prejudice based on wealth, race or creed, and maintained a standard of values that placed a premium upon integrity, decency, and consideration for others."[993] He also recalls how, at West Point, he castigated himself for belittling a young recruit over his profession and vowed to never do so again.[994] Despite the culture of West Point to intimidate new recruits, Eisenhower could only go as far as his conscience would allow,[995] which was rooted in his moral training.

> Of a healthy society the family is not only a portrait in miniature, it is also the vessel of racial continuity through which the living culture can draw nourishment from a warmly human past. Out of it grows the human values which are the substance of social justice, the very essence of democracy: the values of tolerance, sympathetic understanding, self-discipline and self-sacrifice in the common good.. whatever his personal beliefs about God and immortality, each [of the Eisenhower brothers] was to retain all his life long a profound respect for the moral tenets which the parents derived, or thought they derived, from their religion...The boys might say that around the core of mystical nonsense was a good solid husk of common sense. They shucked off the husk and threw away the core.
>
> Davis *Eisenhower*

Eisenhower's observance of religious practice does not seem prominent in his life at West Point, or thereafter. He did not neglect his faith, it simply became more personal. Throughout the war he maintained a strong belief in the divine purpose of the allied forces. His inaugural address as President opened with a prayer to "Almighty God" to guide the way for him and his government.[996]

From a leadership perspective, he admired certain leaders for their character attributes. Notably, he read Washington's farewell address and his speech at Newburgh, which he says "exemplified the human qualities that I frankly idolised."[997]

During the middle part of his career, Eisenhower was fortunate to come into contact with diverse leadership personalities and techniques: Patton, MacArthur, Connor, Pershing and Marshall – a veritable who's who of military leadership. He diligently worked for all of these people who regarded him as outstanding.[998] Yet Eisenhower showed no real signs of deviating from his sense of self. Many of his superior officers regard him as someone that made "human, considerate, well tempered decisions".[999] Their focus on his self-awareness is illuminating.

To some, Eisenhower is perceived as a charismatic leader because of his ability to inspire, and have followers "emulate [his] values, goals and behaviours."[1000] One account attributes charismatic leadership to the contents of on an analysis of some 20,000 letters sent to Eisenhower during his first presidential election campaign.[1001] A prominent University of Columbia sociologist analysed the letters and indicated that the content was consistent with the characteristics of charismatic leadership. Another sociologist advocated that Eisenhower's charisma emanated from his "ordering power".[1002] In this regard, it was claimed that Eisenhower's authority and power as a General and then as a President activates the need in followers for order, as it is the "...order creating, order disclosing, order discovering power..." that appeals to followers' need for order.[1003]

> My good fortune has been a lifetime of continuous association with men and women, widely different, who sometimes in a few minutes by word of mouth, or sometimes over the years by their example, gave others inspiration and guidance.
>
> Eisenhower *Stories I tell friends*

On both accounts, the sociologists take a particularly narrow view of charismatic authority and charisma in general. The devotion that they attribute to

Eisenhower's charisma results more from follower identification with his moral position[1004] than with any "personal abilities" which have a "profound and extraordinary effect"[1005] on them. Eisenhower does not seem to possess any "extraordinary gift".[1006] He certainly does not demonstrate any particularly strong charismatic effect on people prior to his ascendancy to the position of President, which may indicate that his charisma is more a matter of celebrity status.[1007] Devotion and loyalty are not confined to charismatic leadership and could equally be attributed to transformational leadership.[1008] Transformational leaders are "attentive and supportive, but they also inspire and serve as exemplars to followers".[1009] They serve to raise the level of motivation and morality in both followers and themselves.[1010] The classification of Eisenhower being transformational is perhaps more appropriate than charismatic in the social scientific context.

Eisenhower's leadership approach can be described as a combination of maintaining high-quality relationships with others and using a normative behavioural approach. The approach that appealed to Eisenhower seems to concur with that of his mentors - General Marshall:[1011]

The way he exercised leadership coincided nicely with Eisenhower's temperament. He never yelled or shouted, he almost never lost his temper. He built an atmosphere of friendly co-operation and teamwork around him, without losing the distinction between the commander and his staff – there was never any doubt as to who was the boss.[1012]

The observation of Eisenhower adopting the same approach is supported by several authors and first-hand accounts that provide a picture of a person demonstrating a relational approach. For example, during World War II, when he held the position of Supreme Allied Commander, he would refer to his general staff as "the family".[1013] The overriding consensus was that while Eisenhower was highly task motivated, he was equally focussed on consideration for others. In this regard his staff and colleagues regarded him as sincere and eminently likeable. He was widely regarded as "a decent, humane person who tried to display compassion, consideration, and kindness even under the most trying of circumstances."[1014] He was also pragmatic, stating: "as when the pressure mounts and strain increases, everyone begins to show the strain in his makeup. It is up to the commander to conceal his; above all to conceal doubt, fear and distrust".[1015]

The view of Eisenhower as concerned and considerate for followers is also supported by one of his most diligent biographers, Kornitzer, who claims to have read "every book that has been written about Dwight D Eisenhower" (by 1955) and states that he was a man of "profound humility".[1016] The Eisenhower brothers agreed with this view in relation to their brother as President and military commander where they state that he was "...just as humble, just as warm and friendly, just as considerate of others, and just as free of any trace of arrogance..." in either role.[1017] Eisenhower could be characterised as, fundamentally "...a man possessed of an essentially moral vision of human life."[1018] He operated from a position of respect for others and a desire to do what was right under the circumstances.

> Mother was a slave to her friends and neighbours...I think maybe we all learned a degree of the spirit of service for others from Mother, because we all experienced those incidents with her.
>
> Edgar Eisenhower

In an era when heroic leadership dominated, Eisenhower is distinctly post-heroic.[1019] Despite his position of authority, he used people skills to encourage others to participate in the decision-making process.[1020] In his book *Crusade in Europe,* written as an account of the allied operations in World War II, he continually refers to the co-operation required for success and the efforts made to ensure that this occurred. This book focuses on the importance of *"unity, teamwork, allies,* and *partnership"* .[1021] To him it was essential that the team worked effectively, and the best way to ensure that this occurred was to encourage a participatory model and persuade others to the cause: "According to Eisenhower, leadership is the ability to decide what is to be done, and then to get others to *want* to do it."[1022] The key here is his focus on follower motivation. Eisenhower's relational leadership approach emanated from his appreciation, sense of respect and understanding of others. For example, in order to engage the other nation's commanders in WWII "he intended to work with his deputies, not by imposing his will on them, but through persuasion and co-operation, to draw on their talents by establishing a close personal relationship with them."[1023]

It is clear that his attitudes are derived from his family and a community that conformed to a strict moral code. It was this code that formed the basis of Eisenhower's values. The combination of these two leadership approaches bears strong resemblance with the social scientific theory of authentic leadership. This theory bases the effectiveness of leadership on the manner in which leaders possess attributes which followers perceive to be genuine, and that the leader also acts consistently and normatively towards followers.[1024] Eisenhower's leadership is characterised by integrity, normative behaviour, trust, collaboration and consideration. As such, few leaders could be more appropriately labelled authentic than Eisenhower. To followers in both the military and as President his leadership always had overtones of the greater good – from winning a war to overcoming the influence of the military industrial complex. His virtuous background being strongly inculcated in him leading to the eventual perception of a good leader with honourable intent.

Leadership 101

Fortunately, Eisenhower's career provides us with a detailed reflection on his views of leadership, both by himself and through others. Integrity and authenticity were central to his conception. On this he says:

Integrity of character and high purpose or a moral conviction seem to separate out his approach to leadership. This is reinforced when he comments on how a leader should relate to follower.

Coersion, control and manipulation were not part of his arsenal of skills as he recognised that:

"If you pull the string...it will follow wherever you wish. Push it, and it will go nowhere at all."

"I would rather try to persuade a man to go along, because once I have persuaded him he will stick. If I scare him, he will stay just as long as he is scared, and then he is gone."

The fundamental difference here is the need to have followers want to work with you. This form of leadership relies on motivation, persuasion and collaboration rather than power.

Chapter 8 - **The measure of greatness**

Genetics and environmental influences may provide some indication of an individual's characteristics and behaviour but it does not provide any indication of the values, beliefs and attitudes that we develop towards others. It has been proposed that these attributes determine the type of leadership approach which manifests. Research has demonstrated that environmental factors (such as birth order, family size etc) do not provide any reliable indication of the type of leadership approach a leader will exhibit then[1025] this requires that we consider other environmental influences that could explain leadership approach, hence the the role of philosophical influences. What should be apparent at this point is that the role of moral and religious influences tend to have a strong bearing on a person's normative behaviours. This chapter will review the philosophical factors that have acted on the soldier-statesmen and the extent to which the factors determines their leadership approach. It will then be necessary to analyse the cultural context of the different leaders, in particular the role of the culture in which the leaders lived. Finally, the chapter concludes with what we mean by an ethical leader and the factors that contribute to this leadership approach.

Philosophical influences in leadership approach development

The role that social, political, moral and religious philosophy play in the lives of the soldier statesmen indicates that the degree of influence of each has implications for the way in which leaders act towards followers. It has been seen that the influence of social/political philosophy has the tendency to produce more individualised leadership approaches, while moral/religious philosophy tends to produce more socialised leadership approaches. If leadership is a relationship between leader and followers then this suggest that leaders with that display behaviours that are more socially acceptable then they are more likely to be successful in their interpersonal relationships with followers. Fo that reason the more normative behaviours are preferred and so the role of moral philosophy becomes self-evident.

An exposure to moral philosophy has the effect of creating and shaping a more follower-focussed leader with normative behaviours. Normative connotes ethical insofar as it prescribes how leaders behave towards followers. In the social scientific domain, leadership theories tend to present models to improve one's leadership effectiveness in terms of results such as greater efficiency or motivation rather than in terms of follower consideration or moral outcomes. A normative perspective focuses on good leadership as an ethical construct that necessitates ethical leader conduct. This alters our usual conception of leadership from being externally focussed (goal oriented) to internally focussed (person oriented) – "rather than telling people what to *do*, attention should be directed towards telling people what to *be*, or helping them to become more virtuous".[1026] Without the moderating influence of morality, then leadership is merely an instrumental activity. Leaders are expected to be exemplars, to act as role models for groups and to provide correct guidance.[1027] The moral behaviour of a leader is often viewed as representative of followers' values and in some cases as an ideal that followers seek to emulate. The exposure to moral (and by inference religious) philosophy has been demonstrated to result in a leadership approach where normative behaviours are more evident.

Given that leadership is an influence relationship,[1028] or even a sociological relationship,[1029] then the degree of trust and integrity in a leader must play a role in the success of the leaders social interaction with followers.[1030] These ethical elements can be cultivated through an exposure to moral philosophy,[1031] underpinned by the development of an ethical worldview. While a greater exposure to moral philosophy may produce more normative leaders, this raises the issue of what type of leaders do we really want in society. Are we more interested in producing competent, effective leaders who achieve results, or leaders who do the right thing and treat followers with respect? Most would answer that both of these are desirable, but current social scientific literature predominantly describes the former, with the latter being a welcome by-product.

An increased role for morality in leadership would seem more pressing in Western society as it becomes more multicultural and multi-religious (at the same time trending towards becoming more secular).[1032] The adoption of moral philosophy in our school system could be beneficial in this regard to the development of good (that is morally good) leaders.[1033] Moral education at an early stage of human social development would appear appropriate, as the development of a person's morality begins early in life.[1034] At least this is what research has identified – we form our morality through an observation of the world that we live in. If we live in an environment where theft is acceptable then our values around any sort of theft (e.g intellectual) are conditioned in a similar manner. The saying that "every time children are in the presence of adults values are being taught" is apt.

Advocating a focus on moral philosophy in our education system is not a new concept. Plato proposed that we identify those predisposed for leadership roles early in their life and then train them to understand how to deliver "good" to society. This approach has been promoted over time,[1035] yet the presence of moral philosophy education is exiguous at primary/secondary level schooling and of limited availability at the tertiary level. To maximise the potential for ethical leaders to emerge it would seem logical to introduce moral philosophy into our education systems curriculum - the earlier the better.

The question then remains as to whether the exposure to moral philosophy alone is sufficient to engender virtuous conduct and produce more normative leaders. There is a long history on the role of morality training. Aristotle's *Nichomachean ethics* for one proposed that "morality cannot be learned simply by reading a treatise on virtue".[1036] Further, "the spirit of morality, said Aristotle, is awakened through the spirit of another."[1037] As such, moral leadership is *learned* through emulating a model person that conducts them-self in a way in which we learn to behave appropriately. This is intuitively logical – people from backgrounds with poor role models tend to behave unacceptably. Research has in fact identified that a "prodigious patron" is an essential element of moral guidance.[1038] To behave morally we need to see morality in action.

Emulating moral behaviour is but one element. In addition is the requirement to assimilate the moral guidance as "reflective conduct", where a person is able to cognitively adopt the morality.[1039] In other words "monkey see, monkey do", but in the case of us more intelligent primates we also need to understand through reason why the conduct is appropriate. It is not simply a case of emulation but understanding as well.

Finally, moral conduct is not merely being aware of an acceptable code of conduct but adhering to it. Apropos the subject leaders, it is readily identifiable that there were varying degrees of moral guidance exercised by parents and those *in loco parentis*. The degree to which the leaders adopted this conduct and made it their own also varies by degree. However, a sound moral code *must exist* in order for someone to adopt and assimilate it. This is clearly evident in the early life of Washington and Eisenhower, to some extent in de Gaulle's, and almost non-existent in the case of Napoleon. The degree of influence of parents in all cases was quite pronounced and where this acted to instil a moral code the resulting conduct of the leader accorded with the parental influence. It would seem apparent from the review of the soldier statesmen's early lives that the presence of moral philosophy acts as a determinant to the development of normative leadership qualities and the degree to which these have been fostered by patrons and reflected upon by the subject leader can be seen in the degree of normative behaviour exhibited.

The role of culture

One aspect that becomes evident from the analysis of the soldier statesmen's backgrounds and influences is a relationship between their leadership approach and their culture. In the case of the American leaders, they exhibit a more socialised leadership approach, while the French leaders exhibit a more individualised leadership approach. This may be merely coincidence given that there are only four leaders, but it may also indicate that different cultures, and even different periods of time, call for a particular leadership approach. In order to better understand leadership it may also be necessary to better understand the culture and time in which the particular leadership approach develops and succeeds.

Research into leadership has identified that it is affected by the context in which it operates.[1040] Early research proposed that the situation around the leader augments the leadership dyad, that is, leadership is more effective when leaders adapt to follower contingencies .[1041] This work laid the foundation for an appreciation of factors external to the leadership dyad. These external factors are generically termed "context" and describe a range of factors that a leader will consider in relation to their approach to followers.

The changing context in which leadership operates is also changing the way in which leadership is perceived.[1042] The rate of organisational change, globalisation, cultural factors in the workplace or society[1043] in turn change our perception of leadership. For example, as organisations become more globalised, the complexity of dealing with different cultures places more demands on leaders adapting to more diverse requirements. The approach that might work in one culture is not appropriate in another. The organisation that is able to succeed in a different cultural environment is intrinsically linked to the ability of its leaders to culturally adapt.

This observation raises the significance of social, political, moral and religious influences in the development of a persons leadership approach. Would an organisation want ardent nationalists being in senior management positions? The question that arises then is how these people have formed their worldview to become so nationalistic. The demonstration of the connection between philosophical influences and worldview is an indicator of the type of leadership approach that such senior executives hold. With respect to the soldier statesmen it has been observed that there is a distinct difference between the philosophical influences in one culture to another. We have seen that the type of philosophical influences on the French leaders differs markedly to those on the American leaders. It is therefore necessary to understand what role these philosophical influences play in relation to both culture and time.

As such, it could be suggested that there is both a societal and temporal dimension to the role of philosophical influences. The political, social, religious and moral environment differs from country to country and from era to era. Understanding the role that these influences play in the type of worldview formed may be valuable in allowing us to understand the type of leaders that emerge. We only have to look back in time to see obvious examples of the impact of these two dimensions. Prior to the advent of democracy most countries were subject to absolute or hereditary rule. This societal dimension of the political and social philosophy in operation undoubtedly influences how people interacted with each other. This can readily be observed in working lives of people of the time, often in strictly hierarchical organisations led by authoritarian control.

That this suggests is that there is an underlying social, political, moral and religious philosophical context of a society at a particular point in time: a socio-historical context. But this concept is not entirely new. Two leadership theories of the late twentieth and early twenty first century identify that there is a socio-political and socio-economic dimension to leadership. The former has been proposed in an attempt to explain the emergence of destructive leaders,[1044] while the latter has been used to explain the effectiveness of productive narcissists in organisations.[1045] The socio-political context of leadership identifies factors such as the instability in the socio-political environment, a perceived threat from an external source, susceptible cultural values, and/or an absence of checks and balances in the socio-political environment as being preconditions to the emergence of destructive leaders.[1046] For example, if we are to take the socio-political environment of Europe prior to WWII there is a remarkable concurrence between the type of leaders that emerged and the role the socio-political environment played in facilitating their emergence. This gives us cause to reflect on the ability of our socio-political environment today to ensure that such leaders do not reappear. In addition, it has been proposed that the economic environment also plays a role in the type of leader which might emerge and succeed. The productive narcissist proposed by Michael Maccoby succeeds because the dominant mode of production[1047] of a society determines its social character,[1048] and that the matching of the leader type to the social character results in more effective leaders. In this model the productive narcissist succeeds because of the attributes of the leader meeting particular economic realities. The quality of strategic intelligence in productive narcissist seems intimately suited to the rapidly evolving technological environment we are in today. Bothe these theories of leadership advocate a relationship between the social context and another dimension, be it political or economic.

Similarly, in relation to the soldier statesmen a similar environmental context surrounds the leader–follower dyad. The socio-historical context influencing a leader's worldview provides a means of understanding how and why such leaders emerge and become effective. In each case involving the soldier statesmen, it has been observed that the manifestation of their leadership approach is dependent on the particular socio-historical context in which they led. In the case of Washington, the War of Independence sought fundamentally to resolve an injustice, with Washington fulfilling his nation's requirement for a moral champion. Similarly, the French Revolution was an outpouring of individualism that sought to challenge and usurp the status quo, to which someone like Napoleon, the conqueror, was inevitably suited. The same can be said of de Gaulle, the revanchist, opposed to foreign domination, or Eisenhower, the crusader, restoring freedom and justice. Clearly, there was an temporal context around the emergence of these leaders that accorded with the type of leader that emerged. Yet the societal factors were also important – that Napoleon's republican views accorded with those of his countrymen is not mere chance; or that the self-determinism (nationhood) of Washington and his countrymen merged into rebellion; or the aspirations of de Gaulle's restoration of France's grandeur with the needs of the French people for identity and security; or Eisenhower's consolidative and egalitarian approach to the allied powers and his country's democratic and communitarian ethos. Each leader operated in a particular socio-historical context which aligned with their worldview and contributed to their "greatness".[1049] But what exactly do we mean by greatness?

Good and great leadership

We have seen that the Great Man theory of leadership proposes that certain individuals are destined for greatness due to inherent traits that meet the social conditions of the time.[1050] This theory influenced early thinking on leadership to suggest that the leadership of great men was congenital: the notion that leaders were born and not made being the implication. The trait theory of leadership developed to propose a set of personality attributes that defined whether a person would emerge and become effective in a leadership role. The simple conclusion from this is that a great leader is more likely to be endowed with the attributes for great leadership.

The notion that inherent traits are the basis for one being a leader, or even a great leader, requires explication. Even though personal traits, as a basis for leadership, has been marginalised by research in both genetics and personality attributes of leaders,[1051] the belief and likelihood that traits make a difference to one's success in leadership persists. This begs the question whether the soldier statesmen (all great leaders) became leaders, even great leaders, because of inherent characteristics, or because of some other factor. Let's consider each leader's claim to "greatness" in turn.

Napoleon was clearly a highly successful commander of notable talent and was eminent in the military domain. In the political domain he also achieved more than many other French politicians before or since. Of even greater testament to his abilities is the fact that he was able to achieve social and political reform during one of his country's most tumultuous periods. Yet, despite this, he is often derided for his megalomania and bellicosity. This is consistent with an investigation of his background, which reveals a strong focus on personalised power with little moral integrity underpinning his actions. His achievements in warfare and civic reform may be significant, but are moderated by the fact that his country was left defeated and ruined, and countless lives lost. Despite the negative outcome, he is still regarded as a great leader due principally to his exceptional military abilities.

Washington, too, is attributed with being a successful military leader because of his most notable achievement – commanding the Revolutionary Army in the War of Independence. Yet throughout the early part of his career he was hardly a successful military commander. His early campaigns saw him usually on the losing side, where he showed little or no sign of military brilliance. In the political domain he is widely credited with being somewhat of a model, with notable characteristics being his modesty and lack of hubris. It would seem that his greatness as a leader is predominantly due to the manner in which he discharged his role as military commander and President. As such his greatness is linked *both* to his achievements and the moral integrity that he demonstrated in the discharge of his roles.

De Gaulle does not qualify as a military commander of any note in either World War I or II, where he only commanded briefly before defeat in both instances. It is perhaps unfair to say that he was a poor military commander, but it would be true to say that he did not achieve anything to note him as a successful military commander. If anything, his notoriety and self-proclaimed leadership of the French Resistance identified him as a leader and ultimately this led to his widespread recognition (as a result of the allies' success). As a military commander and then civic leader, in both roles he was treated ambivalently by French citizens: he was euphorically received as *Le Général* after the war and then rejected by the population in his quest for the role of President, where his contiguous reigns seemed marked by controversy. His greatness can be attributed to his dedication to his country and the relentless pursuit of the restoration of its international status, or in other words, the moral intent of his leadership.

Eisenhower's success in commanding the victory over the Axis powers was, without question, a significant achievement. Like Washington, this event marked him for greatness. Yet he had no prior military command with which to assess his military abilities. Even though the achievement as Commander-in-Chief is significant, it is not plausible to describe him as a great military commander in the same way as Napoleon is described. Similarly, his achievement of the role of President is also notable and a reason for him being considered a great leader, even though he was considered a mediocre President after leaving office. Although he is regarded as being an effective leader across two distinct domains, there is limited evidence to support a claim that he had exemplary military or political abilities. If anything, his leadership is characterised by the moral integrity of his leadership.

In summary, there is more to these "great leaders" achieving greatness than the achievement in a role, or the performance of the role in a particularly significant historical context. Undoubtedly, it is significant that they led their countries' armed forces and then succeeded in leading their nations. This confirms that they are all great in reputation by virtue of a significant achievement, their status and the rank/position they held. But this is only relevant to greatness *per se*, not to great leadership. If leadership is about how a leader influences followers to achieve a positive outcome, then only three of the soldier statesmen can be labelled as great leaders: Washington, de Gaulle and Eisenhower. The common thread that runs between these soldier statesmen leadership is the *manner* in which they led – the moral integrity or purpose of their leadership. Greatness, under a normative conception, necessitates the inclusion of the ethical nature or purpose of leadership. We cannot simply connect the greatness of a person to their leadership. The leadership has to possess a quality that defines it as great. The very definition of greatness includes the recognition of the moral integrity with which one acts. It only stands to reason that a great leader should be marked by exercising great leadership and that this can only result from the ethical manner in which they lead.

The Great Man and trait theories would support the assertion that all the soldier statesmen simply possess the "right stuff"[1052] to be great (effective) military leaders. Yet three of the four soldier statesmen had no prior success in military command to demonstrate natural leadership ability. Research into the qualities of military leaders has failed to identify a unique set of military leadership traits, and so it is unlikely that they could uniformly possess such qualities if they have not been identified.[1053] Even if a set of traits existed, it would seem that the three identified soldier statesmen would hardly meet the criteria of being great military commanders anyway. Fundamentally, their achievements and status are more determinative of their notoriety than their military abilities.

The same rationale can be applied to each of the soldier statesmen's civic leadership roles. Trait theory would again suggest that these leaders possessed particular attributes that ensured their success. Once again, research into leadership abilities over the past half century has failed to identify a commonly accepted classification of traits for any form of leadership, let alone political leadership. The relevance of identified traits from research is even less applicable when the traits identified have emerged primarily out of the assessment of leaders from, predominantly, commercial environments.[1054]

More important still is how we understand what is meant by "good" or "great leader" and, by inference, "good" or "great leadership". If leadership is about a leader doing something beneficial for followers then good leadership must have an ethical dimension. Leaders must do something of value for followers and not have their leadership based on some intrinsic quality of the leader. A great leader, therefore, approaches leadership with the intention of doing even greater "good" and thereby bringing about a more beneficial result for followers. Rather than attributing greatness to the qualities of the leader, greatness results from the ethical exercise of leadership. In the final analysis a leader exists because of followers and it is only logical that they exist to benefit them.

Afterword

The perception could emerge of the American soldier statesmen as being "better" leaders than the French. This could also be seen as a cultural bias but may also demonstrate a current preference for normative leadership behaviours displayed by the American soldier statesmen. Given the size of the population sample it may be coincidental that both American leaders display such leadership. To discount the presumption of ethnocentricity one only has to consider the outcomes of studies that investigate the relationship between leadership and culture. The most relevant studies ultimately prove inconclusive or contradictory on several aspects.[1055] For example, the Trompenaars Hampden-Turner[1056] study identified Americans as more individualistic (than the French), less likely to display emotions, and highly achievement oriented, whereas the GLOBE project[1057] identified the Anglo (American) group as being more humane-oriented and the Latin Europe (French) group as more self-protective with respect to leadership.[1058] The former study would suggest that this research is not consistent with the cultural norms identified, while the latter supports the research. This would suggest that any bias is more likely to be in relation to leadership theory that promotes normative conduct than with a cultural stereotype, which has, as yet, not been empirically validated.

The other aspect that militates against a cultural bias is the observation in relation to the socio-historical context of leadership. Leadership approaches need to be assessed against the societal and temporal conditions of their time. This may identify the leadership approaches of the French soldier statesmen as entirely appropriate for their time and culture. As such the leadership approaches are more likely to relate to the cultural and temporal factors in operation.

Bibliography

Adams, H.B. (1893) *The Life and Writings of Jared Sparks* Houghton, Mifflin and Company, New York, NY, USA

Adams, J. & Yoder, J.D. (1985) Effective Leadership for Women and Men Ablex Publishing Corp, Norwood, NJ, USA

Adair, J. (1973) Action Centered Leadership Gower Press, Farnborough, Hants, UK

Adair, J. (1974) Training for Leadership Macdonald and Janes, London, UK

Alimo-Metcalfe, B. (1996) An investigation of female and male leadership constructs and empowerment Women in Management Review 10, 2, 3

Alston, M. & Bowles, W. (1998) Research for social workers: an introduction to methods Allen & Unwin, Crows Nest, Australia

Alvesson, M.(1996) Leadership studies: from procedure and abstraction to reflexivity and situation The Leadership Quarterly, 7, 4, 457

Ambrose, S.E. (1990) Eisenhower: Soldier and President Simon & Schuster, New York, NY, USA

Anderson, H.H. (1937) An experimental study of dominative and integrative behavior in children of pre-school age Journal of Social Psychology
8, 335

Anderson, M. & Spellman, B. (1995) On the status of inhibitory mechanisms in cognition: memory retrieval as a model case Psychological Review, 102,1, 68

Aquinas, T. *On the Government of Rulers: De regimine principum* Blythe, J. (trans.)(1997), University of Pennsylvania Press, Philadelphia, PA, USA

Aristotle, *Politics*, Jowlett, B. (transl.)(1977) Harvard University Press, Cambridge, MA, USA

Aristotle *Politics*, Sinclair, T.A.(ed.) Saunders, T.J. (trans.) (1983) Penguin Books, Middlesex, London, UK

Aristotle, The Nichomachean Ethics http://ebooks.adelaide.edu.au/a/aristotle/nicomachean/contents.html, date accessed 2 March 2010

Arvey, R.D., M Rotundo, M., Johnson, W., Zhang, Z. & McGue, M. (2006) The determinants of leadership role occupancy: genetic and personality factors *The Leadership Quarterly* 17, 1

Asser, J., Keynes, S. & Lapidge, M. (1983) *King Alfred the Great: Asser's life of King Alfred and other Contemporary Sources* Penguin Books, London, UK

Aston, N. (2002) *Christianity and Revolutionary Europe: c.1750-1830* Cambridge University Press, Cambridge UK

Augustine of Hippo & Benjamin, *On Free Choice of the will* in Anna, S. & Hackstaff, L.(trans)(1964) Bobbs-Merrill, IN, USA

Aurelius, M. *Meditations* Casaubon, M. (trans)(2005), Cosimo, New York, NY, USA

Aurelius, M. *Meditations* Long, G.(trans)(1997), Dover Publications, Stilwell, UK

Avolio, B. (1999) Are leaders born or made? *Journal of Psychology*, 32, 5, 18

Avolio, B.J. & Bass, B.M. (1987) Transformational Leadership, Charisma and Beyond in Hunt, J.G., Balsa, B.R., Dachler, H.P. & Shrisheim, C.C. (eds) *Emerging Leadership Vistas* Lexington Books, Lexington, MA, USA, 29

Axelrod, A. (2006) *Eisenhower on leadership: Ikes Enduring Lessons on Total Victory Management* Jossey Bass, San Francisco, CA, USA

Baldwin, A.L. (1949) The Effect of Home Environment on Nursery School Behavior *Child Development* 20, 49

Bandura, A. (1977) Social cognitive theory in Pervin, L.A. & John, O.P. (eds) *Handbook of Personality* The Guildford Press, New York, NY, USA

Barnard, C.I. (1938) *The Functions of the Executive* Harvard University Press, Cambridge, MA, USA

Bass, B.M. (1960) *Leadership, Psychology and Organizational Behavior* Greenwood Press, Westport, CT, USA

Bass, B.M. (1970) *Leadership and Performance Beyond Expectation* The Free Press, New York, NY, USA

Bass, B.M. (1990) Bass and Stogdill's *Handbook of Leadership* The Free Press, New York, NY, USA

Bass, B.M. (1999) Two decades of research and development in transformational leadership *European Journal of Work and Organizational Psychology* 8, 1, 9

Bass, B.M. & Riggio, R.E. (2006) *Transformational leadership* Erlbaum, Mahwah, NJ, USA

Bass, B.M. & Steidlmeier, P. (1999) Ethics, Character, and authentic trans-formational leadership behaviour *The Leadership Quarterly* 10, 2, 181

Bassiry, G.R. & Jones, M. (1993) Adam Smith and the Ethics of Modern Capitalism *Journal of Business ethics* 12, 8, 621

Beer, S. (1972) *Brain of the Firm: a Development in Management Cybernetics* Herder & Herder, New York, NY, USA

Benne, K.D. & Sheats, P. (1948) Functional roles of group members *Journal of Social Issues* 4, 2, 41

Bennis, W.G. & Nannus, B. (1985) *Leaders: the Strategies for Taking Charge* Harper & Row, New York, NY, USA

Bentham, J. (1789) *An Introduction to the Principles of Morals and Legislation* Oxford at the Clarendon Press, London, UK

Bentham, J. (1799) *A Fragment on Government: Being an Examination of What is Delivered, on the Subject of Government in General* T Payne, London, UK

Bergson, H. (1917) *L'Évolution Créatrice* Cosimo books, New York, NY, US

Berkovitz, J.R. (2002) *The Shaping of the Jewish Identity in Nineteenth Century France* Wayne State University Press, Detroit, MI, USA

Bourienne, L.A. *Memoirs of Napoleon by Himself Dictated on St Helena*, Memes, J.S.(trans)(1831) Constable & Co Edinburgh, UK

Bourienne, L.A. *Memoirs of Napoleon by Himself Dictated on St Helena*, Phipps, R.W.(trans)(1891) Charles Scribner & Sons, London, UK

Bowers, D.G. & Seashore, S.E. (1966) Predicting organizational effectiveness with a four factor theory of leadership *Administrative Science Quarterly* 2, 2, 238

Bowie, N. (2000) A Kantian theory of leadership *The Leadership and Organization Development Journal* 21,4, 185

Bowlby, J. (1977) The Making and Breaking of Affectional Bonds *The British Journal of Psychiatry* 130,3, 201

Brefenbrenner, U. (1961) Some familial antecedents of responsibility and leadership in adolescents, in Petrullo, L. & Bass, B.M. (eds) *Leadership and Interpersonal Behavior*, Holt, New York, NY, USA

Brennan, J.G. (1967) *The Meaning of Philosophy*, Harper & Row, New York, NY, USA

Bretherton, I. (1992) The Origins of Attachment theory: John Bowlby and Mary Ainsworth *Developmental Psychology* 28, 5, 759

Brookhiser, R. (1996) *Founding Father: Rediscovering George Washington*, Free Press New York, NY, USA

Brookhiser, R. (1996) *Rediscovering George Washington* Free Press, New York, NY, USA

Brookhiser, R. (2008) *George Washington on Leadership* Basic Books New York, NY, USA

Browning, O. (1906) *The Boyhood and Youth of Napoleon* John Lane The Bodley Head, London, UK

Brungardt, C. (1996) The making of leaders: A review of the research in leadership development and education *Journal of Leadership and Organizational Studies* 3, 3, 81

Bryman, A. (1992) *Charisma and Leadership in Organizations* Sage, London, UK

Bryman, A., Collinson, D., Grint, K., Jackson, B. & Uhl-Bien, M. (2011) *The Sage Handbook of Leadership* Sage Publications, London, UK

Burton, D.(ed)(2000) *Research Training for Social Scientists: a Handbook for Postgraduate Research* Sage, Thousand Oaks, CA, USA

Butcher, H.C. (1946) *My Three Years with Eisenhower: the Personal Diary of Captain Harry C Butcher*, USNR Simon & Schuster, New York, NY, USA

Calas, M. & Smircich, L. (1998) *Reading Leadership as a Form of Cultural Analysis* in Hunt, J.G., Baliga, B.R., Dachler, H.P. & Schreisheim, C.A. (eds.) *Emerging Leadership Vistas* Lexington Books, Lexington, MA, USA

Campbell, R. (1969) *Letters from a Stoic: Epistulae Morales as Lucilium* Penguin, London, UK

Carrithers, D.W., Mosher, M.A. Rahe, P.A. (2001) *Montesquieu's Science of Politics: Essays on the Spirit of Laws* Rowman & Littlefield publishers, Lanham, MA, USA

Carlyle, T. (1840) *On Heroes, the Heroic and Hero Worship in History* Chapman & Hall, London, UK

Carlyle, T. (1840) *On Heroes, Hero worship and the heroic in history* in B Kellerman (ed) (1896) *Political Leadership* University of Pittsburgh Press, Pittsburgh, PA, USA

Carney, T.F. (1973) Prosopography: Payoffs and Pitfalls *Phoenix* 27, 2, 156

Cate, C. (1960) *Charles de Gaulle: the last romantic* The Atlantic online at: http://www.theatlantic.com/magazine/archive/1960/11/charles-de-gaulle-the-last-romantic/306916/ date accessed: 14 Oct 2010

Cattaui, G. (1960) *Charles de Gaulle: l'homme et son destin* A Fayard, Paris, France

Cawthorn, D. (2002) *Philosophical Foundations of Leadership* Transaction publishers, New Brunswick, NJ, USA

Cerny, P.G. (1980) *The Politics of Grandeur: Ideological Aspects of de Gaulle's Foreign Policy* Cambridge University Press, Cambridge, UK

Cerny, P.G. (1988) The process of personal leadership: The case of de Gaulle *International Political Science Review* 9, 2, 137

Chandler, D.G. (1966) *Campaigns of Napoleon* Scribner New York, NY, USA

Chandler, D.G. (1973) *Napoleon* Wiedenfeld and Nicolson, London, UK

Chandler, D.G. (2006) *On the Napoleonic Wars* Greenhill Books, Sth Yorkshire, UK

Chandler, S. & Richardson, S. (2005) *100 ways to Motivate Others: how great leaders can produce insane results without driving people crazy* Maurice Basset Publishing ebook online at http://books.google.com.au/ books?id=XdDVsYVM2bEC date accessed 21 Sept 2010

Charlot, J. (1970) *Le phenomene* Gaullist Fayard, Paris, France

Chernow, R. (2011) *Washington: a Life* Penguin, NY, USA

Church, A.J. (2009) *The Story of Early Britain* General Books, online at https://archive.org/details/storyofearlybrit00chur date accessed: 15 August 2010

Cicero *De Re Publica* in Yonge, C.D. (trans.)(2009) Digireads publishing, New York, NY, USA.

Cicero *De Officiis* in Griffin, M.T. & Atkins, E.M. Cicero: On Duties (1991) Cambridge University Press, Cambridge, UK

Ciulla, J.B. Leadership Ethics: mapping the territory in Ciulla in Ciulla, J.B. (2004) (ed) *Ethics: the heart of leadership* Praeger publishers, Westport, CT, USA

Clague, M. (1975) Conceptions of Leadership *Political Theory* 3,4

Clinton, R.J. (1988) *The Making of a Leader: recognizing the lessons and stages of leadership* Navpress, Colorado Springs, CO, USA

Cohler, A.M., Miller, B.C. & Stone H.S.(eds) *Montesquieu The Spirit of the Laws* Cambridge University Press, Cambridge, UK

Cole, G.D.H. (2003) *On the Social Contract* by Jean-Jacques Rousseau Dover Publications, New York, NY, USA

Colish, M.L. (1990) *The Stoic Tradition from Antiquity to Early Middle Ages: stoicism in classical Latin literature* EJ Brill Leiden, The Netherlands

Conger, J.A. (1998) Qualitative research as the cornerstone methodology for understanding leadership *The Leadership Quarterly* 9, 1, 109

Conger, J.A. (1999) Charismatic and transformational leadership in organizations: an insiders perspective on the developing streams of research *The Leadership Quarterly*, 10, 2, 145

Conger, J.A. & Kanungo, R.N. (1987) Toward a behavioral theory of charismatic leadership in organizational settings *Academy of Management Review* 12, 4, 637

Connelly, O. (2006) *Blundering to Glory: Napoleon's military campaigns* Rowman & Littlefield London, UK

Cook, D. (1983) *Charles de Gaulle* General publishing company, Toronto, Canada

Copleston, F.C. (2003) *A History of Philosophy – Greece and Rome* (volume 1) Continuum International Publishing, London, UK

Crawley, A. (1969) *De Gaulle: a biography* Collins, London, UK

Crebbin, W. (1999) Revisioning learning – contributions of postmodernism, constructivism and neurological research Association of the Active Australian Researchers, *Abstracts Paper* Cre000462

Cress, D.A. (1987) *Jean Jacques Rousseau: The Basic Political Writings*, Hackett Publishing Co, Indianapolis, IN, USA

Crist, F.R. (1989) Hegel's conservative liberalism *Journal of Political Science* 22, 4, 717

Crombie, I.M. (1963) *An Examination of Plato's doctrines* Routledge & Kegan, London, UK

Crook, C. & Garratt, D. *The Positivist Paradigm in Social Science Research* in B Somekh & C Lewin (eds.)(2005) Research methods in the social sciences Sage, London, UK

Cudd, A. (2007) *Stanford Encyclopedia of Philosophy* online at http://plato. stanford.edu/entries/contractarianism/ date accessed 11 Feb 2010

Cunliffe, M. (1960) *Washington: man and monument*, New American Library of World Literature, New York, NY, USA

Curran, C.E. (2002) *Catholic Social Teaching 1891-Present: a historical, theological and ethical analysis*, Georgetown University Press, Washington DC, USA

Curtis, L. (1945) *World War: its cause and cure* Oxford University Press, London, UK

Curtis, M. (1959) *Three Against the Third Republic Transaction Publishers* New Brunswick, NJ, USA

Dancy, J., Sosa, E., Steup, M. (2010) *A Companion to Epistemology* (vol IV) Wiley-Blackwell, Sussex, UK

Danoff, B. (2005) Lincoln and Tocqueville on democratic leadership and self-interest properly understood *The Review of Politics* 67, 4, 687

Danserau, F., Graen, G. & Haga, W. (1975) A vertical dyad linkage approach to leadership within formal organizations: a longitudinal investigation of the role making process *Organizational Behavior and Human Performance* 13, 46

Dansette, A. (1939) *Napoleon: Emperor of the French*, Fayard, Paris, France

Davies, B. (1982) *An Introduction to the Philosophy of Religion* Oxford University Press, Oxford, UK

Davies, T. (1997) *Humanism*, Routledge, London, UK

Davis, K.S. (1945) *Soldier of Democracy* Country life press, Garden City, NY, USA

Day, C.M. (1981) Promotions of health care personnel in hospitals: heuristic decision making *Dissertation Abstracts International* 43, 3, 1290

Day, D.V., Gronn, P.& Salas, E. (2006) Leadership in team-based organizations: on the threshold of a new era *The Leadership Quarterly* 17, 3, 211

de Gaulle, C. (1865) *The Celts of the Nineteenth Century: an appeal to the living representatives of the Celtic race* Davenport Mason, J. Tenby, London, UK

de Gaulle, C. (1955) *The Complete War Memoirs of Charles de Gaulle*, Simon & Schuster New York, NY, USA

de Gaulle, C. (2002) *Discorde chez l'ennemi* Eden, R.(trans)(2002) The Enemy's House Divided University of North Carolina Press, Chapel Hill, London, UK

de Gaulle, C. (1935) Le *fil de l'épee* Hopkins, G.(trans)(1960) Criterion Books, New York, NY, USA de Tocqueville, A. *Democracy in America*, Goldhammer, A. (trans.) (2004) Literary Classic of the United States Inc, New York, NY, USA

Deene, K. *French composers after the Franco-Prussian War (1870-1): a prosopographical study* in Keats-Rohan, K.S.B. (ed) (2007) Prosopography approaches and applications: a handbook The unit for prosopographical research, Linacre College, University of Oxford, UK

Dewey, J. (1996) *Theory of the Moral life* Irvington Publishers, New York, NY, USA

Driver, J. *Normative Ethics* in Jackson, F. & Smith, M. (eds.)(2008) *The Oxford companion to contemporary philosophy* Oxford University Press, Oxford, UK

Dudden, F.H. (1905) *Gregory the Great: His place in history and thought* Russell & Russell, New York, NY, USA

Dupre, B. (2007) *50 Philosophy Ideas You Really Need to Know*, Quercus, London, UK

Ebenstein, W. & A.O. (1991) *Great Political Thinkers: Plato to the present* Holt, Fort Worth, TX, USA

Eisenhower, D.D. (1968) *At Ease: stories I tell to friends* Robert Hale Limited, London, UK

Eisenhower, D.D. (1948) *Crusade in Europe* Doubleday Dell Publishing Group, New York, NY, USA.

Elby. A (2009) Defining Personal Epistemology: A response to Hofer and Pintrich (1997) and Sandoval (2005) *The Journal of the Learning Sciences* 18, 138

Elcock, H. (2001) *Political Leadership* Edward Elgar Publishing, Cheltenham, London, UK

Ellis, J.J. (2004) *His Excellency: George Washington* Random House, New York, NY, USA

Ellis, P.B. (1993) *Celtic Dawn: the dream of Celtic unity* Constable & Co, London, UK

Englund, S. (2004) *Napoleon: a Political life* Scribner, New York, NY, USA

Evensky, J. (2005) Adam Smith's Theory of Moral sentiments: On morals and why they matter to a liberal society of free people and free markets *Journal of Economic Perspectives* 19, 3, 109

Fairholm, G.W. (1991) *Values Leadership: Towards a new philosophy of leadership* Praegar, New York, NY, USA

Farneworth, E. (2010) *The Works of Nicholas Machiavel* T.Davies, Covent Garden, London, UK

Fauvelet de Bourienne, L.A. *Memoirs of Napoleon by himself dictated on St Helena* Memes, J.S.(trans)(1831) Constable & Co, Edinburgh, UK

Fiedler, F. A contingency model of leadership effectiveness in Berkowitz, L. (ed)(1964) *Advances in Experimental Social Psychology* Academic Press, New York, NY, USA

Fink, H. (1981) *Social Philosophy* Methuen & Co, London, UK

Finley, M.I. (ed) (1988) *The Legacy of Greece: a new appraisal* Clarendon Press, Oxford University Press, London, UK

Flavell, J.H. (1979) Metacognition and cognitive monitoring – a new area of cognitive development inquiry *American Psychologist* 34, 10, 906

Fleischaker, S. (2004) *On Adam Smith's Wealth of Nations: a philosophical companion* Princeton University Press, Princeton, NJ, USA

Fleishmann, E.A. (1953) The description of supervisory behavior *Journal of Applied Psychology* 67, 523

Fleishman, E.A. & Harris, E.A. (1962) Patterns of leadership behavior related to employee grievances and turnover *Personnel Psychology* 15, 43

Fortin, E.L. St Augustine in Strauss, L. & Cropsey, J. (eds.) (1987) *History of Political Philosophy* University of Chicago Press, Chicago, IL, USA

Foucault, M. *Ethics, Subjectivity and Truth* Vol.1 Rabinow, P. (ed)(1983) The *Essential Works of Foucault (1954-1984)* NY Press, New York, NY, USA

Fournier, A. (1911) *Napoleon I: a Biography* Longmans Green & Co, London, UK

Fox, E.W. (1963) Appearance and reality in the recent French elections *Virginia Quarterly Review* 39, 2, 184

Frankfort, H., Frankfort, H.A., Wilson, J.A. & Jacobsen, T. (1946) *Before Philosophy: the Intellectual Adventures of Ancient Man* University of Chicago Press, Chicago, IL, USA

Freeman, D.S. (1968) *Washington*, Charles Scribner's Sons, New York, NY, USA (an abridged biography of the seven volume Freeman, D.S (1948) *George Washington* Charles Scribner's Sons, New York, NY, USA.)

French, J.R.P. & Raven, B. The *Bases of Social Power* in D Cartwright, D. (ed)(1959) *Studies in Social Power* Institute for Social Research, town, MI, USA

Galton, F. (1869) *Hereditary Genius: an inquiry into its laws and consequences* Macmillan, London, UK

Galton, F. (1876) The History of Twins as a Criterion of the Relative Powers of Nature v Nurture *The Journal of the anthropological institute of Great Britain and Ireland* 5, 391

Gardner, J.W. (1993) *On Leadership* The Free Press Macmillan Inc, New York, NY, USA

Gardner W.L., Avolio B.J., Luthans, F., May D.R., Walumbwa F. (2005) "Can you see the real me?" A self-based model of authentic leader and follower development *The Leadership Quarterly* 16, 343

Garten, J.E. (2005) B-*schools: only a C+ in ethics* BusinessWeek edition 3949 5 Sept, 110

Gerritsen, A. (2008) Prosopography and its Potential for middle period research *Journal of Song Yuan Studies* 38, 3

Gibbons, T.C. (1986) *Revisiting the Question of Born vs Made: Towards a theory of development of transformational leaders,* Doctoral dissertation, Fielding Institute, Santa Barbara, CA, USA.

Gini, A. (1997) Moral leadership and business ethics *Journal of Leadership and Organizational Studies* 4, 4, 73

Goethals G.R. & Sorenson G.J. (2005) *The Quest for a General Theory of Leadership* Edward Elgar Publishing, Northampton, MA, USA

Goethals, G., Sorrenson, G.J. & MacGregor Burns, J. (eds.) (2004) *Encyclopedia of Leadership* Sage Publications, Thousand Oaks, CA, USA

Goetzel, V.J. & M.G. (1962) *Cradles of Eminence* Littlewodd Brown & Co, Boston, MA, USA

Golan, R. (1999) *Modernity and Nostalgia: art and politics in France between the wars* Yale Publications, New Haven, CT, USA

Goleman, D. (2009) *Working with Emotional Intelligence: why it matters more than IQ*, Bantam Books, Bloomsbury Publishing, London, UK

Goodman, M. *The Emergence of Christianity* in A Hastings (1999)(ed) A *world history of Christianity* Cassell, London UK

Gourgaud, G. (1932) *The St Helena Journal of General Baron Gourgaud* John Lane The Bodley Head Ltd, London, UK

Graen, G.B. & Uhl-Bien, M. (1995) Relationship-based approach to leadership: Development of Leader-member Exchange (LMX) Theory of Leadership over 25 years: applying a multi-level, multi-domain perspective *The Leadership Quarterly* 6, 2, 219

Graen, G.B. & Scandura, T.A. (1987) Towards a psychology of dyadic organizing *Research in Organizational Behavior* 9, 175

Grayling, A.C. (ed) (1996) *Philosophy: a guide through the subject*, Oxford University Press, London, UK

Green, V.H.H. (1971) *From St Augustine to William Temple; eight studies in Christian leadership* Books for Library Press, Freeport, NY, USA

Greenleaf, R.K. (1977) *Servant Leadership: A journey into the nature of legitimate power and greatness* Paulist Press, Mahwah, NJ, USA

Griffiths, R. (2010) *The Pen and the Cross: Catholicism and English Literature*, 1850-2000 Continuum International Publishing, London, UK

Gronn, P. & Ribbins, P. (1996) Leaders in context: post positivist approaches to understanding educational leadership *Educational Administration Quarterly* 32, 2, 465

Gunther, J. (1952) *Eisenhower: the man and the symbol* Hamish Hamilton, London, UK

Hackman, M.S. & Johnson, C.E. (2009) *Leadership: a communications perspective* (5th ed) Waveland, Long Grove, IL, USA

Hackman, J.R. & Wageman, R. (2005) A theory of team coaching *Academy of Management Review* 30, 2, 269

Hadas, M. (1958) *The Stoic Philosophy of Seneca: essays and letters of Seneca* Doubleday & Co, Garden City, NY, USA

Hales, E. (1961) *The Emperor and the Pope: the story of Napoleon and Pius VII* Doubleday & Co, Garden City, NY, USA

Hall, C.S. *The Genetics of Behavior* in Stevens, S.S.(1951)(ed) *Handbook of experimental psychology* (vol.2) John Wiley & Sons, New York, NY, USA

Hall, R. (2004) *Political Thinkers* Routlege, London, UK

Hall, V.M. (1976) *George Washington: the character and influence of one man*, Foundation for American Christian education, San Francisco, CA, USA

Hallet, D., Chandler, M.J. & Krettenauer, T. (2002) Disentangling the course of epistemological development: parsing knowledge by epistemic content *New Ideas in Psychology* 20, 2, 285

Halpin, A.W. & Winer, B.J. *A Factorial Study of the Leader Behavior Descriptions* in Stogdill, R. & Coons, E. (1957)(eds) *Leader behavior: Its description and measurement* Columbus Ohio State University Bureau of Business research Columbus, OH, USA

Harris, J. (1998) *The Nurture Assumption: why children turn out the way they do* The Free Press, New York, NY, USA

Harrison, J.A. (1906) *George Washington: patriot, soldier, statesman* GP Putnam's Sons, New York, NY, USA

Hatch, A. (1944) *General Ike* Henry Holt & Co, New York, NY, USA

Hatch, A. (1960) *The de Gaulle Nobody Knows: an intimate biography of Charles de Gaulle* Hawthorn books Inc, New York, NY, USA

Hayibor, S., Agle, B.R., Sears, G.J., Sonnenfeld, A.W. & Ward, A. (2011) Value congruence and charismatic leadership in CEO-Top manager relationships: an empirical investigation *Journal of Business Ethics* 102, 2, 237

Hawkins, F. (transl.) (1646) *Youths Behavior, or Decency in Conversation amongst Men* W. Wilson, London, UK

Hegel, G.W.F., *Philosophy of Right* Knox, T.M. (1967)(trans) Clarendon Press, Oxford, UK

Henry, L. Napoleon's War Maxims with his Social and Political Thoughts in McErlean, J. (1996)(ed) Napoleon's *Little red book* Poniard Publishing, Ontario, Canada

Herold, J.C. (1955)(ed) *The Mind of Napoleon – a selection from his written and spoken words* Columbia University Press, New York, NY, USA

Hersey, P. & Blanchard, K. (1982) Leadership styles: attitudes and behaviors *Training and Development Journal* 36, 5, 50

Hershey, P. & Blanchard, K. (1969) Lifecycle theory of leadership *Training and Development Journal* 23, 5, 26

Higginbotham, D. (2004) *George Washington: Uniting a nation* Rowman & Littlefield, Lanham, MD, USA

Hirsch, E.D. (1976) *The Aims of Interpretation* The University of Chicago Press, Chicago, IL, USA

Hodgkinson, C. (1983) *The Philosophy of Leadership* Basil Blackwell publisher Ltd Oxford UK

Hofer, B.K. & Pintrich, P.R. (1997) The development of epistemological theories: beliefs about knowledge and knowing and their relation to learning *Review of Educational Research* 67, 1, 88

Hoffman, S. & Hoffman, I. *The Will to Grandeur: de Gaulle as political artist* In Rustow, D.A. (1970)(ed) *Philosophers and Kings: Studies in leadership* George Braziller, New York, NY, USA

Hoffman, L., Rosen, S. & Lippitt, R. (1960) Parental coercive, child autonomy, and the child's role at school *Sociometry* 23, 15

Hofstede, G. (1994) The business of international business is culture *International Business Review* 3, 1, 1

Hogan, R. & Kaiser, R. (2004) What we know about leadership *Review of General Psychology* 9,2, 169

Hogan, R., Curphy, G.J. & Hogan, J. (1994) What we know about leadership: effectiveness and personality *American Psychologist* 49, 493

Hollander, E. (1964) *Leaders, Groups and Influence* Oxford University Press, New York, NY, USA

Hollander, E.P. (1958) Conformity Status and idiosyncrasy credit *Psychological Review* 65, 2, 120

Hollander, E.P. & Julian, J.W. (1969) Contemporary trends in the analysis of leadership processes *Psychological Bulletin* 7, 5, 387

Holt, T. (2009) *Moral Philosophy* online at http://www.moralphilosophy. info/ date accessed 2 August 2011

House, R.J. (1974) A path-goal theory of leader effectiveness *Administrative Science Quarterly*, 16, 321

House, R.J. (1976) A 1976 theory of charismatic leadership in Hunt, J.G. & Rowlands, J.R. (eds) (1976) *Leadership: The cutting edge: a symposium held at the Southern Illinois University* Southern University Press, Carbondale, IL, USA

House, R.J. (1988) *Leadership research: some forgotten, ignored or overlooked findings* in Shrisheim, C.C. (eds) (1986) *Emerging leadership vistas: international symposium on leadership and managerial behavior* Lexington Books, Lexington, MA, USA

House, R.J & Baetz, M.L. (1979) Leadership: some empirical generalizations and new research directions in BM Straw (ed.) *Research in Organizational Behavior* Faculty of Management Studies, University of Toronto, Toronto, Canada, 1, 399

House, R.J. & Javidan, M. Overview of GLOBE in House, R.J. Hanges, P.J. Javidan, M. Dorfman, P.W. & Gupta, V. & assoc. (eds)(2004) *Culture, Leadership and Organizations: The GLOBE study of 62 societies*, Thousand Oaks Publishers, Thousand Oaks, CA, USA

House, R.J. & Aditya, R.N. (1997) The social scientific study of leadership: quo vadis? *Journal of Management* 23, 3, 409

House R.J. & Mitchell, R.R. (1974) Path-goal theory of leadership *Journal of Contemporary Business* 3, 81

Howell, J.M. & Avolio, B.J. (1992) The ethics of charismatic leadership: Submission or liberation? *Academy of Management Executive* 6, 43

Hughes, E.J. (1963) *The Ordeal of Power: A political memoir of the Eisenhower Years* Atheneum, town, NY USA

Hughes, S. *Social Philosophy* online at http://onlinephilosophyclub.com/social-philosophy.php, date accessed 18 August 2009

Hyde, A.M. (1868) *The American Boys life of Washington* James Miller, New York, NY, USA

Inwood, M.J. (1998) *Hegel* Routledge, London, UK

Irving, W. (1859) *Life of George Washington* vol. XIV, Da Capo Press, New York, NY, USA.

Jackson, M.C. (2002) *Systems approaches to management* Kluwer Academic publishers, New York, NY, USA

Janowitz, M. (1960) *The Professional soldier: a social and political portrait* Free Press of Glencoe, Glencie, IL, USA

Jenkins, W.O. (1947) A review of leadership studies with particular reference to military problems *Psychological Bulletin* 44, 1, 54

Joorman, J., Hertel, P., Brozovich, F. & Gotlib, I. (2005) Remembering the good, forgetting the bad: intentional forgetting of emotional material in depression *Journal of Abnormal Psychology* 114, 4, 640

Judge,T.A., Illies, R., Bono,J.E. & Gerhardt, M.W. (2002) Personality and leadership: a qualitative and quantitative review *Journal of Applied Psychology* 87, 765

Judge, T.A. & Piccolo, R.F. (2004) Transformational and transactional leadership: A meta-analytic test of their relative validity *Journal of Applied Psychology* 89, 755–768

Kain, P.J. (1993) *Marx and modern political theory: from Hobbes to contemp-orary feminism* Rowman & Littlefield publishers, Lanham, MA, USA

Kant, I. *Critique of practical reason* Kingsmill, T.(ed)(2014) University of Adelaide, South Australia, Aust online at http://ebooks.adelaide.edu.au/k/kant/immanuel/k16pra/

Kardash, C.M. (1996) Effects of pre-existing beliefs, epistemological beliefs, and need for cognition on interpretation of controversial issues *Journal of Educational Psychology* 88, 2, 260

Katz, D. & Kahn, R.L. (1978) *The Social Psychology of Organizations* (2nd ed) John Wiley & Sons, New York, NY, USA

Katz, J. (1998) *Out of the Ghetto* Syracuse University Press, New York, NY, USA

Keithly, D. & Tritten, J. (1997) A charismatic dimension of military leadership *Journal of Political and Military Sociology* 25, 139

Kellerman, B. (2008) *Followership: how followers are creating change and changing leaders* Harvard Business School publishing, Boston, MA, USA

Kennedy, E. (2007) Bergson's philosophy and French political doctrines: Sorrel, Maurras, Péguy and de Gaulle *Government and Opposition* 15, 1, 75

Kerr, S. & Jermier, J.M. (1978) Substitutes for leadership: their meaning and measurement *Organizational Behavior and Human Performance* 22, 3, 375

Kets de Vries, M.F.K. (1985) Narcissism and leadership: an object relations perspective *Human Relations* 38, 6, 583

Kim, K. (1993) Internalism and Externalism in epistemology *American Philosophical Quarterly* 30, 4, 303

Kirkland, C.M. (1857) *Memoirs of Washington* Appleton, NY, USA

Kirkpatrick, S.A. & Locke, E.A. (1991) Leadership: do traits matter? *Academy of management Executive* 5, 2, 50

Kitchener, R.F. (2002) Folk epistemology: an introduction *New Ideas in Psychology* 20, 2, 89

Kitchener, R.F. (1983) Cognition, metacognition, and epistemic condition *Human Development* 26, 22

Kitchener, K.S. & King, P.M. (1981) Reflective judgement: concepts of justification and their relationship to age and education *Journal of Applied Development Psychology* 2, 89, 116

Knutsen, T.L. (1997) *A History of International Relations Theory* Manchester University Press, Manchester, UK

Kohlberg, L. (2008) The development of children's orientation towards a moral order *Human Development* 51, 8

Kohlberg, L. (1975) The cognitive-developmental approach to moral education *The Phi Delta Kappa* 56, 10, 670

Kornitzer, B. (1955) *The Great American Heritage: the story of the five Eisenhower brothers* Farrar Straus and Cudahy Inc, New York, NY, USA

Kouzes, J.M. & Posner, B.Z. (eds) (2004) *Christian reflections on the Leadership Challenge* Jossey Bass, San Francisco, CA, USA

Kramer, F.A. (1992) *Perspectives on Leadership from Homers Odyssey Business and the contemporary world* John Wiley & Sons Inc, Summer 1992

Kramer, R. (1999) Trust and distrust in organizations: emerging perspectives, enduring questions *Annual Review of Psychology* 50, 569.

Krishnan, V.R. (2001) Value systems of transformational leaders *Leadership and Organizational Development Journal* 22, 3, 126

Kuhn, D., Cheney, R. & Weinstock, M. (2000) The development of epistemological understanding *Cognitive Development* 15, 309

L'Estrange, R. (1818) *Seneca Morals: by way of abstract* Sherwood, Neely and Jone's, London, UK

Lacouture, J. (1990) *De Gaulle: the rebel* (1890-1944) O'Brien, P. (trans) (1993) WW Norton & Co, New York, NY, USA

Larson, J. (1968) *Eisenhower: the president nobody knew* Popular Library, New York, NY, USA

Lawlor, L. & Leonard, V.M.(2011) Henri Bergson in *The Stanford Encyclopedia of Philosophy* Zalta, E.N. (ed.) online at URL = http://plato.stanford.edu/archives/win2011/entries/bergson/ date accessed 25 January 2010

Ledwidge, B. (1982) *De Gaulle* Wiedenfeld & Nicholson, London, UK

Lee, R.A. (1981) *Dwight D Eisenhower: soldier & statesman* Nelson Hall, Chicago, IL, USA

Lenski, G. (1991) Positivism's future: and sociology's The Canadian *Journal of Sociology* 16, 2, 188

Lenzer, G. (1998) *Comte and Positivism: the essential readings* Transaction publishers, New Brunswick, NJ, USA

Leonard, H.S. (2003) Leadership development for the postmodern, postindustrial information age *Consulting Psychology Journal: Practice and Research* 55, 1, 11

Littell, E. & R.S.(1849) *Littell's Living Age* Volume 21, T.H Carter & Co, Boston, MA, USA

Locke, J. (2002) *The Second Treatise of Government and a Letter Concerning Toleration* (Thrift edition) Courier Dover Publications, Mineola, NY, USA

Loehlin, J.C. & Nichols, J. (1976) *Heredity, Environment and Personality* University of Texas, Austin, TX, USA

Long, A.A. (ed) (1999) *The Cambridge Companion to Early Greek Philosophy* Cambridge University Press, New York, NY, USA

Lord, R.G., De Vader, C.L. & Alliger, G.M. (1986) A Meta-Analysis of the Relation Between Personality Traits and Leadership Perceptions: An Application of Validity Generalization Procedures *Journal of Applied Psychology* 71, 3, 402

Lord, R.G. & Maher, K.J. (1991) *Leadership and Information Processing: linking perceptions and performance* Unwin Hyman, Boston, MA, USA

Lyon, P. (1974) *Eisenhower – portrait of a hero* Little Brown & Co, Boston, MA, USA

Maccoby, M. (2007) *Narcissistic Leaders: who succeeds who fails* Harvard Business School Publishing, Boston, MA, USA

Maccoby, M. (2003) *The Productive Narcissist: the promise and perils of visionary leadership* New York, NY, USA

Maccoby, M. (2007) *The Leaders We Need: and what makes us follow* Harvard Business School Press, Boston, MA, USA

MacGregor Burns, J. & Dunn, S. (2004) *George Washington* Times Books Henry Holt & co, New York, NY, USA

MacGregor Burns, J. (1978) *Leadership* Harper, New York, NY, USA

Machiavelli, N. *The Prince* Bondanella, P. & Musa, M. (transl.) (1979) Oxford University Press, Oxford, UK

Machiavelli, N. (1854) *The History of Florence and of the Affairs of Italy from the Earliest Times to the Death of Lorenzo the Magnificent* HG Bohn Publishers, Covent Garden, London, UK.

MacIntyre, A. (1997) *A Short History of Ethics: a history of moral philosophy from the Homeric age to the twentieth century*, Routledge, London, UK

Mackenzie, J. (2011) Positivism and constructivism, truth and "truth" *Educational Philosophy and Theory* 43, 5, 534

MacLeod Currie, H. (1973) *The Individual and the State* Dent, London, UK

Madelin, L. (1935) *Napoleon* Dunod, Paris, France

Mahoney, D.J. (2000) *De Gaulle: Statesmanship, Grandeur and Modern Democracy* Transaction Publishing, New Brunswick, NJ, USA.

Maller, J.B. (1931) Size of family and personality of offspring *Journal of Social Psychology* 2, 1, 3

Martinko, M.J. & Gardner, W.L. (1984) The observation of high-performing educational managers: methodological issues and managerial implications in Hunt, J.G., Hosking, D., Schriesheim, C.A. & Stewart, R. (eds) (1984) *Leaders and Managers: international perspectives on managerial behavior and Leadership* Pergamon Press, New York, NY, USA.

Marx, K. & Engels, F. (1848) *The Communist Manifesto* Cosimo Classics, New York, NY, USA

Masson, F. & Piaggi, G. (1895) *Napoleon inconnu papier inédits* 1769-1793, National Library, Paris, France

Matthews, G., Deary, I.J. & Whiteman, M.C. (2003) *Personality Traits* Cambridge University Press, Cambridge, UK

Matviko, J.W. (ed.) (2005) *The American President in Popular Culture* Greenwood Publishing Group, Westport, CT, USA

Maxwell, J.C. (2003) *Running with Giants: what the old testament heroes wanted you to know about life and leadership* Warner Books, New York, NY, USA

Mayer, J.D. & Salovey, P. (1995) Emotional intelligence and the construction and regulation of feelings *Applied and Preventive Psychology* 4, 3, 197

Mazlish, B. James Mills and the Utilitarians in Rustow, D.A. (ed)(1970) *Philosophers and Kings: Studies in leadership* George Braziller Inc, New York, NY, USA

McCall, M.W. (1976) *Leadership research: choosing gods and devils on the run Journal of Occupational Psychology* 49, 3, 139

McCormick, M.J., Martiniko, M.J. (2004) Identifying leader social cognitions: integrating the causal reasoning perspective into social cognitive theory *Journal of Leadership and Organizational Studies* 10, 2

McCrae, R.R. & Costa, P.T. (1997) Personality trait structure as a human universal *American Psychologist* 52 509

McCrae, R.R. & Costa, P.T. (1987) Validation of the Five-Factor Model of Personality Across Instruments and Observers *Journal of Personality and Social Psychology* 52

McCrimmon, M. (2009) Post-heroic leadership: how to succeed in the 21st century *Canadian Manager* 34, 3, 10

McCullogh, D. (2008) *Timeless Leadership: a conversation with David McCullough* Harvard Business Review, March, 45

McGinn, B. (1994) *Antichrist: two thousand years of fascination with evil* Harper, New York, NY, USA

McGrath, J.E. (1962) *Leadership Behavior: some requirements for leadership training* US Civil Service Commission, Office of Career Development, Washington DC, USA

M'Guire, E.C. (1836) *The Religious Opinions and Character of Washington* Harper & Brothers, New York, NY, USA

Meade, W. (1857) *Old Churches, Ministers and Families of Virginia*, Applewood Books, Bedford, MA, USA

Meade, W. Rassmussen, S. & Tilton, W. (1999) *Washington – the man behind the myth* University of Virginia Press, Charlottesville, VA, USA

Medhurst, M.J. & Eisenhower, D.D. (1993) *Dwight D Eisenhower: Strategic Communicator* Greenwood Press, Westport, CT, USA

Merriam, S.B. (1998) *Qualitative Research and Case Study Applications in Education* Jossey-Bass, San Francisco, CA, USA

Meyer, C.T. (1947) The assertive behavior of children as related to parent behavior *Journal of Home Economics* 39, 77

Michalski, R.L. & Shackelford, T.K. (2002) An attempted replication of the relationship between birth order and personality *Journal of Research in Personality* 36, 2, 182

Mill, J.S. (1848) *Principles of Political Economy* CC Little and J Brown (Google books edition), London, UK

Mill, J.S. (1861) *Considerations on Representative Government* in D Thompson, D. (1976) *John Stuart Mill and Representative Government* Princeton University Press, Princeton, NJ, USA

Miller, D. (2003) *Political Philosophy: a very short introduction* Oxford University Press, Oxford, UK

Milne, A.J. (1973) Bentham's principle of utility and legal philosophy *Northern Ireland Legal Quarterly* 24, 3, 276

Molé, M. (1814) Le Comte Molé: 1781-1855: sa vie, ses mémoires Paris, France

Monk, R. & Raphael, F.(eds) (2000) The Great Philosophers Phoenix, London, UK

Montaigne, M. Of Physiognomy Frame, D.M.(1958)(transl.) The Complete essays of Montaigne Stanford university Press, Stanford, USA

Morgeson, F.P., Scott DeRue, D. & Karam, E.P. (2009) Leadership in teams: a functional approach to understanding leadership structures and processes Journal of Management 20, 10, 1

Mortensen, K. (2008) Persuasion IQ: the 10 skills you need to get exactly what you want Amacom, Broadway, NY, USA.

Mroczek, D.K. & Little, T.D. (eds) (2008) Handbook of Personality Development Psychology Press, New York, NY, USA

Murat, A. (2008) La Tour du Pin en Son Temps Via Romana, Versailles, France

Murphy, L.B. Social factors in child development in Newcomb, T.M. & Hartley, E.L. (eds)(1974) Readings in Social Psychology Holt, New York, NY, USA

Murphy, A.J. (1941) A study of the leadership process American Sociological Review 6, 674

Mumford, M.D., Zaccaro, S.J., Connelly, M.S. & Marks, M.A. (2000) Leadership skills: conclusions and future directions The Leadership Quarterly 11, 1, 155

Nafe, R.W. (1930) A psychological description of leadership Journal of Social Psychology 1, 248

Nahavandi, A. (2006) The Art and Science of Leadership (4th ed) Pearson Prentice Hall, Sydney Australia

Nalon, D., Daglish, C., Brownlee, J. & Hatcher, C. (2004) How do epistemological beliefs contribute to leadership behavior, and changes required to meet the needs of today's business challenges? Proceedings 17th Annual Small Enterprise Association of Australia and New Zealand Conference, Brisbane, Queensland, 9

Nanus, B. (1992) Visionary Leadership John Wiley & Sons San Francisco CA, USA

Naugle, D.K. (2002) Worldview: the history of a concept Eerdman Publishing, Grand Rapids, MI, USA

Neal, S. (1978) The Eisenhowers: reluctant dynasty Doubleday & Co, New York, NY, USA

Neale, J. (1958) Essays in Elizabethan History Jonathan Cape, London, UK

Nietzsche, F. Menschliches, Allzumenschliches in M Faber & S Lehmann (1985) Human, All-too-human - a book for free spirits Penguin, London, UK

Nietzsche, F. Thus Spake Zarathustra in A Nietzsche Reader Hollingdale, R.J. (trans.)(1977) Penguin, London, UK.

Norman, W. (1963) Toward an adequate taxonomy of personality attributes: replicated factor structure in peer nominated personality ratings Journal of Abnormal Psychology 66, 774.

Northouse, P.G. (2010) Leadership: Theory and Practice (5th ed.) Sage, New York, NY, USA

Norton, D.F. (2009) The Cambridge Companion to Hume Cambridge University Press, Cambridge, UK

Nystedt, L. (1997) Who should rule? Does personality matter? European Journal of Personality 11, 1, 1

Ogg, F.A. (ed.) (2010) A Source Book of Mediaeval History: Documents Illustrative of European Life and Institutions from the German Invasions to the Renaissance Kessinger Publishers, New York, NY, USA

Olivecrona, K. (1975) The will of the sovereign: some reflections on Bentham's concept of "a law" The Journal of Jurisprudence 20, 95

Ory, P. (1987) La nouvelle droite fin de siècle in Nouvelle histoire des idées politiques Hachette, Pluriel, France

Outram, D. (1995) The Enlightenment Cambridge University Press, Cambridge, UK

Padilla, A., Hogan, R. & Kaiser, R.B. (2007) The toxic triangle, destructive leaders, susceptible followers and conducive environments The Leadership Quarterly, 18, 3, 176

Pajares, M.F. (1992) Teachers beliefs and educational research: cleaning up a messy construct Review of Educational Research 62, 311

Parke Custis, G.W. (1859) Lossing B.J. (ed) Recollections and Private Memoirs of the Life and Character of Washington William H Moore, Washington DC, USA

Palmer, G.B. (1996) Toward A Theory of Cultural Linguistics University of Texas Press, TX, USA

Parry, T. (1998) Grounded theory and social process: a new direction for leadership research The Leadership Quarterly 9, 1, 85

Pastore, N. (1949) The Nature Nurture Controversy Kings Crown Press, Columbia University, New York, NY, USA

Paulding, J.K. (1848) A Life of Washington George Clark & son, Dublin, Ireland, UK

Peckham, H.H. (1958) The War of Independence: a military history University of Chicago Press, Chicago, IL, USA

Pearce, T. (2010) From 'circumstance' to 'environment': Herbert Spencer and the idea of the organism-environment interaction Studies in history and philosophy of biological and biomedical sciences 41, 248

Perret, G. (1999) Eisenhower Random House, New York, NY, USA

Perry, M., Chase, M., Jacob, M.C. & Jacob, J.R. (2009) Western Civilization: ideas, politics and society Houghton Mifflin Harcourt, New York, NY, USA

Perry, W.G. (1970) Forms of Intellectual and Ethical Development in the College Years: a scheme Holt Reinhart and Winston, New York, NY, USA

Phillipson, N. Adam Smith as civic moralist in Hont, I. & Ignatieff, M. (eds) (1983) Wealth and virtue Cambridge University Press, Cambridge, UK.

Philo, G. & Walton, P. (1973) Max Weber on self-interest and domination Social Theory and Practice 2, 335

Pierce, J.L. & Newstrom, J.W. On the meaning of leadership in Pierce, J.L. & Newstrom, J.W. (2010) Leadership and the Leadership process McGraw Hill (5th edn) New York, NY, USA

Piotrowski, C. & Armstrong, T.R. (1989) The CEO: an analysis of the Telecast 'Pinnacle' Psychological Reports 65, 2, 437

Plato The Republic Lee, H.D.P. (trans.) (2009) Plain Label books, London, UK

Plato The Trial and Death of Socrates B Jowlett (trans.) (2010) Chartwell Books, New York, NY, USA

Plomin, R., De Fries, R. & McClearn, G.E. (1990) Behavioral Genetics: a primer Times Books, New York, NY, USA.

Podsakoff, P.M., Mackenzie, S.B., Moorman, R.H. & Fetter, R. (1990) Transformational leader behaviors and their effects on followers trust in leader, satisfaction, and organisational citizenship behaviors The Leadership Quarterly 1, 2, 109

Pojman, L.P. & Feister, J. (2011) Ethics: Discovering right and wrong Wadsworth, Belmont, CA, USA

Pollele, M.R. (2007) Fifty Great Leaders and the Worlds they made Westport, CT, USA

Popper, M. (2001) Hypnotic Leadership: Leaders, Followers and the loss of self Praegar Publishers, Westport, CT, USA

Posner, G., Strike, K., Hewson, P. & Gertzog, W. (1982) Accommodation of a scientific conception: Towards a theory of conceptual change Science Education 66, 2, 211

Price, T. (2008) An Introduction to Leadership Ethics Cambridge University Press, Cambridge, NY, USA

Price, T. Philosophy in Goethals G., Sorrenson G.J., MacGregor Burns J. (eds) (2004) Encyclopaedia of Leadership Sage Publications, Thousand Oaks, CA, USA

Ptolemy of Lucca (with portions attributed to Thomas Aquinas) De Regimine Principum, Blythe, J. (trans)(1997) *On the government of Rulers: De regimine principum*, University of Pennsylvania Press, Philadelphia, PA, USA

Rachels, J. & S. (2010) The Elements of Moral Philosophy McGraw Hill, New York, NY, USA

Rachels, J. (1971) God and human attitudes Religious Studies 334

Rafferty, A.E. & Griffin, M.A. (2004) Dimensions of transformational leadership: conceptual and empirical extensions The Leadership Quarterly, 15, 329

Ragoff, M.A. (1996) A comparison of constitutionalism in France and the United States Maine Law Review 49, 21, 22

Ramage, M. & Shipp, K. (2009) Systems Thinkers Springer, London, UK

Rassmussen, W.M.S. & Tilton, R.S. (1999) George Washington – the man behind the myths University Press of Virginia, Charlottesville, VI, USA

Ratcliffe, B. (1981) Prelude to Fame: an account of the early life of Napoleon up to the battle of Montenotte Warne, London, UK

Reicher, S., Haslam, S.A. & Hopkins, N. (2005) Social identity and the dynamics of leadership: Leaders and followers as collaborative agents The Leadership Quarterly 16, 547

Richards, J. (1980) Consul of God: the life and times of Gregory the Great Routledge, London, UK

Richardson, J.D. (1897) Compilation of Messages and Papers of the President Bureau of National Literature New York, NY, USA

Robinson, S. (1996) Trust and the breach of the psychological contract Administrative Science Quarterly 41, 574.

Rosenthal, S.A. & Pittinsky, T.L. (2006) Narcissistic Leadership The Leadership Quarterly 17, 617

Rossides, D.W. (1998) Social Theory: Its Origins, History, and Contemporary Relevance General Hall Inc, New York, NY, USA

Rost, J.C. (1993) Leadership for the Twenty First Century Praeger publishers, Westport, CT, USA

Ruggiero, T. (ed) Political Philosophy online at http://www.philosophical society.com/Political%20Philosophy.htm#polphil-def date accessed 22 September 2009

Samier, E.A. & Stanley, A. (2008) Political Approaches to Educational Administration and Leadership Routledge London, UK

Sandoval, W.A. (2005) Understanding students' practical epistemologies and their influence on learning through inquiry Science Education 89, 634

Sandoval, W.A. (2009) In defense of clarity in the study of personal epistemology The Journal of the Learning Sciences 18, 150

Sarros, J.C. & Santora, J.C. (2001) Leaders and values: a cross cultural study Leadership and Organizational Development Journal 22, 5, 243

Sashkin, M. (1987) A new vision for leadership Journal of Management Development, 6, 4, 19

Sashkin, M. & Rosenbach, W.E. (1998) A new vision of leadership in W.E. Rosenbach, W.E. & Taylor, R.L. (eds) Contemporary Issues in Leadership Westview Press, Boulder, CO, USA

Shamir, B., House, R.J., & Arthur, M.B. (1993) The motivational effects of charismatic leadership: a self-concept based theory Organization Science, 4,4, 577

Shamir, B. & Howell, J. Organizational and contextual influences on the emergence and effectiveness of charismatic leadership The Leadership Quarterly 10, 2, 257

Scheurich, J. (1997) Research Method in the Postmodern Routledge, London, UK

Schommer, M. (1990) Effects of beliefs about the nature of knowledge on comprehension Journal of Educational Psychology 82, 498

Schommer, M. (2004) Explaining the epistemological belief system: introducing the embedded systemic model and coordinated research approach Educational Psychologist 39,1, 24

Schommer, M., Crouse, A. & Rhodes, N. (1992) Epistemological beliefs and mathematical text comprehension: believing it is simple does not make it so Journal of Educational Psychology 84, 435

Schommer, M. (1993) Epistemological development and academic performance among secondary school students Journal of Educational Psychology 85, 406

Schroeder, J.F. (1855) Maxims of Washington: political, social, moral and religious D Appleton & Co, New York, NY, USA

Schroeder, W. & Huebert, H. (2001) Mennonites Historical Atlas Springfield Publisher, Manitoba, Canada

Schultz, D.P. & S.E. (1998) Psychology and Work Today: an introduction to Industrial and Organizational Psychology Prentice Hall, Upper Saddle River, NJ, USA

Schultz, D.P. & S.E. (2012) A History of Modern Psychology Wadsworth, Belmont, CA, USA

Sellars, J. (2006) Stoicism University of California Press, Berkeley, LA, USA

Shamir, B. (1992) Attribution of influence and charisma to the leader: the romance of leadership revisited Journal of Applied Social Psychology 22, 5, 386.

Shamir, B., House, R.J. & Authur, M.B. (1993) The motivational effects of charismatic leadership: a self-concept based theory Organizational Science 4,4, 577

Shamir, B. & Howell, J. (1999) Organizational and contextual influences on the emergence and effectiveness of charismatic leadership The Leadership Quarterly 10, 2, 257

Sharma, U. & S.K. (2006) Western Political Thought Atlantic Publishers, New Delhi, India

Shennan, A. (1993) De Gaulle, Routledge, New York, NY, USA.

Shils, E. (1965) Charisma, order and status American Sociological Review 30, 204

Shoenbrun, D. (1966) The Three Lives of Charles de Gaulle Hamish Hamilton, London, UK

Shorter Oxford English Dictionary (6th ed) Oxford University Press, Oxford, UK

Shoup, J. (2002) A Prosopography of 12 Influential Leaders: a study on developing exemplary leaders University of California Riverside, doctoral dissertation

Shoup, J. (2005) A Collective Biography of Twelve World Class Leaders University Press of America, Lanham, Maryland, USA

Shriberg, A. & D. (2002) Practicing Leadership: principles and applications John Wiley & Sons, New York, NY, USA

Simola, S., Barling, J. & Turner, N. (2012) Transformational leaders and leaders mode of care reasoning Journal of Business Ethics 108, 2, 229

Skinner, Q. (1994) The Foundation of Modern Political Thought Cambridge University Press, Cambridge, UK

Slaughter, P. (1886) Christianity the Key to the Character and Career of Washington Whittaker, New York, NY, USA

Smirchich, L. & Morgan, G. (1982) Leadership: the management of meaning Journal of Applied Behavioral Science 18, 3, 257

Smith, A. (1759) The Theory of Moral Sentiments version at http://www.ibiblio.org/ml/libri/s/SmithA_MoralSentiments_p.pdf date accessed 15 July 2009

Smith, A. (1843) An Inquiry into the Nature and Causes of the Wealth of Nations online version at http://www.gutenberg.org/files/3300/3300-h/3300-h.htm date accessed 16 Sept 2010

Snow, C.P. (1959) The Two Cultures Cambridge University Press, Cambridge, UK.

Snyder, L.L. (1968) The New Nationalism Transaction publishers, New Brunswick, NJ, USA

Sparks, J. (1834) The Writings of George Washington being his correspondence, addresses, messages and other papers, official and private volume 6, American Stationers Company, Boston, MA, USA

Sparks, J. (1860) The Life of George Washington Little Brown, Boston, MA, USA

Spencer, H. (1896) The Study of Sociology D. Appleton & Co, New York, NY, USA

Spielvogel, J.J. (2008) Western Civilization (1300-1815), Wadsworth, Belmont, CA, USA

Stogdill, R. (1974) Handbook of Leadership: a survey of theory and research Free Press, New York, NY USA

Stogdill, R.M. (1948) Personal factors associated with leadership: a survey of the literature Journal of Psychology 25 35

Stone, L. (1971) Prosopography Daedalus, 100

Strauss, A. & Corbin, J. (1998) Basics of Qualitative Research: Grounded procedures and techniques Sage, Thousand Oaks, CA, USA

Strauss, L. & Cropsey, J. (1987) The History of Political Philosophy The University of Chicago Press, Chicago, IL, USA

Strauss, L. (1989) An Introduction to Political Philosophy: ten essays Wayne

State University Press, Detroit, MI, USA

Strong, P.M. Commentary: On Qualitative methods and leadership research in Hunt, J.G., Hosking, D., Schriesheim, C.A. & Stewart, R. (eds) (1984) Leaders and managers: international perspectives on managerial behavior and Leadership Pergamon Press, New York, NY, USA

Sutton, M. (2002) Nationalism, Positivism and Catholicism: The Politics of Charles Maurras and French Catholics 1890-1914 Cambridge University Press, Cambridge, UK

Swift, A. (2006) Political Philosophy: a beginners guide for students and politicians Polity, Cambridge, UK

Szacki, J. (1979) History of Sociological Thought Alswich press, London, UK

Tatsch, J.H. (1931) Facts about George Washington as a Freemason Macoy publishing and Masonic supply Co. New York, NY, USA

Thompson, D. (1976) John Stuart Mill and Representative Government Princeton University Press, Princeton, NJ, USA

Thoms, J.C. (2008), Ethical integrity in leadership and organizational moral culture Leadership, 4, 419

Tickle, E.L., Brownlee, J. & Nalon, D. (2005) Personal epistemological beliefs and transformational leadership behaviours The Journal of Management Development 24, 1

Tournoux, J. (1966) Petain and de Gaulle Coburn, O.(trans) Viking, New York, NY, USA

Trompenaars, F. & Hampden-Turner, C. (1997) Riding the Waves of Culture – understanding cultural diversity in business Nicholas Brearley Publishing, London, UK

Tucker, R.C. (1978) The Marx Engels Reader (2nd edn) WW Norton & Co Inc, New York, NY, USA

Turner, J.C. Towards a Cognitive Redefinition of the Social Group in Tajfel, H. (ed) (2008) Social identity and intergroup relations Cambridge University Press, Cambridge, UK

Varaki, B.S. (2203) Epistemological beliefs and leadership style among school principals International Education Journal 4, 3, 224

Velasquez, M.G. (192) Business Ethics: Concepts and Cases Prentice Hall, New York, NY, USA

Verboven, K., Carlier, M., Dumolyn, J. A Short Manual to the Art of Prosopography in Keats-Rohan, K.S.B. (ed.) (2007) Prosopography approaches and applications: a handbook The unit for prosopographical research, Linacre College, University of Oxford, UK

von Bertalanffy, K.L. (1950) An outline of general system theory British Journal for the Philosophy of Science, 1,2, 134

von Clausewicz, C. (1832) On War online version at http://books.google.com.au/books?id=agomkmvimc4C date accessed 29 Oct 2010

Vroom, V.H. (1973) Research: a new look at managerial decision-making Organizational Dynamics 1, 4, 68

Vroom, V.H.& Yetton, P.W. (1973) Leadership and decision making Organisational Dynamics 28, 4, 82

Vroom, V.H. & Jago, A.G. (1978) On the validity of the Vroom-Yetton model Journal of Applied Psychology 63, 2, 151

Waclawski, J. (2001) Abraham, Martin and John: where have all the great leaders gone? The Industrial-Organizational Psychologist 38, 1, 70.

Walker, M.C. The theory and Meta-theory of Leadership: the important but contested nature of theory in Goethals, G.R. & Sorenson, G.J. (2005) The Quest for a General Theory of Leadership Edward Elgar Publishing, Northampton MA, USA.

Washington, H.A. (1861) The Writings of Thomas Jefferson Derby & Jackson, New York, NY, USA

Weber, E. (1962) Action Française; Royalism And Reaction In Twentieth-Century France Stanford University Press, Stanford, CA, USA

Weber, M. (1922) Roth, G. & Wittich, C. (eds.) (1968) Economy and Society: an outline of interpretative sociology University of California Press, Berkley, CA, USA

Weber, M. The Protestant Ethic and the Spirit of Capitalism in Parsons, T. (trans) (2003) Dover Publications, New York, NY

Werth, A. (1965) de Gaulle, a Political Biography Penguin books, Hamonds-worth, UK

West, L. (1996) Beyond Fragments: adults, motivation and higher education, a biographical analysis Taylor & Francis, London, UK

Winkler, I. (2009) Contemporary Leadership Theories Springer, London, UK

White, S (2003) Cicero, Marcus Tullius in Craig, E. (ed.) Routledge Encyclopedia of Philosophy Routledge, London, UK, online at http://www.rep.routledge.com.ezproxy.libadfa.adfa.edu.au:2048/article/A031SECT1 date accessed 16 November 2009

Whitelaw, N. (1991) A Biography of General Charles de Gaulle: "I am France" Dillon Press, New York, NY, USA

Whitmore, E. (2003) Epistemological beliefs and the information seeking behaviour of undergraduates Library of Information Science Research 25, 127

Wiggam, A.E. (1931) The Biology of Leadership Business Leadership, Pitman, New York, NY, USA

Wilbur, W. (1973) The Making of George Washington De Land, Fla

Willner, A.R. (1968) Charismatic Political Leadership: a theory Centre for International studies Princeton, NJ, USA

Willner, A.R. (1984) The Spellbinders: Charismatic political leadership Yale University Press, New Haven, USA

Wren, J.T. A Quest for a Grand Theory of Leadership in Goethals, G.R. & Sorenson, G.L.J. (2005) The quest for a general theory of leadership Edward Elgar Publishing, Northampton, MA, USA

Wren, J.T. (2007) Inventing Leadership Edward Elgar Publishing, Northamp-ton, MA, USA

Wren, J.T., Hicks, D.A., Price, T.L. (2004) Modern Classics on Leadership E Elgar publishing, Northampton, MA, USA

Yagil, D. (1998) Charismatic leadership and organizational hierarchy: Attribution of charisma to close and distant followers The Leadership Quarterly 9, 2, 161.

Yammarino, F.J. & Bass, B.M. Long term forecasting of transformational leadership and its effects among naval officers: some preliminary findings in Clark, K.E. & Clark, M.B.(eds)(1989) Measures of leadership Leadership Library of America, NJ, USA

Young, N. (1910) The Growth of Napoleon: a study in environment J.Murray, London, UK

Young, N. (1932) George Washington Duckworth, London, UK

Yukl, G. (1989) Managerial leadership: a review of theory and research Journal of Management 15, 2, 254

Yukl, G. (2006) Leadership in Organisations Prentice Hall, New York, NY, USA

Yukl, G. (1999) An evaluation of conceptual weaknesses in transformational and charismatic leadership theories The Leadership Quarterly 10, 2, 285

Zaccaro, S.J. (2007) Trait-based perspectives of leadership American Psychologist 62, 1, 6

Zaccaro, S.J., Rittman, A.L. & Marks, M.A. (2001) Team Leadership The Leadership Quarterly 12, 4, 451

Zaccaro S.J., Kemp, C. & Bader, P. (2004) Leadership traits and attributes in Antonanakis, J., Cianciolo, A.T. & Sternberg, R.J. (eds) The Nature of Leadership Sage, Thousand Oaks, CA, USA

Zand, D. (1972) Trust and managerial problem solving Administrative Science Quarterly 17, 299

Zaleznik, A. (1977) Managers and Leaders: are they different? in H Levinson (ed) (1989) Designing and managing your career Harvard Business Press, Boston, MA, USA, 64

Zeller, E. (2000) Outlines of the History of Greek Philosophy Routledge, London, UK

Zetzel, J.E.G.(ed.)(1995) *De Re Publica – selections Marcus Tulius* Cicero Cambridge University Press, Cambridge, UK

Zhang, Z., Illies, R., Arvey, R.D. (2009) Beyond genetic explanations for leadership: the moderating role of the social environment Organizational Behavior and Human decision processes 110, 118

Znaniecki, F. (1939) Social groups as products of participating individuals The American Journal of Sociology 44, 6, 799

Zuckert, C. (2005) Tocqueville – 200 years The Review of Politics 67, 4, 597

Index

[1] Namely, the trait perspective of leadership such that they were simply endowed with the traits of "Great Men".

[2] Gini, A. (1997) *Moral leadership and business ethics* Journal of Leadership and Organisational Studies 4, 4, 73.

[3] Smirchich & Morgan, op.cit, 257; Hollander, E.P. & Julian, J.W. (1969) Contemporary trends in the analysis of leadership processes *Psychological Bulletin* 7, 5, 387; Stogdill, *op.cit.* 35.

[4] Bass, *Bass and Stogdill's Handbook of Leadership op. cit.* 19; Rost, *op.cit.* 102.

[5] Although the earliest appearance of this term is unclear it did appear in the modern conscience with the writing of Carl von Clausewicz's famous military treatise *On War (1832)*. Von Clausewicz refers to the necessity of the merger between military skills of the General and the political skills of the Statesman as essential to the success of a societal leader in wartime: "To conduct a whole war, or its greater act, which we call campaigns, to a successful conclusion, there must be an intimate knowledge of State policy in its highest relations. The conduct of the war and the policy of the State here coincide, and the General becomes the Statesman." von Clausewicz, C. (1832) On War online version at http://books.google.com.au/books?id=agomkmvimc4C date accessed 29 Oct 2010, 74. The modern parlance for the term "soldier statesman" is attributed to either military men who act as statesmen, in accordance with von Clausewicz's description, or ex military men who enter politics.

[6] Good examples of this can be seen in certain US corporations such as Apple, Enron, GE, where gifted chief executive officers (CEOs) assume an almost messianic status in their organisations, yet their leadership abilities are somewhat idiosyncratic and hardly ideal models.

[7] Ragoff, M.A. (1996) A comparison of constitutionalism in France and the United States *Maine Law Review* 49, 21, 26.

[8] Plato, *The Republic*

[9] Notably Plato in early Greece and Stuart Mill and Carlyle in the nineteenth century.

[10] Carlyle, T. (1840) *On Heroes, the Heroic and Hero Worship in History* Chapman & Hall, London, UK, 285. Ironically, the term "environment" is attributed to Thomas Carlyle but was coined as "an environment of circumstance" being related to nature, whereas when we talk of environmental factors we are referring to nurture: see Pearce T. (2010) *From 'circumstance' to 'environment': Herbert Spencer and the idea of the organism-environment interaction* Studies in History and Philosophy of Biological and Biomedical Sciences, 41, 248.

[11] Mill, J.S. (1848) *Principles of political economy* (Google books edition) CC Little and J Brown, London, UK, 379.

[12] Galton, F. (1892) *Hereditary Genius: an inquiry into its laws and consequences* Macmillan, London, UK. (Note: work was written in 1869 but not generally available – the 1892 account is commonly available).

[13] Spencer, H. (1881) *The Study of Sociology* D. Appleton & Co, New York, NY, USA, 34.

[14] *ibid.* 181

[15] Day, C.M. (1981) Promotions of health care personnel in hospitals: heuristic decision making *Dissertation Abstracts International* 43,3,1290.

[16] Maller J.B. (1931) Size of family and personality of offspring *Journal of Social Psychology* 2, 1, 3.

[17] Bass, *Bass and Stogdill's Handbook of Leadership, op.cit.* 807-810; Bass B.M. (1960) *Leadership, Psychology and Organisational Behaviour* Greenwood Press, Westport, CT, USA; Hoffman, L., Rosen, S., Lippitt, R. (1960) *Parental coercive, child autonomy, and the child's role at school* Sociometry 23, 15; Zaleznik A. (1977) Managers and Leaders: are they different? in Levinson, H. (ed.) (1989) *Designing and Managing Your Career* Harvard Business Press, Boston, MA, USA, 64; Bogardus, E.S. (1934) *Leaders and Leadership* Appleton-Century, New York, NY, USA; Anderson, H.H. (1937) *An experimental study of dominative and integrative behaviour in children of pre-school age* Journal of Social Psychology 8, 335; Baldwin, A.L. (1949) *The effect of home environment on nursery school behaviour* Child Development 20, 49; Meyer, C.T. (1947) The assertive behaviour of children as related to parent behaviour *Journal of Home Economics* 39, 77; Avolio, *op.cit.* 18;.

[18] Bass, *Bass and Stogdill's Handbook of Leadership, op.cit.* 810 citing Murphy: Murphy, L.B. (1947) Social factors in child development in Newcomb, T.M. & Hartley, E.L. (eds) *Readings in Social Psychology* Holt, NY, USA.

[19] *ibid.* 810 citing Willner: Willner, A.R. (1968) *Charismatic Political Leadership: a theory* Centre for International Studies, Princeton, NJ, USA.

[20] *ibid.* 811-812: Bass provides details of several studies in this regard.

[21] *ibid.*

[22] Michalski, R.L. & Shackelford, T.K. (2002) An attempted replication of the relationship between birth order and personality *Journal of Research in Personality* 36, 2, 182. Note that while consistent variations have been found in personality between siblings, the predominance of characteristics aligning with the five factor model for first and last born does not provide a sufficiently high concurrence with requirements advocated in leadership research.

[23] Kirkpatrick & Locke, *op.cit.* 50 & 55 – where intelligence is described as cognitive ability and persistence as tenacity.

[24] Bass, *Bass and Stogdill's Handbook of Leadership, op.cit.* 810.

[25] *ibid.* 808.

[26] *ibid.* 197

[27] *ibid.* 197, 809

[28] Zaleznik *op.cit.* 64.

[29] *ibid.*

[30] Bass, *Bass and Stogdill's Handbook of Leadership, op.cit.* 810 citing Willner, *ibid.*

[31] *ibid.* 810

[32] *ibid.*

[33] In terms of the classification used charismatic leadership could be either an individual or adaptive approach. However, the point here is that an environmental factor has been touted as a precursor to the identification of a certain mode of leadership.

[34] Willner, A.R. (1984) *The Spellbinders: Charismatic political leadership* Yale University Press, New Haven CT, USA, 14.

[35] Shamir, B., House, R.J. & Arthur, M.B. (1993) The motivational effects of charismatic leadership: a self-concept based theory *Organizational Science* 4,4, 577; Hayibor, S., Agle, B.R., Sears, G.J., Sonnenfeld, A.W.& Ward, A. (2011) Value congruence and charismatic leadership in CEO-Top manager relationships: an empirical investigation *Journal of Business Ethics* 102, 2, 237.

[36] Loehlin, J.C. & Nichols, J. (1976) *Heredity, Environment and Personality* University of Texas, Austin, TX, USA; Bouchard, T.J. (1999) Genes, environment and personality in Ceci, S.J. & Williams, W.M. (eds) *The Nature-Nurture Debate: the essential readings* Oxford-Blackwell Publishing, Oxford, UK, 98; Mroczek, D.K. & Little, T.D. (2008) *Handbook of Personality Development* Routledge, New York, NY, USA.

[37] Arvey, R.D., Rotundo, M., Johnson, W., Zhang, Z. & McGue, M. (2006) The determinants of leadership role occupancy: genetic and personality factors *The Leadership Quarterly* 17, 1-20.

[38] Avolio, B. (1999) Are leaders born or made? *The Journal of Psychology* 32, 5, 18; Judge, T.A., Illies, R., Bono, J.E., Gerhardt, M.W. (2002) Personality and leadership: a qualitative and quantitative review *Journal of Applied Psychology* 87, 765.

[39] House & Atidya, *op.cit.* 419.

[40] Bandura, A. (1977) Social cognitive theory in Pervin, L.A. & John, O.P. (eds) *Handbook of personality* The Guildford Press, New York, NY, USA, 154; Bowlby, J. (1977) The making and breaking of affectional bonds *The British Journal of Psychiatry* 130,3,201; Bretherton, I. (1992) The origins of Attachment theory: John Bowlby and Mary Ainsworth *Developmental Psychology* 28, 5, 759

[41] Boag, S. (2011) Explanation in personality psychology: "verbal magic" and the five factor model *Philosophical Psychology* 24, 2, 223; Harris J., *op.cit.*

[42] Nystedt, L. (1997) Who should rule? Does personality matter? *European Journal of Personality* 11, 1, 1; Zhang, Z., Illies, R. & Arvey, R.D. (2009) Beyond genetic explanations for leadership: the moderating role of the social environment *Organizational Behaviour and Human Decision Processes* 110, 118.

[43] Harris, *op.cit.* 356-359.

[44] Brungardt, C. (1996) The making of leaders: A review of the research in leadership development and education *Journal of Leadership & Organizational Studies* 3, 3, 81.

[45] Whitmire, *op.cit.* 5.

[46] Kardash, C.M. (1996) Effects of pre-existing beliefs, epistemological beliefs, and need for cognition on interpretation of controversial issues *Journal of Educational Psychology* 88, 2, 260, 261.

[47] Perry, W.G. (1970) *Forms of Intellectual and Ethical Development in the College Years: a scheme* Holt Reinhart and Winston, New York, NY, USA; Kitchener, K.S. & King, P.M. (1981) Reflective judgement: concepts of justification and their relationship to age and education *Journal of Applied Development Psychology* 2, 89, 116; Schommer, M. (1993) Epistemological development and academic performance among secondary school students *Journal of Educational Psychology* 85, 406.

[48] Hofer & Pintrich, op.cit; Sandoval, *op.cit.* 634; Elby, A. (2009) Defining Personal Epistemology: A response to Hofer and Pintrich (1997) and Sandoval (2005) *The Journal of the Learning Sciences* 18, 138.

[49] Posner, G., Strike, K., Hewson, P. & Gertzog, W. (1982) Accommodation of a scientific conception: Towards a theory of conceptual change *Science Education* 66, 2, 211.

[50] Hallet, D., Chandler, M.J. & Krettenauer, T. (2002) Disentangling the course of epistemological development: parsing knowledge by epistemic content *New Ideas in Psychology* 20, 2, 285 – emphasis added.

[51] Pajares, M.F. (1992) Teachers beliefs and educational research: cleaning up a messy construct *Review of Educational Research* 62, 311.

[52] Schommer, M. (2004) Explaining the epistemological belief system: introducing the embedded systemic model and coordinated research approach *Educational Psychologist* 39,1, 24

[53] Schommer-Aitkins *ibid.*, 23 citing Boffenbrenner, U. (1979) *The Ecology of Human Development* Harvard University Press, Cambridge MA, USA.

[54] Note: worldview and world view are both valid uses of the same term.

[55] Naugle, D.K. (2002) *Worldview: the history of a concept* Eerdman Publishing, Grand Rapids, MI, USA, 56: Naugle traces the derivation of the word to the German *weltanschauung* and attributes its initial use to Immanuel Kant who saw it as one's "sense perception of the world"(59). Kant's *Critique of Judgement* (1790) describes worldview thus: "If the human mind is to *be able to even think* the given infinite without contradiction, it must have within itself a power which is super-sensible, whose ideas of noumenon cannot be intuited but can yet be regarded as the substrate underlying what is mere appearance, namely, our intuition of the world (*weltanschauung)*" (58)

[56] *Shorter Oxford English Dictionary* (6th edn) Oxford University Press, Oxford, UK.

[57] Tickle, E.L., Brownlee, J. & Nalon, D. (2005) Personal epistemological beliefs and transformational leadership behaviours *The Journal of Management Development* 24, 1 citing Burns, Leadership, *op.cit*, Krishnan, V.R. (2001) Value systems of transformational leaders *Leadership and Organizational Development Journal* 22, 3, 126; Sarros, J.C. & Santora, J.C. (2001) Leaders and values: a cross cultural study *Leadership and Organizational Development Journal* 22, 5, 243.

[58] *ibid.*, 6; internalist and externalist perspectives are described in Kim, K. (1993) Internalism and externalism in epistemology *American Philosophical Quarterly* 30, 4, 303.

[59] Hughes, S. *Social Philosophy*; Fink, *op.cit.* 3.

[60] *ibid.*

[61] Strauss, L. & Cropsey, J. (1987) *The History of Political Philosophy*, Chicago, IL, USA, 4-5; Strauss, L. (1989) *An Introduction to Political Philosophy: ten essays* Wayne State University Press, Detroit, MI, USA, 6.

[62] Miller, D. (2003) *Political Philosophy: a very short introduction* Oxford University Press, Oxford, UK, 2.

[63] Swift, A. (2006) *Political Philosophy: a beginner's guide for students and politicians* Polity, Cambridge, UK, 5.

[64] *ibid.*3.

[65] Miller, *op.cit.* 4.

[66] Swift, *op.cit.* 5.

[67] Ruggiero, T. (ed.) philosophical society.com *Political Philosophy*.

[68] Rachels, J. & S. (2010) *The Elements of Moral Philosophy* McGraw Hill Higher Education, New York, NY, USA, 1.

[69] *ibid.* 13.

[70] Rachels, *op.cit.* 49.

[71] Holt, T. (2009) *Moral Philosophy*.

[72] Shriberg et al, *op.cit.* 231

[73] There is some contention over Platos birth date so this is an approximation based on current evidence.

[74] Plato *The Republic* HDP Lee (trans.) (1987) (2nd ed.) Penguin Books, London, UK, xix: (Plato is widely acknowledged as being the first ancient Greek philosopher to propose such a philosophy but some would credit Socrates with this epithet.)

[75] *ibid*

[76] Plato *The Republic, op.cit,* 333

[77] JT Wren (2007) *Inventing leadership* Edward Elgar Publishing, Northampton, MA, USA, 16

[78] *Ibid:* These were basically "universal truths", such as "Beauty" or "Good".

[79] *ibid*

[80] Wren *op.cit.,* 17

[81] A Shriberg, *op.cit.* 233

[82] Plato, *op.cit.* 334

[83] Cawthorn, *op.cit.* 9 citing from *The Republic* (FM Cornford trans.)

[84] R Monk & F Raphael (eds) (2000) *The Great Philosophers* Phoenix, London, UK, 71

[85] Contractarianism being the legitimate political or moral authority of government over the polity: A Cudd (2007) *Stanford Encyclopaedia of Philosophy*

[86] Goethals, Sorrenson, MacGregor Burns, *op.cit.* 1197

[87] Cawthorn, *op.cit.* 17

[88] Aristotle, *Politics* B Jowlett (transl.) (1977) Harvard University Press, Cambridge, MA, USA, 68

[89] Wren, *op.cit.* 54

[90] Aristotle, *op.cit.* 6

[91] Wren, *op.cit.* 52

[92] *ibid*

[93] Goethals & Sorrenson, *op.cit.* 126

[94] Aristotle *op.cit.* 1

[95] Aristotle, *op.cit. 114*

[96] Goethals, Sorrenson, MacGregor Burns, *op.cit.* 1197

[97] *ibid.* 63

[98] *ibid.* 124

[99] J Sellars (2006) *Stoicism*, University of California Press, Berkeley LA,USA, 1-4

[100] ML Colish (1990) *The stoic tradition from antiquity to early Middle Ages: stoicism in classical latin literature* Leiden, NY, USA, 136

[101] Sellars, *op.cit.* 2

[102] *ibid.* 122: Although the latin *virtus* approximates with "virtue" in English, the Greek equivalent of virtue *arete* is perhaps the most accurate equivalent which connotes "moral excellence", or acting as an outstanding example.

[103] Campbell, *op.cit.* 16

[104] S White (2003) *Cicero, Marcus Tullius* in E. Craig (ed.) Routledge Encyclopedia of Philosophy Routledge, London, UK.

[105] White, *op.cit.*

[106] Colish, *Pauline theology and stoic philosophy op.cit.* 82

[107] R Hall (2004) *Political Thinkers* Routlege, London, UK, 145

[108] *ibid*

[109] J.E.G Zetzel (Ed.) (1995) *De Re Publica – selections Marcus Tulius Cicero* Cambridge University Press, NY, USA, 13

[110] White, *op.cit.*

[111] Zetzel, *op.cit.*14

[112] CD Yonge (transl.) (2009) *The republic and the laws*, Digireads publishing - Cicero *De Re Publica*: Book V:VI

[113] *ibid.* 67

[114] *ibid.* 68-70

[115] Sellars, *op.cit.* 13

[116] R Campbell (1969) *Letters from a stoic: epistulae morales as Lucilium* Penguin, London, UK, 18

[117] R L'Estrange (1818) *Seneca Morals: by way of abstract*, Sherwood, Neely and Jone's, London, UK, 109

[118] This is not an original concept by any means. Cicero advocated *malis minus est semper eligendum* in *De Officiis*, which is a direct attribution to a quotation by Plato: – "between the best of all, which is to do injustice and not be punished, and the worst of all, which is to suffer injustice without the power of retaliation; and justice...as the lesser evil..." *Republic* Book II

[119] Colish, *op.cit.*, 39

[120] *ibid.* 48

[121] Goethals, Sorrenson, McGregor Burns, *op.cit.*, 1373

[122] *ibid.* 651-2

[123] Cawthorn, *op.cit.* 27

[124] T Williams (transl) *On Free Choice of the will* Hackett Publishing Company Indiana, USA, xiv

[125] Fitzgerald & Cavadini *op.cit.* 659

[126] Gini, *op.cit.* 71 paraphrasing Augustine as "regardless of the outcome, the first and final job of leadership is the attempt to serve the needs and well being of the people being

led".

[127] Also known as *Liber Pastoralis Curae*: FH Dudden (1905) *Gregory the Great: His place in history and thought* Russell & Russell, NY, USA, 228

[128] J Richards (1980) *Consul of God: the life and times of Gregory the Great* Routledge and Keegan, London, UK, 261

[129] *ibid.* 162

[130] FA Ogg (ed.) (2010) *A Source Book of Mediaeval History: Documents Illustrative of European Life and Institutions from the German Invasions to the Renaissance* Kessinger Publishers, New York, USA, 92 (note: while the instruction applied principally to clerical leadership Gregory used the term "ruler" in general). The source of Pastoral Care/Rule is J P Migne *Pastrologae Cursus Completus* First series, Vol LXXVII, Col 12-127 *passim*.

[131] Richards *op.cit.* 143 citing *Regula Pastoralis*

[132] This text was subsequently adopted by King Alfred (the Great) (849-899CE), resurrected as *Regula Pastoralis* (c.890CE). See AJ Church (2009) *The story of Early Britain* General Books, UK, 221. The text for this work can be found at Ogg, *op.cit.* 191-195; K Davis (trans.) *Pastoral Care*, University of Bucknell, UK

[133] Morgan, *op.cit.* 455

[134] James Blythe attributes major works such as "*On the government of rulers (De Regimine Principum)*" to Ptolemy of Lucca (1236-1327).

[135] Fink, *op.cit.* 15

[136] *ibid.* 16

[137] Cawthorn, *op.cit.* 32

[138] *Cawthorn, op.cit.* 16

[139] Wren, *op.cit.* 30; J Blythe (trans) (1997) *On the government of Rulers: De regimine principum*, University of Pennsylvania Press, UK: Blythe and Wren attribute this work to Bartholomew of Lucca (c. 1236-1327) and that only parts of the work were written by Aquinas, namely *On Kingship, to the king of Cyprus* (Book 1).

[140] Blythe, *op.cit.* 29

[141] *ibid.* 34

[142] Wren, *op.cit.* 55

[143] A Shriberg, *op.cit.* 234

[144] Cawthorn, *op.cit.* 38

[145] *ibid.*

[146] Blythe, *op.cit.* vii

[147] *ibid.*

[148] *ibid.* 4

[149] *ibid.* ix

[150] *ibid.* 6,42

[151] Q Skinner (1994) *The Foundation of modern political thought* Cambridge University Press, Cambridge, UK, 53

[152] L Strauss *Marsilius of Padua* in L Strauss & J Cropsey (eds) *op.cit.* 281

[153] *ibid.* 280

[154] Skinner, *op.cit.* 59

[155] J Szacki, *op.cit.* 29

[156] Goethals, Sorrenson, McGregor, *op.cit.* 1197

[157] Bass, *Bass & Stogdill's Handbook of Leadership, op.cit.* 161

[158] Virtuous here is in the English sense of the word even though the *Virtù* that Machiavelli prescribes for a leader is more closely related to the qualities such as adroitness, persistence, strength, foresight.

[159] Goethals & Sorrenson, *op.cit.* 127

[160] Machiavelli, *op.cit.* 59

[161] *ibid.*

[162] Machiavelli's wrote several works of relevance to this aspect such as *The Art of War* and the *Discourse on reforming the Government of Florence*

[163] Bass, *Bass & Stogdill's Handbook of Leadership, op.cit.* 160

[164] Machiavelli, *op.cit.* 15, 60

[165] *ibid.* 62

[166] Cawthorn, *op.cit.* 42

[167] Goethals & Sorrenson, *op.cit.* 80.

[168] *ibid.*

[169] B Russell (1979) *The history of Western Philosophy: and its connection with political and social circumstances from the earliest times to the present day* Book Club Associates/Allen & Unwin London, UK, 532 ; M Nussbaum (2006) *Frontiers of Justice*, Belknap Press, Cambridge MA, USA, 39

[170] T Hobbes (2011) *Leviathan* in AP Martinich & B Battiste (1994) (eds.), Broadview Press, NY, USA, 125

[171] B Dupre (2007) *50 philosophy ideas you really need to know*, Quercus, London, UK, 185

[172] *ibid.* 159

[173] Russell, *op.cit.* 573; Fink, *op.cit.* 33

[174] *ibid*

[175] Fink, *op.cit.* 40-44

[176] J Locke (2002) *The Second Treatise of Government and a letter concerning toleration* Dover Thrift edition Courier Dover Publications ,Mineola NY, USA, 2

[177] Dupre, *op.cit.* 186

[178] Cawthorn, *op.cit.* 63

[179] *ibid.* 64

[180] JT Wren, *op.cit.,* 300

[181] GDH Cole (2003) *On the Social Contract by Jean-Jacques Rousseau* Dover Publications, New York, USA 9

[182] Cole (Rousseau *Contrat Social*), *op.cit.* 36

[183] Goethals, Sorrenson, McGregor, *op.cit.*1198

[184] notably Plato & Locke

[185] DA Cress (1987) *On the social contract*, Hackett Publishing Co, IN USA, 10

[186] *ibid*. 56: This applied equally to one of his French contemporaries - the writer and philosopher François-Marie Arouet, also known as Voltaire, whose social philosophies at the time were as influential.

[187] It is also necessary to consult *The Groundwork of the metaphysic of morals* (1785) for some of the detail discussed herein.

[188] Stanford Encyclopaedia of Philosophy

[189] J Driver *Normative ethics* in F Jackson & M Smith (eds.) (2008) *The Oxford companion to contemporary philosophy* , Oxford Handbooks Online, 31-32

[190] From a deontological perspective

[191] T Price (2008) *An introduction to leadership ethics* Cambridge University Press, USA, 38-39

[192] *ibid*

[193] That is, there is a single moral obligation or duty imposed to act morally.

[194] N Bowie (2000) *A Kantian Theory of Leadership* The Leadership and Organisation development Journal, 21,4, 185

[195] Goethals et al, *Encyclopedia of leadership, op.cit.* 466

[196] AJ Milne (1973) *Bentham's principle of utility and legal philosophy* Northern Ireland legal quarterly, 24, 3, 276

[197] J Bentham (1789) *An introduction to the Principles of morals and legislation* Oxford at the Clarendon Press London.

[198] J Bentham (1799) *A fragment on government: being an examination of what is deliverered, on the subject of government in general* T Payne, London, UK ii

[199] H Fink, *op.cit.*, 67

[200] K Olivecrona (1975) *The will of the sovereign: some reflections on Bentham's concept of "a law"* The Journal of Jurisprudence, 20, 95

[201] Bentham *op.cit.* Ch.III, para II

[202] *ibid*. Ch.I, para I

[203] B Mazlish (1970) *James Mills and the Utilitarians* in DA Rustow (ed) *Philosophers and Kings: Studies in leadership* George Braziller Inc NY, USA, 466

[204] Fink, *op.cit.* 72; JS Mill (1861) *Considerations on Representative Government* cited from D Thompson (1976) *John Stuart Mill and Representative Government* Princeton University Press, Princeton, USA, Chapter 2.

[205] Mill identifies his characterisation of utilitarianism in his work *Utilitarianism (1863)*

[206] *ibid:* which occurred in 1832

[207] *ibid*.472

[208] H Fink, *op.cit.* 73

[209] Wren, *op.cit.*, 253

[210] *ibid*. 259

[211] JS Mill (1861) *Considerations on Representative Government* cited from D Thompson (1976) *John Stuart Mill and Representative Government* Princeton University Press, Princeton, USA: cited in Wren, *ibid*

[212] *ibid.*

[213] A de Tocqueville (1865) A Goldhammer (transl.) (2004) *Democracy in America*, Penguin Putnam USA, 3

[214] B Danoff (2005) *Lincoln and Tocqueville on democratic leadership and self-interest properly understood* The Review of Politics, 67, 4, 687

[215] *ibid.* 706

[216] Tocqueville, *op.cit.* 226

[217] *ibid.* 503

[218] Danoff, *op.cit.* 690

[219] Tocqueville, *op.cit.* 611

[220] *ibid.*

[221] Danoff, *op.cit.* 694

[222] Fink, *op.cit.*, 74

[223] Up to this time the divide between the cavalry and the infantry, for example, was predominantly based on birth – if you were of noble or semi-noble ancestry you rode into battle, if you were not, you walked.

[224] C Zuckert (2005) *Tocqueville – 200 years* The Review of Politics, 67, 4, 597

[225] MJ Inwood (1998) *Hegel* Routledge, London, UK, xxxi

[226] EA Samier A Stanley (2008) *Political approaches to educational administration and leadership* Routledge NY, USA, 46

[227] Inwood, *op.cit.* xxxii

[228] Fink *op.cit.* 74

[229] *ibid.* 78

[230] *ibid.* 80

[231] FR Crist (1989*) Hegels conservative liberalism* Journal of Political science 22, 4, 718

[232] Cawthorn, *op.cit.* 81; T Price, *op.cit.*, 95

[233] Cristi *op.cit.* 738

[234] JT Wren, *op.cit.*, 299

[235] M Popper(2001) *Hypnotic leadership: Leaders, Followers and the loss of self* Praegar Publishers, CT, USA, 90

[236] *ibid.*

[237] Samier & Stanley, *op.cit.* 48

[238] Cristi, *op.cit.* 726

[239] *ibid.* 738

[240] Although in *Elements of the Philosophy of Right* he acknowledges the rationale of divine rights he discounts it as being based on a "…misunderstanding connected with the idea." T.M Knox (1967) (transl) *Hegel's Philosophy of Right* Clarendon Press, Oxford, UK,

[241] JT Wren, DA Hicks, TL Price (2004) *Modern Classics on leadership*, E Elgar publishing, Northampton MA USA, 249; Cawthorn, *op.cit.*, 84,

[242] *ibid.* 84

[243] J Evensky (2005) *Adam Smith's Theory of Moral sentiments: On morals and why they matter to a liberal society of free people and free markets* Journal of Economic Perspectives, 19, 3, 109

[244] *ibid.* 110: Smith was professor of moral philosophy at the University of Glasgow.

[245] A Smith (1759) *The theory of moral sentiments*, online version (Mobi classics), 3-4

[246] Smith, *op.cit.* 8

[247] *ibid.* 9-10

[248] *ibid.*

[249] GR Bassiry & M Jones (1993) *Adam Smith and the ethics of modern capitalism* Journal of Business ethics, 12, 8, 621

[250] *ibid.* 622

[251] S Fleischaker (2004) *On Adam Smith's wealth of nations: a philosophical companion* Princeton University Press, NJ, USA, 237

[252] *ibid.* 237-239

[253] *ibid.* 238

[254] A Smith (1843) *An inquiry into the nature and causes of the wealth of nations* online version (mobi classics) Book 1, Chapter XI, 107

[255] *ibid.* Book IV, Chapter III, 201

[256] Fleischacker, *op.cit.* 238

[257] *ibid.*

[258] Some of the concepts proposed by Smith in *A Theory of Moral Sentiments* were amplified in the works of the late nineteenth century work *Creative Evolution (1917)* by Henri Bergson (1859-1941). Bergson uses the term "intuition" to reflect the development of a feeling of concern for others.

[259] *ibid.*

[260] K Marx & F Engels (1848) *The Communist Manifesto*, Cosimo Classics, NY, USA, 54

[261] *ibid.* 14

[262] Cawthorn, *op.cit.* 95 citing *The Communist manifesto*

[263] W & AO Ebenstein (1991) *Great political thinkers: Plato to the present* Harcourt Brace Publications, TX, USA, 721.

[264] MR Pollele (2007) *Fifty great leaders and the worlds they made*, Westport, USA, 93

[265] *ibid*, 94

[266] Cawthorn, *op.cit.* 102

[267] Nietzsche *Thus Spake Zarathustra* in RJ Hollingdale (transl.) A Nietzsche Reader Penguin, London, UK, 225

[268] *ibid.* 109

[269] T Davies (1997) *Humanism*, Routledge, London, UK 36

[270] Cawthorn, *op.cit.* 104

[271] *ibid*; T Parsons, *op.cit.*, 111

[272] M Weber *The protestant ethic and the spirit of capitalism* T Parsons (2003) (trans.) Dover Publications, NY, xvii

[273] G Philo & P Walton (1973) *Max Weber on self-interest and domination* Social Theory and practice,2, 335-345

[274] Goethals et al, *Encyclopedia of Leadership*, *op.cit.* 163

[275] H Elcock (2001) *Political leadership* Edward Elgar Publishing Cheltenham London, UK, 28

[276] *ibid.* 31

[277] M Weber (1922) *Economy and Society: an outline of interpretative sociology* in G Roth & C Wittich (eds.) (1968) Bedminster Press, NY, USA, 241

[278] While numerous leadership texts cite this quotation it is nearly impossible to locate it in a credible biography. It may be a paraphrasing of another statement by Napoleon in relation to the leader's role in maintaining morale, but at the very least it should appear in the book of Napoleon's maxims by Henry, which it does not.

[279] Nietzsche, F. (1878) Menschliches, Allzumenschliches in Faber, M. & Lehmann, S. (1985) *Human, All-too-human - a book for free spirits*, Penguin, London, UK, 58.

[280] Browning, O. (1906) *The Boyhood and Youth of Napoleon* John Lane The Bodley Head, London, UK, 5.

[281] Englund, S. (2004) *Napoleon: a political life* Scribner, New York, NY, USA, 13

[282] Fournier, A. (1911) *Napoleon I: a Biography* Longmans Green & Co, London, UK, 13.

[283] *ibid.*

[284] Young, N. (1910) *The Growth of Napoleon: a study in environment*, J Murray London, UK, 80.

[285] The French version of his name will be used hereafter.

[286] Fauvelet de Bourienne, L.A. *Memoirs of Napoleon by himself dictated on St Helena* Memes, J.S.(trans)(1831) Constable & Co, Edinburgh, UK, 7.

[287] Browning, *op.cit.* 8.

[288] S Englund, *op.cit.* 14.

[289] Bourienne, *op.cit.* 5.

[290] Madelin, L. (1935) *Napoleon* Dunod, Paris, France, 23-24.

[291] Browning *op.cit.* 25; McLynn, *op.cit.* 8.

[292] Englund, op.cit. 14.

[293] *ibid.* 11.

[294] Gourgaud, G. (1932) *The St Helena Journal of General Baron Gourgaud* John Lane The Bodley Head Ltd, London, UK, 274.

[295] *ibid.* 13.

[296] Bourienne, *op.cit.* 11.

[297] *ibid.* 4.

[298] Browning, *op.cit.* 4.

[299] *ibid.*

[300] Young, *op.cit.*, 85.

[301] Browning, *op.cit.* 41.

[302] Young, *op.cit.* 272.

[303] This is not the derivation of the name of the order but is a coincidental similarity. They were known to be one of the "least religious" orders.

[304] Bourienne, *op.cit.* 10.

[305] Browning, *op.cit.* 13.

[306] *ibid.* 50.

[307] Bourienne, *op.cit.* 10.

[308] *ibid.* 8, 13.

[309] Browning, *op.cit.* 13.

[310] This is widely cited by biographers but Browning alleges it to be apocryphal: Browning *op. cit.* 19.

[311] McLynn, *op.cit.* 25.

[312] Englund, *op.cit.* 23.

[313] Browning, *op.cit.* 76 (no other detail on this has been obtained).

[314] Young, *op.cit.* 122; McLynn, *op.cit.* 31.

[315] Chandler, D.G. (1966) *Campaigns of Napoleon* Scribner New York, NY, USA: this paragraph's facts are taken primarily from this source and a composite of the biographies on Napoleon.

[316] Chandler, D.G. (2006) *On the Napoleonic Wars* Greenhill Books, Sth Yorkshire, UK.

[317] McLynn, *op.cit.* 664.

[318] Englund, *op.cit.* 461.

[319] Young, *op.cit.* 84.

[320] *ibid.*

[321] *ibid.* 86.

[322] *ibid.*

[323] *ibid.*

[324] Fournier, *op.cit.* 1.

[325] McLynn, *op.cit.* 19.

[326] Young, *op.cit.* 25: citing Boswell's *History of Corsica*.

[327] McLynn, *op.cit.* 19.

[328] Later reinstated under protest.

[329] Battle of Lodi, 1796.

[330] Connelly, O. (2006) *Blundering to glory: Napoleon's military campaigns* Rowman & Littlefield, London, UK, 26; Englund, *op.cit.* 108.

[331] Bourienne, *op.cit.* 11.

[332] Madelin, *op.cit.* 33-35.

[333] McLynn, *op.cit.* 28.

[334] McLynn, *op.cit.* 5.

[335] Fournier, *op.cit.* 1.

[336] *ibid.*

[337] *ibid.* 32.

[338] Madelin, *op.cit.* 40; Young, *op.cit.* 145; McLynn, *op.cit.* 33.

[339] *ibid.* 40.

[340] Young, *op.cit.* 127.

[341] The book had widespread influence in Europe and commenced the *Sturm und drang* movement, a reactionary force against the ideals of the enlightenment. It captured the feeling of the time that saw empiricism and rationalism as oppressive and not representative of the human experience.

[342] Fournier, *op.cit.* 16.

[343] *ibid.*

[344] Buonaparte, N. (1786) *Dissertation sur l'autorite royale* from the translation in Young, *op.cit.* 127-8.

[345] *ibid.*

[346] Englund, *op.cit.* 30.

[347] He was in fact charged on one occasion but was able to avoid prosecution by demonstrating his allegiance to France.

[348] Fournier, *op.cit.* 21.

[349] Englund, *op.cit.* 31

[350] Rose, *op.cit.* 199.

[351] *ibid.*

[352] *ibid.*

[353] Englund, *op.cit.* 25.

[354] Madelin, *op.cit.* 36.

[355] A fraternity of lieutenants of the French Army.

[356] Englund, *op.cit.* 30.

[357] *ibid.* 31.

[358] Rose, *op.cit.* 14.

[359] *ibid.* 175.

[360] McLynn, *op.cit.* 36.

[361] Ratcliffe, B. (1981) *Prelude to Fame: an account of the early life of Napoleon up to the battle of Montenotte* Warne, London, UK, 13.

[362] Fournier, *op.cit.* 19.

[363] Englund, *op.cit.* 30.

[364] *ibid.* 21. In a conversation in 1803, Napoleon was quoted as saying of Rousseau: "Bah! Jean Jacques! Now that you mention him, let me tell you that in my eyes he is a mere chatterbox – or, if you like that better, a rather eloquent ideologist. I never cared for him and, what is more, I never could quite understand him. It's true I didn't have the courage to read all of him, because he seemed, on the whole, boring." Herold, J.C. (ed.) (1955) *The mind of Napoleon – a selection from his written and spoken words* Columbia University Press, New York, NY, USA, 70.

[365] Young, *op.cit.* 125;

[366] McLynn, *op.cit.* 38.

[367] Englund, *op.cit.* 9.

[368] McLynn, *op.cit.* 45.

[369] *ibid.* 46.

[370] Fournier, *op.cit.* 33.

[371] Rose, *op.cit.* 57.

[372] Bonaparte, N. (1790) Essay response to Academy de Lyons on topic "What are the most important truths and feelings to instil into men for their happiness?"

[373] Madelin, *op.cit.* 43.

[374] *ibid.*

[375] Fournier, *op.cit.* 34.

[376] Fournier citing Masson & Biagi *Napoleon innconu*, 214; 285.

[377] *ibid.*

[378] *ibid.* xlv.

[379] *ibid.* iii.

[380] Machiavelli, N. (1854) *The History of Florence and of the Affairs of Italy from the Earliest Times to the Death of Lorenzo the Magnificent* HG Bohn Publishers, Covent Garden, London, UK, Ch.1, (unpaginated).

[381] *Farneworth, op.cit.* iii.

[382] *ibid.* iv.

[383] *ibid.* iv.

[384] Englund, *op.cit.* 30.

[385] *ibid.* 29.

[386] Henry, *op.cit.* 137.

[387] McLynn, *op.cit.* 26.

[388] Henry, *op.cit.* maxim 121.

[389] Herold, *op.cit.* 73.

[390] Henry, *op.cit.* maxim 122.

[391] *ibid.* maxim 126: yet in contradiction he stated in 1800 that "..the nation should beware of a militarist government: I should advise it to choose a civilian magistrate." Herold, *op.cit.* 77.

[392] *ibid.* maxim 78.

393 *ibid.* maxim 258.

394 In a statement made in 1801 Napoleon's views are quite clear: "The grand order that rules the world must also regulate each of its parts. At the center of a society, like the sun, is the government..in the social system, nothing must be left to individual caprice." Herold, *op.cit.* 87.

395 McLynn, *op.cit.* 27.

396 Madelin, *op.cit.* 36.

397 *ibid.*

398 Young, *op.cit.* 131.

399 *ibid.*

400 *ibid.*

401 Outram, D. (1995) *The Enlightenment* Cambridge University Press, Cambridge, UK, 114

402 McLynn, *op.cit.* 249.

403 Englund, *op.cit.* 35.

404 *ibid.*

405 *ibid.*

406 *ibid.*

407 Napoleon stated in 1819 that his father was in fact not devout and had even written irreligious poetry. Toward the end of his father's life he found God – something which Napoleon saw as hypocritical and despicable. Herold, *op.cit.* 33

408 Browning, *op.cit.* 13.

409 F McLynn, *op.cit.* 27.

410 *ibid.*

411 *ibid.*

412 *ibid.*

413 Gourgaud, *op.ct.* 259.

414 Englund, *op.cit.* 31.

415 Aston, N. (2002) *Christianity and Revolutionary Europe: c.1750-1830* Cambridge University Press, Cambridge UK, 255, citing Napoleon's personal correspondence to Lucien (1801).

416 Rose, *op.cit.* 128.

417 Cole, *op.cit.* 31

418 Englund, *op.cit.* 31.

419 Bonaparte *Refutation to Roustan op.cit.*

420 Berkovitz, J.R. (2002) *The shaping of the Jewish identity in nineteenth century France* Wayne State University Press, Detroit MI, USA, 83; McLynn, F. *op.cit.* 436.

421 Gourgaud, *op.cit.* 259.

422 Henry, *op.cit.* maxim 269.

423 Henry, *op.cit.* maxim 272.

[424] Browning, *op.cit.* 19.

[425] Gourgaud, *op.cit.* 259.

[426] Rose, *op.cit.* 270.

[427] *ibid.* 193.

[428] *ibid.*

[429] *ibid.* 215.

[430] McLynn, *op.cit.* 25.

[431] McLynn, *op.cit.* 33.

[432] Young, *op.cit.* 167-178.

[433] Young, *op.cit.* 121.

[434] Snyder, L.L. (1968) *The new nationalism* Transaction publishers, New Brunswick, NJ, USA, 34; Chandler, D.G. (1973) *Napoleon* Wiedenfeld and Nicolson, London, UK, 6.

[435] McLynn, *op.cit.* 28.

[436] *ibid.* 36.

[437] Gourgaud, *op.cit.* 267.

[438] Bourienne, *op.cit.* Ch III (Phipps version).

[439] Chandler, *op.cit.* 179.

[440] McLynn, *op.cit.* 162-3.

[441] Gourgaud, *op.cit.* 119.

[442] *ibid.*

[443] Henry, *op.cit.* maxim 311; McGlynn, *op.cit.* 139.

[444] McGlynn, *op.cit.* 113 (stated to General Marmont).

[445] One only has to see the paintings from this era such as Jacques-Louis David's *Napoleon crossing the Alps* or Jean Baptiste Mauzaisse's *Napoleon the lawmaker* or Antoine-Jean Gros's *Napoleon visting the plague-stricken at Jaffa*.

[446] Statement by Napoleon recorded by the recipient Mathieu Molé in Molé, M. (1814) *Le Comte Molé: 1781-1855: sa vie, ses mémoires*, Paris, France, vol.1, 86.

[447] Rose, *op.cit.* 29: He said, "I know when to change the lion-skin for that of a fox."

[448] Dansette, A. (1939) *Napoleon: Emperor of the French*, Fayard, Paris, France, 56-57.

[449] Several authors imply this without specifically characterising him as such.

[450] Washington *Letter to General Howe*, Headquarters West Point, 1779 in Sparks, J. (1834) *The writings of George Washington being his correspondence, addresses, messages and other papers, official and private*, volume 6, American Stationers Company, Boston, MA, USA, 324.

[451] Aristotle, *The Nichomachean Ethics* http://ebooks.adelaide.edu.au/a/aristotle/nicomachean/contents.html, date accessed 2 March 2010.

[452] Freeman, D.S. (1968) *Washington*, Charles Scribner's Sons, New York, NY, USA, 4; an abridged biography of the seven volume Freeman, D.S (1948) *George Washington* Charles Scribner's Sons, New York, NY, USA.

[453] *ibid.*

[454] Cunliffe, M. (1960) *Washington: man and monument*, New American Library of World Literature, New York, NY, USA, 32

[455] Young, N. (1932) *George Washington* Duckworth, London, UK 24.

[456] Ellis, J. (2004) *His Excellency: George Washington* Random House, New York, NY, USA 7.

[457] *ibid.*

[458] Young (1932), *op.cit.* 25.

[459] *ibid.*

[460] Cunliffe, *op.cit.* 37.

[461] Sparks, J. (1860) *The life of George Washington*, Little Brown, Boston, MA, USA, 492.

[462] *ibid.*

[463] Cunliffe, *op.cit.* 33.

[464] Brookhiser, R. (1996) *Founding father: Rediscovering George Washington* Free Press, New York, NY, USA, 162; Cunliffe, *op.cit.* 38, Freeman, *op.cit.*5.

[465] Freeman, *op.cit.* 9.

[466] Irving, W. (1859) *Life of George Washington* Da Capo Press, New York, NY, USA, 29.

[467] *ibid.*

[468] Freeman, *op.cit.* 5.

[469] *ibid.*

[470] *ibid.* 10.

[471] Sparks, *The Life of George Washington*, *op.cit.* 7.

[472] *ibid.* 12-13.

[473] The son of Lord Fairfax.

[474] *ibid.* 14.

[475] *ibid.*

[476] Ellis, *op.cit.* 12.

[477] *ibid.* 32.

[478] Sparks, *op.cit.* 19.

[479] Also known as the battle of Fort Necessity.

[480] McGregor Burns & Dunn, *op.cit.* 9: It is claimed that this incident precipitated the commencement of the French-Indian Wars of 1754-56.

[481] Sparks, *The Life of George Washington*, *op.cit.* 55.

[482] Ellis, *op.cit.* 18, citing Abbot, W.W., Twohig, D. & Chase, P.D. (1983-95) *The papers of George Washington: Colonial series*, 352-52 – Washington to William Fitzhugh, 15 November 1754.

[483] Sparks, *The Life of George Washington*, *op.cit.* 65.

[484] *ibid.* 68.

[485] Young (1932), *op.cit.* 83

[486] Sparks, *op.cit.* 95.

[487] Young (1932), op.cit. 86

[488] Ellis, *op.cit.* 12; Sparks, *op.cit.* 83.

[489] MacGregor Burns, J. & Dunn, S. (2004) *George Washington* Times Books Henry Holt & co, NY, USA, 12.

[490] Several accounts exist of bullet holes through his clothing.

[491] Ellis, *op.cit.* 15.

[492] Sparks, *op.cit.* 98.

[493] Young (1932), *op.cit.* 78.

[494] Freeman, *op.cit.* 2.

[495] Young (1932), *op.cit.* 89ff.

[496] Sparks, *op.cit.* 108.

[497] Young (1932), *op.cit.* 21.

[498] *ibid.*

[499] a.k.a. *Stamps Act.*

[500] Sparks, *op.cit.* 108.

[501] *ibid.* 109.

[502] Meade, W. Rassmussen, S. & Tilton, W. (1999) *Washington – the man behind the myth*, University of Virginia Press, Charlottesville, VA, USA, 294.

[503] Young (1932), *op.cit.* 87.

[504] Higginbotham, D. (2004) *George Washington: Uniting a nation* Rowman & Littlefield, Lanham, MD, USA, 29.

[505] Peckham, H.H. (1958) *The War of Independence: a military history* University of Chicago Press, Chicago, IL, USA, 178ff.

[506] Sparks, *The Life of George Washington, op.cit.* 354.

[507] *ibid.* 400ff.

[508] Washington notably undertook the role of Commander of the Army for no pay.

[509] Young (1932), *op.cit.* 25.

[510] *ibid.* 26.

[511] *ibid.*

[512] *ibid.* 28.

[513] *ibid.* 21.

[514] As opposed to the popular myth that he threw a silver dollar across the Potomac: Matviko, J.W. (ed.) (2005) *The American President in Popular Culture* Greenwood Publishing Group, Westport, CT, USA, 61.

[515] Rassmussen, W.M.S. & Tilton, R.S. (1999) *George Washington – the man behind the myths* University Press of Virginia, Charlottesville, VI, USA, 93.

[516] Hyde, A.M. (1868) *The American Boy's Life of Washington* James Miller, New York, NY, USA, 31.

[517] Kirkland, C.M. (1857) *Memoirs of Washington*, Appleton, NY, USA, 55.

[518] Ellis, *op.cit.* 8.

[519] Kirkland, *op.cit.* 34.

[520] *ibid.*

[521] *ibid.*

[522] Freeman, *op.cit.* xiii.

[523] *ibid.* 9.

[524] *ibid.*

[525] Kirkland, *op.cit.* 80.

[526] *ibid.*

[527] *ibid.* 78.

[528] Ellis, *op.cit.* 18.

[529] *ibid.* 12.

[530] Burns & Dunn, *op.cit.* 10: the authors state: "why the preoccupation – no, obsession with rank?"; Young (1932), *op.cit.* 70.

[531] Cunliffe, *op.cit.* 38. Anne was the daughter of the wealthy Colonel William Fairfax of Belvoir, one of the most prominent persons and families in Virginia, and cousin of Lord Thomas Fairfax of London, who was to become the single largest landholder, by Royal decree, in the new colony.

[532] Burns & Dunn, *op.cit.* 12.

[533] *ibid.*12.

[534] Freeman, *op.cit.* xiii, citing Richard Hartwell.

[535] *ibid.* 10, Ellis, *op.cit.* 38.

[536] Ellis, *op.cit.* 39.

[537] Meade, *op.cit.* 37-38.

[538] Brookhiser, R. (1996) *Rediscovering George Washington* Free Press, New York, NY, USA, 122.

[539] *ibid.*

[540] *ibid.*

[541] *ibid.* 149.

[542] *ibid.* 148.

[543] MacGregor Burns & Dunn, *op.cit.* 155.

[544] Richardson, J.D. (1897) *Compilation of Messages and Papers of the President* Bureau of National Literature, New York, NY, USA, 1; 56.

[545] Schroeder, J.F. (1855) *Maxims of Washington: political, social, moral and religious* D Appleton & Co, New York, NY, USA, 17.

[546] MacGregor Burns & Dunn, *op.cit.*154.

[547] *ibid.* 308.

[548] 5 April 1732: although there is evidence that he was baptised again in 1765 by Rev. J Gano in the Potomac River as an Anglican: *Time Life,* 5 Sept 1932.

[549] The family Bible owned by his mother is still in existence and has been widely commented on in relation to the family's use, as noted previously.

[550] Law mandated that early Virginian settlers (c.1624) adopt the Anglican faith: "Religion in early Virginia"

[551] Sparkes, *The Life of George Washington, op.cit.* 492.

[552] Freeman, *op.cit.* 15.

[553] Ellis, *op.cit.* 45.

[554] Freeman, *op.cit.* 32.

[555] *ibid.* 15.

[556] Meade, W. (1857) *Old Churches, Ministers and Families of Virginia*, Applewood books, Bedford, MA, USA; Schroeder, *op.cit.* 340, citing John Marshall; Slaughter, P. (1886) *Christianity the key to the character and career of Washington*, Whittaker, NY, USA; McGuire, E.C. (1836) *The Religious Opinions and Character of Washington*, Harper & Brothers, New York, NY, USA.

[557] *ibid.*13.

[558] McGuire, *op.cit.* 58.

[559] Schroeder, *op. cit.* 347.

[560] Parke-Custis, G.W. (1859) Lossing, B.J. (ed.) *Recollections and Private memoirs of the Life and Character of Washington*, William H Moore, Washington DC, USA.

[561] Kirkland, *op.cit.* 477.

[562] Hall, V.M. (1976) *George Washington: the character and influence of one man*, Foundation for American Christian Education, San Francisco, CA, USA, 254-271.

[563] Schroeder, *op.cit.* 342.

[564] Accounts differ as to the exact age.

[565] Harrison, *op.cit.* 13. The "rules" have been attributed to Jesuit Scholars in 1595 and a French manual on good manners from the seventeenth century.

[566] Brookhiser, *Rediscovering George Washington, op.cit.* 127: Hawkins, F. (trans.) (1646) *Youths behaviour, or Decency in Conversation amongst Men,* W.Wilson, London, UK.

[567] Harrison, *op.cit.* 15.

[568] Ellis, *op.cit.* 9.

[569] Harrison, *op.cit*, 16.

[570] Burns & Dunn, *op.cit.* 5.

[571] Kirkland, *op.cit.* 70.

[572] Burns & Dunn, *op. cit.* 13.

[573] Chief Justice of the King's Bench of England

[574] *ibid.* 14.

[575] *ibid.* 19.

[576] Brookhiser, *Founding Father, op.cit.* 123.

[577] Chernow (2011) *Washington: a life* Penguin, New York, NY, USA, 13.

[578] Brookhiser, *Rediscovering George Washington, op.cit.* 122.

[579] *ibid.* 123.

[580] *ibid.* 109.

[581] Colish, *op.cit.* 39.

[582] Freeman, *op.cit.* 15.

[583] Tatsch, J.H. (1931) *Facts about George Washington as a Freemason* Macoy Publishing and Masonic Supply Co. New York, NY, USA, 3; Cunliffe, *op.cit.* 43; Brookhiser, *Rediscovering George Washington*, *op.cit.* 144, 151; Freeman, *op.cit.* 32.

[584] *ibid.*

[585] *ibid.*

[586] *ibid.*

[587] Schroeder, *op.cit.* 314.

[588] The *"Rules of Civility"* (*Youth's Behavior*) and the discipline of his mother were two factors in reinforcing this.

[589] Freeman, *op.cit.* 9.

[590] Washington, H.A. (1861) *The writings of Thomas Jefferson* HW Derby, New York, NY, USA, 286.

[591] Sparkes, *The Life of George Washington*, *op.cit.* 539.

[592] *ibid.*

[593] Paulding, *op.cit.* 19; Brookhiser, *op.cit.* 137.

[594] Cunliffe, *op.cit.* 32.

[595] MacGregor Burns & Dunn, *op.cit.* 10.

[596] Brookhiser, *op.cit.* 128.

[597] *ibid.* 151.

[598] *ibid.* 122.

[599] Paulding, *op.cit.* 256.

[600] Richardson, *op.cit.* I: 205-16.

[601] Custis, *op.cit.* 35:416.

[602] Brookhiser, *op.cit.* 133.

[603] MacGregor & Dunn, *op.cit.* 151.

[604] Brookhiser, *op.cit.* 130.

[605] *ibid.*

[606] MacGregor Burns & Dunn, *op.cit.* 13.

[607] Schroeder, *op.cit.* 244.

[608] Brookhiser (1997) *Founding Father*, *op.cit.* 6.

[609] *ibid.*

[610] Schroeder, *op.cit.* 79.

[611] MacGregor Burns & Dunn, *op.cit.* 151.

[612] Brookhiser, R. (2008) *George Washington on leadership* Basic Books, New York, NY, USA, 56.

[613] Thoms, J.C. (2008), Ethical integrity in leadership and organizational moral culture *Leadership*, 4, 420

[614] de Gaulle, C. *Le fil de l'épee (The Edge of the Sword),* Hopkins, G.(trans.)(1935) Criterion Books, New York, NY, USA, 31: The actual translation in this book is "Training for war is, first and foremost, training in leadership, and it is literally true, for armies as well as for nations, that where the leadership is good, the rest shall be added unto them". The last part of this quotation has an unusual turn of phrase — "the rest shall be added unto them". The original French for this is "*tout le reste sera donne par surcrôit*" which is better translated as "the rest will follow".

[615] Plato, *The Republic, op.cit.* 121. Plato proposed that certain individuals are, by their nature, suited for leadership. The rarest individuals, those with characters of gold, should be selected as leaders, while those with characters of iron or bronze should be left to other roles.

[616] Hatch, A. (1960) *The de Gaulle Nobody Knows: an intimate biography of Charles de Gaulle* Hawthorn books Inc, New York, NY, USA, 19.

[617] Sources are divided on whether the original etymology of de Gaulle is de Gaule.

[618] Lacouture, J. *De Gaulle: the rebel (1890-1944),* O'Brien, P.(trans.)(1990) WW Norton & Co, New York, NY, USA 5.

[619] Cook, D. (1983) *Charles de Gaulle*, General publishing company, Toronto, Canada, 26.

[620] Hatch, *op.cit.* 19; Cook, *op. cit.*

[621] Ledwidge, B. (1982) *De Gaulle* Wiedenfeld & Nicholson, London, UK, 10.

[622] Crawley, A. (1969) *De Gaulle: a biography* Collins, London, UK 13; Lacouture, *op.cit.* 104-105.

[623] *ibid.* 11.

[624] *ibid.*

[625] Lacouture, *op.cit.* 4.

[626] de Gaulle, C. (1955) *The Complete War Memoirs of Charles de Gaulle*, Simon & Schuster, New York, NY, USA, 3; Lacouture, *op.cit.* 7; Bonheur, G. (1945) *Le Glaive nu: Charles de Gaulle et son destin*, Trois Collines, Geneva, Switzerland, 25.

[627] Cook, *op.cit.* 7.

[628] de Gaulle, *War Memoirs, op.cit.* 3.

[629] Lacouture, *op.cit.* 5.

[630] *ibid.*

[631] Hatch, *op.cit.* 15.

[632] Lacouture, *op.cit.* 9.

[633] *ibid.* 8.

[634] Hatch, *op.cit.* 24.

[635] *ibid*; Cook. *op.cit.* 28.

[636] Hatch, *op.cit.* 23.

[637] Cook, *op.cit.* 29.

[638] Cattaui, *op.cit.* 22, Hatch, *op.cit.* 23.

[639] notably Lacouture.

[640] Cattaui, G. (1960) *Charles de Gaulle: l'homme et son destin*, A Fayard, Paris, France, 11.

[641] The period between 1890 and the commencement of World War I which was a period of peace, industriousness and innovation in France.

[642] Cook, *op.cit.* 432 from de Gaulle's *Memoirs of Hope*.

[643] Hatch, *op.cit.* 21.

[644] *ibid.*

[645] Crawley, *op.cit.* 14.

[646] Hatch, *op.cit.* 16.

[647] *ibid.*

[648] Cook. *op.cit.* 26.

[649] Ledwidge, *op.cit.* 12.

[650] Cook, *op.cit.* 27.

[651] Lacouture, *op.cit.* 9.

[652] Hatch, *op.cit.* 21.

[653] *ibid.* 8.

[654] *ibid.* 3.

[655] *ibid.* 16: Ledwidge indicates it as 111/121.

[656] Cook, *op.cit.* 28.

[657] *ibid.* 21.

[658] *ibid.* 20.

[659] Lacouture, *op.cit.* 19. Also, this Regiment had existed from the Napoleonic era and had been glorious at Austerlitz, Wagram and in Moscow, 16.

[660] *ibid.* 29.

[661] *ibid.* 30.

[662] *ibid.* 38.

[663] Hatch, *op.cit.* 37.

[664] *ibid.*

[665] Cook, *op.cit.* 31.

[666] *ibid.* 42.

[667] Lacouture, *op.cit.*236 (Chronology).

[668] Cook, *op.cit.* 32.

[669] *ibid.* 34.

[670] *ibid.*

[671] Lacouture, *op.cit.* 88.

[672] Cook, *op.cit.* 36.

[673] Lacouture, *op.cit.* 89-93.

[674] *ibid.* 94-100.

[675] Hatch, *op.cit.* 62. Now known as the Secrétariat général de la défense et de la sécurité nationale (SGDN)

[676] Lacouture, *op.cit.* 129-130; *ibid.* 67-68.

[677] *ibid.* 75.

[678] *ibid.* 183 (provisional appointment).

[679] *ibid.* 243.

[680] Cook, *op.cit.* 324.

[681] Crawley, *op.cit.* 17; Lacouture cites an account of his sister, *op.cit.* 6.

[682] *ibid.*

[683] Whitelaw, N. (1991) *A biography of General Charles de Gaulle: "I am France"* Dillon Press, New York, NY, USA, 10.

[684] C de Gaulle, *War Memoirs, op.cit.* 1.

[685] *ibid.*

[686] Cattaui, *op.cit.* 22.

[687] Lacouture, *op.cit.* 8.

[688] B Ledwidge, *op.cit.* 5.

[689] *ibid.*

[690] *ibid.*

[691] de Gaulle, C. *The Celts of the Nineteenth Century: an appeal to the living representatives of the Celtic race,* Davenport Mason, J.(trans.)(1865), Tenby, London. UK.

[692] Ellis, P.B. (1993) *Celtic Dawn: the dream of Celtic unity* Constable & Co, London, UK, 78.

[693] Werth, A. (1965) *de Gaulle, a political biography* Penguin books, Hammondsworth, UK, 69; Jackson, *op.cit.* 113; Lacouture, *op.cit.* 26; Cattaui, *op.cit.* 48; Ellis., J.J. *op.cit.* 24; Crawley, *op.cit.* 18.

[694] Ledwidge, *op.cit.* 8, 26.

[695] *ibid.* 9.

[696] *ibid.*

[697] Crawley, *op.cit.* 27.

[698] de Gaulle *War memoirs, op.cit.* 10.

[699] Hatch, *op.cit.* 31.

[700] Crawley, *op.cit.* 27.

[701] Lacouture, *op.cit.* 186 (this author uses the words: aloof, arrogant, authoritarian, egocentric and self-assured). On one occasion in the trenches in World War I, a fellow officer remarked that he believed de Gaulle would achieve something great for France, to which de Gaulle simply replied "Yes, I think so too.": Tournoux, J. *Pétain and de Gaulle*, Coburn, O. (trans.)(1966) Viking, New York, NY, USA, 50.

[702] Lacouture, *op.cit.* 4.

[703] Jackson, *op.cit.* 5, citing de Gaulle's *War Memoirs*.

[704] Jackson, *op.cit.* 123; Lacouture, *op.cit.* 27;Ledwidge, *op.cit.* 8; Werth, *op.cit.* 60

[705] Werth, *op.cit.* 65.

[706] Weber, E. (1962) *Action Française; Royalism And Reaction In Twentieth-Century France*, Stanford University Press, Stanford, CA, USA, 3: The Dreyfuss affair involved the conviction of a French officer for revealing military secrets to the enemy. The charges were found to be false, yet the government continued to try and imprison Dreyfuss until he was pardoned due to intense political pressure and civil outrage.

[707] Jackson, *op.cit.* 122.

[708] Weber, *op.cit.* 3.

[709] Weber, *op.cit.* 51-52; Golan, R. (1999) *Modernity and Nostalgia: art and politics in France between the wars* Yale Publications, New Haven, CT, USA, 24: citing Maurras's *Enquête sur la monarchie (1900)*.

[710] *ibid.* 46.

[711] Ory, P. op.cit., 463.

[712] Social Catholicism is the "application of Catholic principles to the economic and political problems of modern industrial civilisations": Moon, P.T. (1921) The Social Catholic movement in France under the Third Republic *The Catholic Historical Review* 7, 1. Coincidentally, Social Catholicism emerged around the same time as *L'Action Française*. In 1891 Pope Leo XIII issued the *Rerum Novarum* (*How to abolish poverty*). It acted largely as a moderator against the liberalist ideologies being proposed and to in-ject the role of justice back into the social order. This was a major step for the Church to take and a significant departure from standard non-interventionist protocol. For the first time the Church commented on the ills of industrialisation and socialism, criti-cising labour conflicts and social justice and instability. Rather than the usual aphor-isms of "do unto others", the Church actively commented on the fairness of labour markets and the moderation of capitalist principles: Curran, C.E. (2002) *Catholic social teaching 1891-present: a historical, theological and ethical analysis,* Georgetown Uni-versity Press, Washington DC, USA.

Ory, P. (1987) *La nouvelle droite fin de siècle* in *Nouvelle histoire des idées politiques*, Hachette, Pluriel, France, 463.

[713] *de Gaulle and L'action Française* L'Internaute, 12 April 2010.

[714] This observation is not entirely accurate. De Gaulle was also heavily influenced by the historian Jacques Bainville who advocated that German unity must be destroyed to render them impotent – see Werth, *op.cit.* 69

[715] Jackson, *op.cit.* 121.

[716] Crawley, *op.cit.* 21.

[717] Werth, *op.cit.* 60.

[718] Sutton, M. (2002) *Nationalism, Positivism and Catholicism: The Politics of Charles Maurras and French Catholics 1890-1914* Cambridge University Press, Cambridge, UK, 58ff.

[719] Griffiths, R. (2010) *The Pen and the Cross: Catholicism and English Literature, 1850-2000* Continuum International Publishing, London, UK, 142.

[720] Werth, *op.cit.* 68.

[721] Lacouture, *op.cit.* 26.

[722] Ory indicates that he is credited with popularising the word "nationalism" in France, *op.cit.* 460.

[723] Golan, *op.cit.* 24.

[724] Jackson, *op.cit.* 70.

[725] Curtis, M. (1959) *Three against the Third Republic* Transaction Publishers, New Brunswick, NJ, USA, 108.

[726] *ibid.*

[727] *ibid.*

[728] Lacouture, *op.cit.* 108.

[729] Hatch, *op.cit.* 24; Lacouture, *op.cit.* 26; Bonheur, *op.cit.* 25.

[730] de Gaulle, *Le fil de l'épee, op.cit.* 20.

[731] Kennedy, E. (2007) Bergson's philosophy and French political doctrines: Sorrel, Maurras, Péguy and de Gaulle *Government and Opposition* 15, 1, 75.

[732] Shoenbrun, D. (1966) *The three lives of Charles de Gaulle* Hamish Hamilton London, UK, 75.

[733] Ledwidge, *op.cit.* 8.

[734] Jackson, *op.cit.* 102.

[735] de Gaulle, *Le fil de l'épee, op.cit.* 20.

[736] *ibid.* 58.

[737] Werth, *op.cit.* 69; Ledwidge, *op.cit.* 8; Lacouture, *op.cit.* 26 Jackson, *op.cit.* 110

[738] de Gaulle, *France and her army, op.cit.* 6: "mother, see your sons, who fought so much!"

[739] Written by de Gaulle at age 14.

[740] Ledwidge, *op.cit.* 15.

[741] Crawley, *op.cit.* 22.

[742] Shoenbrun, *op.cit.* xiv: resistant is a tradition of French heroes who opposed subjugation.

[743] *ibid.*

[744] *ibid.*

[745] Lacouture, *op.cit.* 27.

[746] *ibid.*

[747] *ibid.*

[748] Murat, A. (2008) *La Tour du Pin en Son Temps* Via Romana, Versailles, France, 290.

[749] de Gaulle, *Le fil de l'épee, op.cit.* 58; Cattaui, *op.cit.* 49.

[750] *ibid.* 42.

[751] de Gaulle, C. *La discorde chez l'ennemi (The enemy's house divided),* Eden, R.(trans.) (2002) University of North Carolina Press, North Carolina, Chapel Hill, London, UK, xxxviii.

[752] de Gaulle, *Le fil de l'épee, op.cit.* 41.

[753] *ibid.* 21.

[754] de Gaulle, *La discorde chez l'ennemi, op.cit.* xxxvi.

[755] *ibid.* 4.

[756] *ibid.* 6.

[757] Ledwidge, *op.cit.* 3; Werth, *op.cit.* 65.

[758] Crawley, *op.cit.* 18.

[759] Jackson, *op.cit.* 106.

[760] *ibid.*

[761] de Gaulle, *Le fil de l'épee, op.cit.* 64.

[762] *ibid.* 65.

[763] *ibid.*

[764] *ibid.*

[765] *ibid.* 56.

[766] *ibid.* 42.

[767] *ibid.* 41.

[768] *ibid.*

[769] *ibid.* 42.

[770] *ibid.* 43.

[771] Cattaui, *op.cit.* 305.

[772] *ibid.* 259.

[773] Shennan, A. (1993) *De Gaulle,* Routledge, New York, NY, USA, 2.

[774] General Faidherbe became known not only for his successes and valour but his defiance during the Franco-Prussian War when, even after Napoleon III had capitulated, he refused to lower the French flag.

[775] The practical joke went along the following lines: one night a calling card was delivered to his parents' home indicating that a famous person would call on them that evening. When his parents went to the front door they found Charles dressed in military uniform announcing himself as General Faidherbe. Ledwidge, *op.cit.* 12

[776] Crawley, *op.cit.* 13; Lacouture, *op.cit.* 8; Hatch, *op.cit.* 22.

[777] de Gaulle *War memoirs op.cit.* 4.

[778] Jackson, *op.cit.* 111.

[779] Cate, C. (1960) *Charles de Gaulle: the last romantic* The Atlantic.

[780] de Gaulle, *The Celts of the Nineteenth Century: op.cit,* 7: (note: the author is Charles de Gaulle's uncle).

[781] Hatch, *op.cit.* 25.

[782] de Gaulle, *Le fil de l'épee, op.cit.* 43.

[783] Lacouture, *op.cit.* 113.

[784] Cook, *op.cit.* 17

[785] Cerny, P.G. (1988) The process of personal leadership: The case of de Gaulle *International Political Science Review* 9, 2, 137.

[786] Lacouture, *op.cit.* 191.

[787] France's President at the time.

[788] *ibid.*

[789] Lacouture, *op.cit.*186; Shoenbrun, *op.cit.* 79.

[790] Jackson, *op.cit.* 101.

[791] Crawley, *op.cit.* 28, citing a woman who had known de Gaulle for many years who would say that she felt that "Charles regarded her sex either as a source of pleasure or a waste of time." Yet in 1945, when in power, he gave women the right to vote (although this may have been no more than populist politics): Werth *op.cit.* 64.

[792] Jackson, *op.cit.* 113.

[793] *ibid.* 114.

[794] de Gaulle, *Le fil de l'épee*, 104.

[795] Jackson, *op.cit.* 114, 118.

[796] de Gaulle, *Le fil de l'épee*, 106.

[797] Lacouture, *op.cit.* 198.

[798] Cook, *op.cit.* 17.

[799] de Gaulle, *Le fil de l'épee*, *op.cit.* 41.

[800] The latter two appear to be derived from his familiarity with Bergson.

[801] Cook, *op.cit.* 83.

[802] Jackson, *op.cit.* 18. Cook, *op.cit.* 15

[803] Cook, *op.cit.* 15.

[804] Cerny, P.G. (1980) *The politics of grandeur: ideological aspects of de Gaulle's foreign policy* Cambridge University Press, Cambridge, UK, 64.

[805] Cook, *op.cit.* 16.

[806] Hatch, *op.cit.* 16.

[807] Cook, *op.cit.* 21.

[808] Fox, E.W. (1963) Appearance and reality in the recent French elections *Virginia Quarterly Review* 39, 2, 184.

[809] Cerny, *The process of personal leadership, op.cit.* 139; Schoenbrun, *op.cit.* 84, 165.

[810] Cerny, *The Politics of Grandeur, op.cit.* 64.

[811] Clague, *op.cit.* 423.

[812] Mahoney, D.J. (2000) *De Gaulle: Statesmanship, grandeur and modern democracy* Transaction Publishing, Brunswick, NJ, USA: the authors cites Wolfgang Mommsen, Julien Freund, Raymond Aaron and Allan Bloom as proposing this parallel.

[813] de Gaulle, *Le fil de l'épee, ibid.* 57.

[814] *ibid.*

[815] *ibid.* 30.

[816] Cattaui, *op.cit.* 311.

[817] Cerny, *The Politics of Grandeur, op.cit.* 3.

[818] *ibid.* 56.

[819] Nanus, *Visionary Leadership*, op.cit. 3-5.

[820] Sashkin, op.cit. 26; Sashkin, M. & Rosenbach, W.E. (1998) A new vision of leadership in W.E. Rosenbach, W.E. & Taylor, R.L. (eds) *Contemporary Issues in Leadership* Westview Press, Boulder, CO, USA, 222

[821] Charlot, J. (1970) *Le Phenomene* Gaullist Fayard, Paris, France, 436

[822] Bass *Leadership and Performance Beyond Expectation op.cit.* 26-27; Cerny, *The process of personal leadership, op.cit.* 131. The particular aspect of transformational leadership which Bass ascribes conforms to the functional approach.

[823] Cook, *op.cit.* 15; de Gaulle, *Le fil de l'épee, op.cit.* 62.

[824] Ambrose, S.E. (1990) *Eisenhower: soldier and president* Simon & Schuster New York, NY, USA, 81.

[825] Aristotle *Politics,* Sinclair, T.A.(ed.) Saunders, T.J. (trans.) (1983) Penguin Books, Middlesex, London, UK, 182.

[826] *ibid.* 11 (his name was reversed by his mother early in his life).

[827] There were in fact seven children but one son died after birth.

[828] Ambrose, *op.cit.* 15.

[829] Davis, *op.cit.* 36.

[830] *ibid.* 38.

[831] Kornitzer, B. (1955) *The Great American Heritage: the story of the five Eisenhower brothers* Farrar Straus and Cudahy Inc New York, NY, USA 23: Note: even though there were six surviving brothers, one brother, Roy, died in 1942 prior to this book being written.

[832] *ibid.* 19.

[833] Davis, *op.cit.* 41.

[834] Lee, R.A. (1981) *Dwight D Eisenhower: soldier & statesman* Nelson Hall, Chicago MA, USA, 10.

[835] Davis, *op.cit.* 46.

[836] Wild Bill was the town Marshall of Abilene in 1871. His presence as Marshall is cited in Eisenhower's autobiography: Eisenhower, D.D. (1968) *At Ease: stories I tell to friends* Robert Hale Limited, London, UK, 88.

[837] Lyon, P. (1974) *Eisenhower – portrait of a hero* Little Brown & Co, Boston, MA, USA, 33.

[838] *ibid.*

[839] Eisenhower, *op.cit.* 2.

[840] Gunther, J. (1952) *Eisenhower: the man and the symbol* Hamish Hamilton, London, UK 27; Ambrose, *op.cit.* 19; Eisenhower, *op.cit.* 39-41.

[841] Neal, S. (1978) *The Eisenhowers: reluctant dynasty* Doubleday & Co New York, NY, USA 12.

[842] Eisenhower, *op.cit.* 32.

[843] Medhurst, M.J. (1993) *Dwight D Eisenhower: Strategic Communicator* Greenwood Press, Westport, CT, USA, 7.

[844] Ambrose, *op.cit.* 17.

[845] *ibid*; Eisenhower, *op.cit.* 70.

[846] Eisenhower, *op.cit.* 70.

[847] Ambrose, *op.cit.* 11.

[848] Davis, K.S. (1945) *Soldier of democracy* Country Life Press, Garden City, NY, USA. 48; Lyon, *op.cit.* 39; Neal, *op.cit.* 15.

[849] Kornitzer, *op.cit.* 45.

[850] Ambrose, *op.cit.* 18.

[851] *ibid.*

[852] Lyon, *op.cit.* 38.

[853] Gunther, *op.cit.* 59.

[854] Lyon, *op.cit.* 40.

[855] Lee, *op.cit.* 11; Eisenhower, *op.cit.* 36.

[856] *ibid.* 4.

[857] Eisenhower, *op.cit.* 37.

[858] *ibid.* 22.

[859] Eisenhower, *op.cit.* 7.

[860] Lyon, *op.cit.* 44.

[861] Eisenhower, *op.cit.* 7.

[862] Ambrose, *op.cit.* 27.

[863] Eisenhower, *op.cit.* 16.

[864] Lyon, *op.cit.* 46.

[865] *ibid.*

[866] Ambrose, *op.cit.* 30.

[867] Several authors make note of the importance of playing football in the army hierarchy and that coaching identified one as being more of a leader than the role of quarterback.

[868] Ambrose , *op.cit.* 33.

[869] *ibid.*

[870] *ibid.*

[871] *ibid.*

[872] *ibid.* 37.

[873] *ibid.* 40.

[874] *ibid.* 42.

[875] *ibid.*

[876] *ibid.* 43.

[877] *ibid.* 44.

[878] MacArthur's fitness report, 1930, Eisenhower Museum and Library, Abilene, Texas, USA.

[879] Ambrose, *op.cit.* 44.

[880] *ibid.* 61.

[881] *ibid.*

[882] *ibid.* 72.

[883] *ibid.* 75.

[884] Medhurst, *op.cit.* 193.

[885] Davis, *op.cit.* 13.

[886] *ibid.* The surname is Germanic, originally Eisenhauer: Gunther, *op.cit.* 50: literally a hewer of iron or an iron craftsman; David, *op.cit.* 10, states that the family would translate it as "iron striker".

[887] Then known as the Eisenhauers.

[888] Lee, *op.cit.* 2; Davis, *op.cit.* 11.

[889] Schroeder, W. & Huebert, H. (2001) *Mennonites Historical Atlas* Springfield Publisher, Manitoba, Canada, iii.

[890] Particularly during the 30 year war 1618-1648: Davis, *op.cit.* 11.

[891] Lee, *op.cit.* 3.

[892] Gunther, *op.cit.* 50.

[893] Davis, *op.cit.* 13, the River Brethren became the Brethren of Christ.

[894] *ibid.* 52.

[895] *ibid.*

[896] *ibid.* 32.

[897] Lyons, *op.cit.* 34.

[898] Gunther, *op.cit.* 57.

[899] Kornitzer, *op.cit.* 25-27.

[900] *ibid.*

[901] *ibid.* 19.

[902] *ibid.* 58.

[903] Ambrose, *op.cit.* 11.

[904] *ibid.* 12.

[905] *ibid.*

[906] *ibid.*

[907] *ibid.*

[908] Kornitzer, *op.cit.* 46.

[909] Hatch, A. (1944) *General Ike* Henry Holt & Co, New York, NY, USA, 15.

[910] Eisenhower, *op.cit.* 16.

[911] Ambrose. *op.cit.*16.

[912] Eisenhower, *op.cit.* 51.

[913] *ibid.*

[914] Ambrose, *op.cit.* 21.

[915] Lee, *op.cit.* 14.

[916] Ambrose, *op.cit.* 11.

[917] His next brother should have been named Paul but he died in infancy.

[918] Eisenhower, *op.cit.* 34.

[919] *ibid.*

[920] A detailed account of the Eisenhower brothers is covered in Kornitzer's work cited previously.

[921] Kornitzer, *op.cit.* 27.

[922] Eisenhower, *op.cit.* 34.

[923] Eisenhower, *op.cit.* 38.

[924] *ibid.* 37.

[925] *ibid.* 76.

[926] Lee, *op.cit.* 18.

[927] *ibid.*

[928] *ibid.* 19.

[929] *ibid.*

[930] Eisenhower, *op.cit.* 40.

[931] *ibid.*

[932] *ibid.*

[933] *ibid.*

[934] *ibid.*

[935] *ibid.* 41.

[936] *ibid.*

[937] Lee, *op.cit.* 18.

[938] Ambrose, *op.cit.* 21; Lee, *op.cit.* 18.

[939] Eisenhower, *op.cit.* 64; Neal, *op.cit.* 17.

[940] Eisenhower, *ibid.* 16.

[941] Perret, G. (1999) *Eisenhower* Random House, New York, NY USA, 33-34; Eisenhower, *op.cit.* 88.

[942] Lee, *op.cit.* 21

[943] Gunther, *op.cit.* 59.

[944] *ibid.*

[945] *ibid.* 41.

[946] Lee, *op.cit.* 24.

[947] Lyon, *op.cit.* 41.

[948] *ibid.* 38, Gunther, *op.cit.* 57.

[949] Hatch, *op.cit,* 15.

[950] Gunther, *op.cit.* 52.

[951] Hatch, *op.cit.* 13.

[952] Lee, *op.cit.* 30.

[953] Gunther, *op.cit.* 60.

[954] Ambrose, *op.cit.* 26.

[955] Lyon, *op.cit.* 45.

[956] Gunther, *op.cit.* 59.

[957] Hatch, *op.cit.* 31.

[958] Lee, *op.cit.* 30.

[959] Davis, *op.cit.* 49.

[960] Medhurst *op.cit.* 5.

[961] Davis, *op.cit.* 6.

[962] *ibid.* 13.

[963] *ibid.* 64.

[964] Neal, *op.cit.* 13; Davis, *op.cit.* 48.

[965] Gunther, *op.cit.* 27.

[966] Janowitz, M. (1960) *The Professional soldier: a social and political portrait* Free Press of Glencoe, Glencoe, IL, USA, 133.

[967] Lee, *op.cit.* 30.

[968] Janowitz, *op.cit.* 133.

[969] Eisenhower, *op.cit.* 4.

[970] *ibid.* 12.

[971] Eisenhower, *op.cit.* 32.

[972] *ibid.* 52.

[973] *ibid.*

[974] *ibid.* 41

[975] Neal, *op.cit.* 12-13.

[976] Lyons, *op.cit.* 38.

[977] *ibid.*

[978] *ibid.* 42.

[979] *ibid.* 45

[980] *ibid.*

[981] Medhurst, *op.cit.* 12

[982] *ibid.* 11

[983] *ibid.*

[984] *ibid.* 12.

[985] Eisenhower, *op.cit.* 4.

[986] Medhurst, *op.cit.* 12.

[987] Lyon, *op.cit.* 45.

[988] Eisenhower, *op.cit.* 24.

[989] Ambrose, *op.cit.* 26; Neal, *op.cit.* 27.

[990] Lee, *op.cit.*36.

[991] Lyon, *op.cit.* 46.

[992] Davis, *op.cit.* 49.

[993] Eisenhower, *op.cit.* 18.

[994] *ibid.*

[995] *ibid.*

[996] Medhurst, *op.cit.* 159.

[997] *ibid.*41.

[998] *ibid.* 44.

[999] *ibid.* 34.

[1000] House, *A 1976 theory of charismatic leadership* op.cit.

[1001] Medhurst, *op.cit.* 17.

[1002] *ibid.*

[1003] Shils, E. (1965) Charisma, order and status *American Sociological Review* 30, 204.

[1004] House, *A 1976 Theory of charismatic leadership*, *op.cit.* 194: House advocates that followers adopt a "strong conviction in the moral righteousness of the leader's belief" but that "self confidence and dominance (need for power usually based on referent power)" are also necessary. In relation to the latter, the referent power is based predominantly on the moral integrity demonstrated in the case of Eisenhower.

[1005] House, R.J & Baetz, M.L. (1979) *Leadership: some empirical generalisations and new research directions* in BM Straw (ed.) *Research in organisational behaviour*, Faculty of Management Studies, University of Toronto, Toronto, Canada, 1, 399.

[1006] Using the Weberian definition of charisma.

[1007] Bass *Leadership and Performance Beyond Expectation*, *op.cit.* 31.

[1008] See for example the review of charismatic leadership in Conger, J.A. (1999) Charismatic and Transformational leadership in organisations: an insiders perspective on these developing streams of research *op.cit.* 145.

[1009] Bass, B.M. & Riggio, R.E. (2006) *Transformational leadership* Erlbaum, Mahwah, NJ, USA, 225.

[1010] *ibid.* 16: citing J Macgregor Burns *Leadership op.cit.*

[1011] Ambrose, *op.cit.* 62.

[1012] *ibid.* 63.

[1013] *ibid.* 175 citing Butcher, H.C. (1946) *My three years with Eisenhower: the personal diary of Captain Harry C Butcher, USNR* Simon & Schuster, New York, NY, USA.

[1014] Medhurst, *op.cit.* 10.

[1015] Eisenhower, D.D. (1948) *Crusade in Europe*, Doubleday, Dell Publishing Group, New York, NY, USA, 50.

[1016] Kornitzer, *op.cit.* 199.

[1017] *ibid.*

[1018] *ibid.* 11.

[1019] McCrimmon, M. (2009) Post-heroic leadership: how to succeed in the 21ˢᵗ century *Canadian Manager* 34, 3, 10.

[1020] Axelrod, A. (2006) *Eisenhower on leadership: Ike's enduring lessons on total victory management* Jossey Bass, San Francisco, CA, USA, i.

[1021] Medhurst, *op.cit.* 13 (italics added – it is interesting that he uses these aspects to highlight the success of the Americans in World War II)

[1022] Bass, B. & Bass, R. (2008) *The Bass Handbook of Leadership: Theory Research and managerial applications* Free Press, New York, NY, USA, 17 citing Larson, J. (1968) *Eisenhower: the president nobody knew* Popular Library, New York, NY, USA; Bass, *Leadership and Performance Beyond Expectation*, *op.cit.* 17.

[1023] Ambrose, *op.cit.* 90.

[1024] Gardner W.L., Avolio B.J., Luthans, F., May D.R., Walumbwa F. (2005) "Can you see the real me?" A self-based model of authentic leader and follower development *The Leadership Quarterly* 16, 345.

[1025] In relation to the soldier statesmen's lives this correlation has been compiled in Appendix B

[1026] Northouse, *op.cit.* 381

[1027] Turner, J.C. (2008) Towards a cognitive redefinition of the social group in Tajfel, H. (ed.) (2008) *Social identity and intergroup relations* Cambridge University Press, Cambridge, UK, 31-35.

[1028] Stogdill, Personal factors associated with leadership: a survey of the literature *op.cit.* 35.

[1029] Murphy, A.J. (1941) A study of the leadership process *American Sociological Review* 6, 674.

[1030] Kramer, R. (1999) Trust and distrust in organisations: emerging perspectives, enduring questions *Annual Review of Psychology* 50, 569; Robinson, S. (1996) Trust and the breach of the psychological contract *Administrative Science Quarterly* 41, 574.

[1031] For conciseness, "moral philosophy" will be used to encompass the moral elements of religious philosophy. It is recognised that religious philosophy may also contribute to one's leadership approach, but at core it is contended that the moral elements of religion are relevant to leadership rather than the elements of pure dogma. Moral philosophy overlaps to some extent into religious philosophy in relation to ethical issues. Kohlberg, L. (1975) *The cognitive-developmental approach to moral education* The Phi Delta Kappa, 56, 10, 670; Kohlberg, L. (2008) *The development of children's orientation towards a moral order* Human Development 51, 8.

[1032] It is difficult to prove these aspects across numerous societies without an analysis of census data. Given the migration demands of the First World countries, it would seem a reasonable proposition that this claim is true. As for the increasing secularisation, this is a relative observation given the demise of religious institutions' relevance over time.

[1033] Garten, J.E. (2005) B-schools: only a C+ in ethics *Business Week* edition 3949 5 Sept, 110; Noting that leadership can be learned and is not simply innate: Brungardt, C. (1997) The making of leaders: a review of the research in leadership development *Journal of Leadership and Organisational Studies* 3, 81; McCullogh, D. (2008) Timeless Leadership: a conversation with David McCullough *Harvard Business Review* March, 45-49.

[1034] Velasquez, M.G. (192) *Business Ethics: Concepts and Cases* Prentice Hall, Upper Saddle River NJ, USA, 9.

[1035] For example: Harte (1530-1592) proposed that children should be studied in early childhood to determine their aptitude, and subsequently have their education planned: Schultz & Schultz, *op.cit.* 113.

[1036] Gini, *op.cit.* 66.

[1037] *ibid.*

[1038] Shoup, *op.cit.* 42.

[1039] Dewey, J. (1996) *Theory of the Moral Life* Irvington Publishers, NY, USA, 5.

[1040] See previous discussion in the coverage on leadership in Chapter 2, such as the models proposed by Murphy (situational leadership), Hersey & Blanchard (situational leadership II model), Fiedler (contingency theory), House & Mitchell (path goal theory).

[1041] Stogdill, Personal factors associated with leadership: a survey of the literature op.-cit, 35. Note that other works preceded Stogdill's, such as that of Jenkins, *op.cit.* 54.

[1042] Nahavandi, A. (2006) *The Art and Science of Leadership* (4th edn) Pearson Prentice Hall, NJ, USA, 299.

[1043] *ibid.* 299-301.

[1044] Padilla, A. Hogan, R. & Kaiser, R.B. (2007) The toxic triangle, destructive leaders, susceptible followers and conducive environments *The Leadership Quarterly* 18, 3, 176.

[1045] Maccoby, M. (2007) *The Leaders We Need: and what makes us follow* Harvard Business School Press, Boston, MA, USA.

[1046] Padilla et al. *op.cit.* 185-187.

[1047] *ibid.* 6.

[1048] *ibid.* 3-11.

[1049] A good example of this is the "cult of patriotism" which developed in France in the eighteenth century and was to pave the way for nationalistic fervour in Germany in the twentieth, and the accompanying "cult of personality" that ushered in a string of European dictators from Spain to Russia: Curtis, L. (1945) *World War: its cause and cure* Oxford University Press, London, UK, 42. The socio-historical context of Europe in these periods is reflected in the type of political leaders that emerge.

[1050] Carlyle, *op.cit.* 34.

[1051] See Chapter 2 for a discussion of this under "The influences on the development of leadership approach".

[1052] Kirkpatrick & Locke, *op.cit.* 58.

[1053] Jenkins *op. cit.* 54.

[1054] The big five trait classification – Norman, W. (1963) Toward an adequate taxonomy of personality attributes: replicated factor structure in peer nominated personality ratings *Journal of Abnormal Psychology*, 66, 774.

[1055] Notabley the Trompenaars Hampden-Turner study, the GLOBE project, the Hofstede study and Swartz study. The Hofstede and Swartz studies have not been included in the comparison as the former study only surveyed one organisation (i.e. IBM) across a number of countries while the latter study did not include the USA. The Trompenaars and GLOBE studies are the most useful to demonstrate the point of cultural distinction between the two subject cultures.

[1056] F Trompenaars & C Hampden-Turner (1997) *Riding the Waves of Culture – understanding cultural diversity in business* Nicholas Brearley Publishing London UK.

[1057] R House, M Javidan, P Hanges, P Dorfman (2002) *Understanding cultures and implicit leadership theories across the globe: an introduction to project GLOBE* Journal of World Business, 37, 4; RJ House, PJ Hanges, M Javidan, PW Dorfman, V Gupta (2004) *Culture leadership and organisations: The GLOBE study of 62 societies* Sage Publications, CA, USA. Note that the GLOBE study groups countries such that France is considered a Latin Europe country and the USA an Anglo country.

[1058] House, R., Javidan, M., Hanges, P. & Dorfman, P. (2002) Understanding cultures and implicit leadership theories across the globe: an introduction to project GLOBE *Journal of World Business*, 37, 4.

www.ingramcontent.com/pod-product-compliance
Lightning Source LLC
Chambersburg PA
CBHW071203210326
41597CB00016B/1656